MW01284848

Lautner
A-Z

An Exploration of the Complete Built Work
Jan-Richard Kikkert & Tycho Saariste

Contents

In spring 2007, Jan-Richard Kikkert and Tycho Saariste organised the first field trip on the work of the American architect John Lautner. This excursion was part of the architecture master's programme at ArtEZ. Breaking with common practice for educational field trips, Jan-Richard and Tycho had devised a monomaniacal programme, which focused almost exclusively on visiting Lautner houses.

The results of this trip were so encouraging and promising that a plan was devised to visit all of Lautner's works that still exist. Jan-Richard and Tycho kept looking for ways to meet other people involved in Lautner's work, or invite them to come along for part of the trip, such as his daughters, former colleagues and clients or owners of his houses. They shared knowledge and insights with them in their own, enthusiastic way, and these contacts also yielded new information.

In this publication, the large collection of Lautner's houses is reflected by the network of contacts that Jan-Richard and Tycho built up during their quest. Alan Hess's beautiful introduction is an example of this.

Not without symbolism, Jan-Richard and Tycho's grand tour ended in Midgaard, the log cabin where everything started for Lautner. It was five years after the plans for the first field trip were made.

In the years following the trips, all the material was sorted through and described. The personal approach that has characterised this undertaking from the start also emerges in the way in which Jan-Richard and Tycho report on their observations, insights and conversations. It is the story of architects on a mission, with a professional eye for construction, spatial organisation and unorthodox solutions. The final product is a road movie with 144 stops, the story of a unique tour de force, one which Jan-Richard and Tycho, as practicing architects with active professional lives, will most likely be able to undertake only once in their lives.

This accomplishment is undoubtedly due to the irrepressible and contagious enthusiasm that Jan-Richard and Tycho showed constantly. It didn't matter whether they were just coming back from a visit to one or more of Lautner's houses, preparing for a new trip, receiving a response from yet another new contact they had made, managing to track down a Lautner project on Google Earth, or looking for funding to be able to visit a certain project themselves — Jan-Richard and Tycho always radiated a cheerful urgency to take the next step in their odyssey once again.

I have great appreciation for the way in which Jan-Richard and Tycho have been the driving force behind the project from beginning to end. With this project and publication they have contributed in their own way to the series that the ArtEZ Academy of Architecture produces together with ArtEZ Press. The series offers lecturers the opportunity to explore a specific subject — related to teaching — in depth. The fruitful collaboration with Jan Brand and Minke Vos of ArtEZ Press was demonstrated once again by the professional, constructive and critical way in which they helped turn the manuscript into this splendid publication. The hard work and efforts of ArtEZ's Werkplaats Typografie have led once again to a very beautifully designed book. I would like to thank Sabo Day and the supervisors at Werkplaats Typografie for this.

This publication shows that Lautner's work continues to inspire, even though his death, in 1994, put an end to his production. In light of this, I hope this book will encourage the occupants and owners of his houses to keep them in good repair, and that it will be a source of inspiration for new researchers to further explore hitherto ignored aspects of Lautner's work.

First and foremost, however, I hope that architects and students of architecture who come in contact with Lautner's oeuvre through this publication will pass on — in whichever shape or form — what they have learned from Lautner's rich, spatial and unorthodox way of thinking.

Ko Jacobs
*(Head of ArtEZ Academy of Architecture / Master programme in Architecture
Senior Research Fellow in Architecture)*

Introduction
Alan Hess

John Lautner (1911-1994)

Through no fault of his own, John Lautner's contributions to Modern architecture have been widely recognized only in the last ten or fifteen years. Even so, he still remains an enigma for some critics. We still have more to learn - and understand - about how he expanded the boundaries of Modern architecture. After years of indefatigable research, Tycho and Jan-Richard's book adds an invaluable resource for our understanding of Lautner.

The contentiousness around Lautner's work was probably inevitable, given his particular genius. For him, architecture was about finding the creative and perfect solution to the problem without concern for precedent, tradition, or fashion. The business of architecture, of wooing clients, of getting published, of promoting his work was never of much interest to him.

Had Lautner not been so uncompromising in solving architectural problems, had he not been so farsighted and unconcerned for convention, his designs would not have been so incomprehensible to conventional critics and historians. To them, his work seemed only undisciplined and self-indulgent, and Lautner himself never deigned to help them understand it. Brusque and pointed in his public lectures, he railed against critics, bankers, building departments, and clients who conspired to make architecture mundane.

Of course there were many reasons why those critics were unable to understand what he was doing. In their eyes, Lautner had several strikes against him. He was a student of Frank Lloyd Wright, and thus at odds with the International Style that became the prevailing modernist style in the decades after 1950. He was based in Los Angeles, which was, through much of his career, barely on the margins of most critics' awareness. More profoundly, he was a genuine architectural thinker who took to heart the tools of Modernism - new technology, new programs, new ways of living - and

wrested from them (as Claude Bragdon's Sinbad wrested from the logarithmic spiral) their treasures.

Then there was the sheer brilliance and boldness of his designs. The panoramic open air living room under an upswept concrete brim of the Marbrisa house overlooking Acapulco Bay; the jazzy roof/sign of Googie's coffee shop on the bustling Sunset Strip; the structural daring of the Chemosphere house balanced atop a single column on a hillside; the audacity of conjuring human habitations from frozen waves of concrete like those at the Pacific Coast house; the cave-like intimacy of the Mauer house's inglenook, and the dappled forest-like sunlight of the Sheats-Goldstein living room, to name only a few.

Lautner was so far out-of-step with the International Style's rectilinearity that most critical observers in his day could not guess what he was up to. Today, however, we have an advantage over them; Lautner's buildings remain as visionary as ever, but we have finally caught up with him. Today we can comprehend his complex fluid spaces and the forms that shape them because the works of Zaha Hadid, Rem Koolhaas, MVRDV, Thom Mayne, and Frank Gehry have trained our eyes to make those forms understandable, even normative. We can now look at Lautner's work from fifty years ago and see it in a new light. We should never forget, however, that today's architects rely on computer-aided design to create multi-dimensional richness; Lautner, remarkably, accomplished it without that advantage. From his Taliesin training he would conceive a full solution in his mind, and then communicate it to his talented staff (including James Langenheim, Jim Charlton, Bob Marquis, Herb Greene, Guy Zebert, Warren Lawson, Duncan Nicholson, Helena Arahuete, Vaughan Trammell, Julia Strickland, and others over the years) with initial conceptual sketches. Under his eye they would refine them through drawings and scale models, and engineering challenges would be resolved with input by creative engineers such as Andrew Nasser and Richard Bradshaw. For construction Lautner would often return to the same resourceful builders, including Wally Niewiadomski, John de la Vaux, and Roban

Poirier, to help him execute his vision.

Over Lautner's sixty-year career, his designs matched in creativity, boldness, vision, and diversity the most important and free-thinking architects of Modernism. Though the complexity of his spatial designs often rivalled the best of Paul Rudolph, Lautner was closer to the inventiveness of Paolo Soleri and Eero Saarinen. With Oscar Niemeyer he shared the skilful use of free forms permitted by the liquid character of monolithic concrete fabrication. Though they were contemporaries, and both drew on nature for inspiration, their expressions are nonetheless distinct; Niemeyer was a sculptor of concrete, shaping monumental forms (especially at Brasilia) that indelibly marked the image of a place. He borrowed the serpentine forms of his country's coastlines and rivers, and the serrated peaks of mountain ridges to connect his buildings to the landscape and the visual memory of Brazilians. Lautner, in contrast, was more essentially a sculptor of space. Poured concrete gave him the freedom to create free form shells that defined, contained, and guided the interior spaces of his houses; he drew distant views of nature and city into a house as an intimate presence. The exterior form, or monumentality, of a building was of secondary importance to the energy and livability of the interior space.

Nor was Lautner an architect-engineer of concrete in the mould of Pier Luigi Nervi or Felix Candela (though he consulted with Candela on the great roofs of the Silvertop and Hope houses). Their designs revealed the hidden geometries of nature, giving form to the invisible forces of statics and gravity. Lautner was always focused on the creation of human habitation, of spaces that could be lived in, that could magnify the enjoyment of nature, of views, of climate in daily life. The subtle movement of sunlight through a house was always an important consideration; his forms would allow it, reflect it, and shape themselves to that warm touch.

While Lautner bears comparison with these global architects, it must be remembered that he worked in the middle of one of the most creative periods in Los Angeles architecture, one of the most Modern cities in the United States. His home town boasted the singular talents of Charles Eames, Pierre Koenig, A. Quincy Jones, Craig Elwood, Whitney Smith, Douglas Honnold, Armet and Davis, and many other adventurous architects taking advantage of the region's economic boom and freedom to expand the boundaries of Modern architecture. Even in this company, Lautner's work stood out, and evidence of his influence on his colleagues can be seen. They were colleagues and often friends who respected each others' work. He was never ignored by fellow architects.

Nonetheless we are left with the puzzle of why he was noticed but not appreciated by the mainstream for much of his career. It says much more about us than it did about him - and now we are coming around to appreciating what he did and how he did it.

*

In historical context, Lautner rose from one of the longest and most fruitful currents of Modern architecture. This lineage began after the Civil War in the United States, when Philadelphia - the Silicon Valley of its day - became the locus of practical innovations, corporate powerhouses, and social change unfettered by tradition and class. The chief architect of that city was Frank Furness, who conceived a muscular new architecture growing from the technological freedom of industry instead of the academic repetition of Classical orders. So original were Furness' buildings that they attracted the eye of the young Louis Sullivan, who sought employment with Furness in 1873, before he moved to Chicago - where another young architect, Frank Lloyd Wright, similarly sought employment with Sullivan in 1888. Lautner, in turn, joined Wright's Taliesin Fellowship in 1933.

While the work of each of these architects was Modern (in the sense of using and expressing the practical and aesthetic potential of the industrial age), they considered the machine to be a means to achieve an end, not the end itself; architecture was not a machine for living in. Instead the relation of mankind to nature was as important to them as technology; instead of separating humans from their natural habitats, the machine could bring them closer to nature and its spiritual and pleasurable benefits. Nature formed a strong philosophical foundation for these architects; Furness' father was a close friend of the American philosopher Ralph Waldo Emerson, who wrote of Nature as a transcendental truth; Sullivan's axiom 'form ever follows function' likewise grasped an organic principle of cause and effect, the essential relationship of a tree's branches to its leaves; Wright drew on the natural landscape of his buildings for inspiration. And Lautner used the most modern technologies of steel, concrete, glass, and electric mechanisms to create habitations that embodied and celebrated the ancient and enduring habitations of mankind: forests, caves, meadows, eyries, beaches.

Lautner developed his innate appreciation for these natural settings during his youth in northern Michigan's primeval forests on Lake Superior's rocky shore. During his six years working with Wright at Taliesin - both in the lush green landscape of Wisconsin, and the craggy mountains and seasonal blooming of the Arizona desert - the young student absorbed Wright's teachings by doing, by grading roads with tractors, fitting pipes, farming crops, preparing meals for the fellowship, attending weekly musical performances by the likes of Paul Robeson. But by Lautner's own account he did not design much himself while there. He was one of the small group who worked alongside the master in the drafting room, and was sent out to supervise construction on the projects that began to flow into Wright's office after the fame of Fallingwater resurrected his career in 1936; Lautner worked on Herbert Johnson's house, Wingspread, in Racine, Wisconsin, as well as others.

With his young wife, MaryBud, and a growing family, however, Lautner desired to launch his own career, and so moved to Los Angeles in 1938. The western city was a good choice for his progressive architecture. The city was already recovering from the Great Depression, and the film, music, and high tech industries provided open-minded and solvent clients. Modern architecture was already established in the region in the work of Irving

Gill, R. M. Schindler, Richard Neutra, Kem Weber, J. R. Davidson, Lloyd Wright, and F. L. Wright himself. A series of houses - some for Wright clients who could not afford the master's daring but expensive designs - followed. Lautner's work quickly gained respect; by 1940 the eminent historian and Museum of Modern Art curator Henry-Russell Hitchcock pronounced that Lautner's work 'can unashamedly stand comparison with that of his master.'

Once the Second World War was over - and a building boom to house an enormous influx of population was launched - Lautner gained opportunities to try out many of his ideas. Prefabricated housing intrigued many architects, and in the Carling, Polin and Jacobsen houses Lautner developed a system of triangulated steel pylons that could be factory-fabricated, trucked to a site, and erected in just a few days. A roof could be easily suspended from the three pylons, creating a shelter for the construction of the non-structural walls enclosing the house and defining the rooms. The system had the advantage of being adaptable to steep sites in the hills rimming the Los Angeles basin. Brimming with ideas, Lautner developed two other distinct prefabricated systems - wood-skinned bents at the Mauer house in 1946, and lens-shaped steel trusses at the Gantvoort house in 1949 - as solutions to the same challenge of speedy, cost-effective construction.

In the expanding suburban metropolis of Los Angeles, where people's lives were shaped by mobility based on automobile ownership, Lautner's fertile mind found many other in-triguing design possibilities. No building type was too modest if it presented a creative challenge. Humble drive-in restaurants, for example, stood on almost every corner to serve the auto-mobile public, and Lautner designed a series of inventive Coffee Dan's coffee shops (with Douglas Honnold) and Henry's drive-ins culminating in Googie's restaurant (1949) on the Sunset Strip. Sadly, none remain today, though their willingness to lift the most ordinary, everyday buildings to the level of pure architecture remains an inspiration. Googie's was a hit with the public.

Not only did a crop of dynamic young actors (including James Dean) make it their hang-out, its design blending a roof of exposed corrugated steel decking with its sign made the small restaurant stand out to motorists driving by on the commercial strip. It attracted national attention, this time by *House + Home* editor Douglas Haskell, who realised that Lautner was defining a new direction for architecture in a fast-changing world. Googie's angles and rising front wall of glass were far from the austerities of the International Style. It responded instead to the kinetic automobile landscape, the pleasure of the customers inside, and the public's sense that they were living in a new age.

These were common themes in Lautner's work. He solved the problems each building presented in a new way, given the program, site, materials, client, and budget. His bounti-ful imagination never failed. Through the 1940s, 1950s and 1960s he designed a series of modestly-sized middle-class homes such as the Walstrom and Salkin houses. Many were designed on smaller budgets, or designed to be built by the owners themselves, such as the Tolstoy house. He designed the Sheats ap-artment house as his solution to multi-family housing. The Stevens and Rawlins houses were row houses on long, narrow sites; the design challenge was to bring natural light into the centre of the house. Ranch houses (the simple one-story, single-family suburban home) were being built by the thousands across the United States, and Lautner raised this common type into architecture at the Schaffer house by bringing the quality of light and shelter of the site's extant oak grove into the living spaces.

In these early years, Lautner had occa-sional opportunities to build a large house on an ample budget; in 1950 he built a house for aluminium manufacturer Leo Harvey on a hillside site with views across the Los Angeles basin to the sea. Harvey proved to be a difficult client, but in the late 1950s Lautner met his ideal client, Kenneth Reiner. Their collaboration would reshape the trajectory of his career. A wealthy aerospace inventor and entrepreneur, Reiner shared Lautner's curiosity about the new,

about improving things through design. Ostensibly Reiner hired Lautner to design his own house, Silvertop, on the top of the hill overlooking Silverlake reservoir, but their shared enthusiasms turned the project into a laboratory for reinventing the systems, materials, products, and details of the ideal house. Reiner placed the workshops and technicians of his industries at the architect's disposal. It was Lautner's contemporaneous answer to the Case Study House Program that *Arts + Architecture* magazine editor John Entenza was using to put new technology in the service of the average home.

As always it was not simply the technol-ogy that interested Lautner and Reiner; it was putting those inventions to use in creating dynamic spaces for living. So the living room (the size of three ordinary tract houses) was sheltered by a single curving pre-stressed concrete roof, eliminating structural walls or columns. The views on either side beneath the vaulted roof were entirely open through walls of glass - and the side overlooking the lake and mountain views was a curtain of frameless glass panels that slid aside at the push of a button to unite indoors and out. The site's original open hilltop was re-invented as a living space.

The response to Silvertop proved once again that conventional critics did not know what to make of Lautner. While Los Angeles-based writer Esther McCoy could clearly see how he was translating the means and needs of the modern age into a truly modern architecture, the *Saturday Evening Post*'s critic got tangled in old preconceptions, wondering if it was a 'Dream House or Nightmare?'

Silvertop set Lautner on a new course. It brought him to the attention of a class of wealthy clients who thought independently, leading him to a series of large houses on magnificent sites where he could explore his ideas. The Sheats-Goldstein, Elrod, Marbrisa, Hope, Segel, and Pacific Coast houses, for example, each defined, solved, and realised astonishing answers to a range of creative challenges.

Toward the end of his life, Lautner began to achieve the recognition he deserved. Exhibits and books on his work appeared in

Japan and Europe. His own book of his work was published. After his death more books appeared, and in 2008 the Hammer Museum and Getty Research Institute in Los Angeles held an exhibit and symposium on his career. Today when the masters of Los Angeles architecture are listed in academic or popular media, Schindler, Neutra, and Lautner are always named.

The heart of Lautner's artistry was his willingness to put it all on the line each time he took on a new project. He pondered the problem, he studied the site; Leonard Malin, his client on the Chemosphere house, remembers seeing Lautner sitting alone on the precipitous site night after night, until the darkness closed in and only the glowing tip of his cigarette could be seen. True Modern architecture had to be original. Lautner would work through the parameters, over and over, until he arrived at the ideal solution. It was a process and a commitment that took his designs far beyond the conventional. When current technology was insufficient to achieve that ideal, he came as close as it would allow. Fortunately he had the opportunity sometimes to return to a house decades later (as at the Sheats-Goldstein house) and push it even nearer to the ideal he had originally conceived. This is the soul of Modernism.

Serendipity

Jan-Richard Kikkert

It's 25 December 2003, and I'm walking along the quay of Balboa Island in Southern California. I'm here with my wife and child, visiting my brother-in-law, who takes us to a place that's famous for its sumptuous Christmas decorations. There's one house in amongst all the extravagance that's not decorated. In the dark it most resembles an enormous animal that washed ashore with its mouth wide open. I recognize it immediately, even though I can't place it straight away. When I get home, I discover that it is John Lautner's Rawlins house. Lautner is an architect about whom I bought a book at the Architectura & Natura book shop in Amsterdam in 1998, which presents an overview of his body of work that he put together himself. It contains images and text about forty-nine works, supplemented by an interview and a list of works and most important publications. The accidental visit awakened my interest, and when we were in California two years after, I decided to visit the house that most appealed to me in the book, the Sheats-Goldstein residence. Because the owner has his own website, it is easy to write to him. He asks us to come close to sunset, because he has a *Skyspace* by James Turrell in his garden, which is shown to its greatest advantage around that time. Although Goldstein gave us the address, the entrance is fairly well hidden among the dime-a-dozen show-off houses in Beverly Hills. Only a striking gate gives away that something extraordinary is hidden in behind. After we drive straight down a steep hill, the beginning of a covered entrance to another world becomes visible on the left. A narrow corridor leads to a water patio, where a path made of glass stepping stones crosses a pond with large goldfish, forming the entrance to the house. Our host is waiting for us and gives us a tour of the house. Although we recognize it, of course, from the photos in Lautner's book, the house is a complete surprise. Usually, a house that has been photographed well tends to underwhelm in reality, but something else is going on here. Although it was built using the same form language and materials, the house consists of spaces that are very diverse in character, which are connected in such a way as to create a dynamic whole. There is a passage, covered by a wooden roof, which gives access to the water patio, though one's view of it is delayed by a bend in the passage. Here the house seems to consist of only one floor, and the view of Los Angeles is still completely hidden. The front door gives access to a low space where you can choose between three directions. A sharp right takes you to the dining room, which leads to the kitchen, a left brings you into the living room, which has a roof that seems to be folded over the space, and diagonally on the right, a staircase next to a passageway leads down to the master bedroom suite. Although it is impossible to describe the house without mentioning the many motorised elements, like the various glass roofs that slide open at the push of a button, or the television that can rise up from one of the concrete tables, that is not where the essence of the spectacle of this house lies. I have never seen anything like the way in which the spaces, which mostly blend into one another, are defined by their relation to the environment, the way in which they are defined by the different ceilings. The ubiquitous sharp corners in the floor plans, sections and façades and the way in which the terrace is on a subtle incline in order to prevent you from plunging into the depth give you the sense that this is architecture on the edge.

Around three hours later, we're outside again. We're very impressed by the remarkable combination of the exuberant architecture and the intimacy of the spaces.

Dropping in on Lautner unannounced, like my wife Christine and I did on Philip Johnson in 1999, was sadly no longer possible, because he died in 1994. But it was now clear to me that I also wanted to see Lautner's other works. An opportunity presented itself sooner than I had expected. In addition to having my own architectural firm, I have been teaching on various architecture programmes since 1989. One of them is the ArtEZ Academy of Architecture in Arnhem. The school has a rich tradition in terms of field trips. There is a field trip at the end of each year of study, for the whole school plus a handful of teachers. That year we went to Munich, ten hours away by train. During the trip, the director of the academy, Ko Jacobs, asked me to organise a field trip for the third-year students. At that point in their studies, they have already seen a good deal of canonical works, so there is room for something more radical. I decided to focus on one architect, see a whole oeuvre in a short period of time, to showcase how an architect develops throughout a lifetime. The stipulations were clear: a lot of exceptional work, situated relatively close together, in a country where I speak the language, and which is easy to visit in a week. The choice was soon made. Back at home in the Netherlands, it soon became clear to me that the locations of Lautner's work were well hidden. Despite its unsightly, miniscule pictures, Esther McCoy and Barbara Goldstein's *Guide to U.S. Architecture 1940-1980*, published in 1982, had always been an excellent adviser for travelling through the United States, but there were only three buildings by Lautner listed in it: Silvertop [63/116], Chemosphere [76] and Elrod [98/108/110]. David Gebhard and Robert Winter's five-hundred-page *Architecture in Los Angeles: A Complete Guide*, from 1985, was more helpful, as was the later edition from 2003, *An Architectural Guidebook to Los Angeles*. Although it was actually too extensive for field work due to its bulk, this book contained nine other designs by Lautner in addition to Silvertop and Chemosphere. And the 2003 edition has two additional projects compared to the 1985 edition. But that was it, for the time being. There also exists a John Lautner Foundation, which responded dryly to my questions that addresses are not disclosed to the public. For a moment, the idea seemed to stall, until I laid hands on Barbara-Ann Campbell-Lange's 1999 book from the *Big Series* by Taschen: *John Lautner 1911-1994*. Aside from a beautiful selection of works complete with floor plans and clear explanatory texts, there was a copy of a map in the back of the book, drawn by Lautner himself on tracing paper, which marked the names of the clients and the locations of Lautner's work in pencil. Initially done with a stencil, and later simply by hand, it started with his own house, from 1939, and continued up until Malin, from 1958. For some projects, the name had been crossed out and replaced by another one, like the Schaeffer house, a name that was first changed to Palmer and then to Wallace. Luckily Google Earth had been introduced in 2005: maybe it did not work everywhere, and maybe it was not in focus, but it was still very useful. That made it possible to track down houses with a very specific roof shape, like Elrod in Palm Springs. With a treasure map and the floor plans from Lautner's own book, I managed to find one after another of Lautner's projects that were on the map. Not everything was on the map, because at a certain point Lautner had stopped, or because the project was outside the area shown on the map. I undertook a quest to find all the projects that were listed in the back of Lautner's monograph, where I wrote to everyone who I suspected might be able to help me. Many people I spoke to also had Lautner's book and wanted to go with me when the time came. One of the people I emailed was Tycho Saariste, whom I had already asked to join me to visit Villa Karma by Adolf Loos when I finally got permission to go into it. Tycho's father, Rein Saariste, was a lecturer at Delft University of Technology, and had helped many generations of architects start out. I knew they had been in Los Angeles together. Of everyone I had told about my plans, Tycho was the most persistent in wanting to join me. Although he wasn't connected to ArtEZ Arnhem, I realised that the quest I was on would take a very long time if I was on my own, and that enthusiastic help would be very welcome. We were a golden team. During the preparations for the first trip we both looked up addresses and phone numbers; according to our division of roles, I called the inhabitants to convince them of the importance of our visit, while Tycho kept an overview of the appointments we'd made and the travel time between the various houses. We also contacted Judy Lautner and Karol Peterson Lautner, Lautner's two oldest daughters, and his biographers, Frank Escher and Alan Hess, and collaborators such as Helena Arahuete, Duncan Nicholson, Vaughan Trammell and Ken Kellogg. The two of us were only in touch via email.

The inception of the Lautner virus

Tycho Saariste

In 1994, when I was a student at the Faculty of Architecture of Delft University of Technology, I went on a field trip to Los Angeles and San Francisco. The aim of the trip was mainly to visit works by architects like Neutra, Schindler and contemporary architects like Gehry and Morphosis. There was also a description of a number of houses by Lautner, with a small photo, in the L.A. architecture guide. We wrote to the inhabitants on the off chance that they would be willing to show us around. A 'side issue' like this introduces some variation in the programme. For me, discovering Lautner was the highlight of the trip. As a student, I had always been a great admirer of modern houses from the twenties. The foundation for this style was laid in Le Corbusier's spatial houses. After the war, Modernism went in a new direction – I could appreciate its openness and transparency, but I often found the houses too austere and sterile. When I visited Lautner's Wolff House, I found what I was looking for: a house that is spatial, open and transparent, but also offers a sense of privacy, security and warmth. It is a modern form of organic architecture, where it is not the dictates of form, but pragmatic reasons that form the basis of the design. It is never boring and shows that austerity and spatiality can indeed go together with the beginnings of organic architecture. Whatever your opinion of it is, it definitely makes for lovely houses that would be wonderful to live in.

Between 1994 and 1999, a number of books about Lautner's work appeared: first of all, his own monograph, which I was given as a Christmas present in 1998 by my employer at the time, John Bosch. This book was the first to showcase Lautner's versatility. All the houses are different, but almost all of them exhibit unconventional solutions to common problems. The book fueled my fascination and made me want to see more of his work. To this end, I went to L.A. again in late 1999 with two fellow architects, but most of Lautner's work turned out to be impossible to find without extensive research carried out beforehand.

In 2006, I get an email from Jan-Richard. I had got to know him in the eighties when he was studying with my father and visited us regularly. At the time I was still at secondary school myself, but I was already more in-terested in architecture than most teenagers – apparently the apple doesn't fall far from the tree. Jan-Richard writes that he has plans to go to Los Angeles with a group of students to study John Lautner's work, because he knows that I went to Los Angeles at university. I reply immediately: 'I'm coming with you!' The same evening, I get to work with Google Earth, looking for a match between the photos, the floor plans and the satellite photos. During earlier visits, these resources did not exist yet, and it was practically impossible to find the information without contacting the right people. Now there turns out to be a whole host of information available, easy to find on a simple home computer. We both spend long nights searching for the houses, sometimes until deep into the night. We send each other emails when we've found another one. We don't go to sleep unless we've found at least one. Some houses frustrate us because it takes us at least three evenings to find them; others are tracked down within an hour. The Canadian architect Martin Daoust, who has a Lautner Forum and has previously carried out a similar search, turns out to be an invaluable help. Initially he is reticent about giving us information, but after a while, when he notices that we also share new findings, he becomes more forthcoming and gives us important hints about the location of certain houses. It turns out that he himself never got around to visiting Lautner's work. In the end we ask if he is interested in coming with us, but he is seriously ill, which makes travel impossible.

In April 2007, Jan Richard and I travel to Los Angeles with seven students and a teacher, Machiel Spaan. We visit a large part of Lautner's work on this trip. In the years that follow, we take seven more trips to the American continent. These became beautiful expeditions that deserve to be described. There are already several books about Lautner, but we have chosen to write down our personal experiences, and at the same time, to give a complete overview of all of Lautner's built works for the first time.

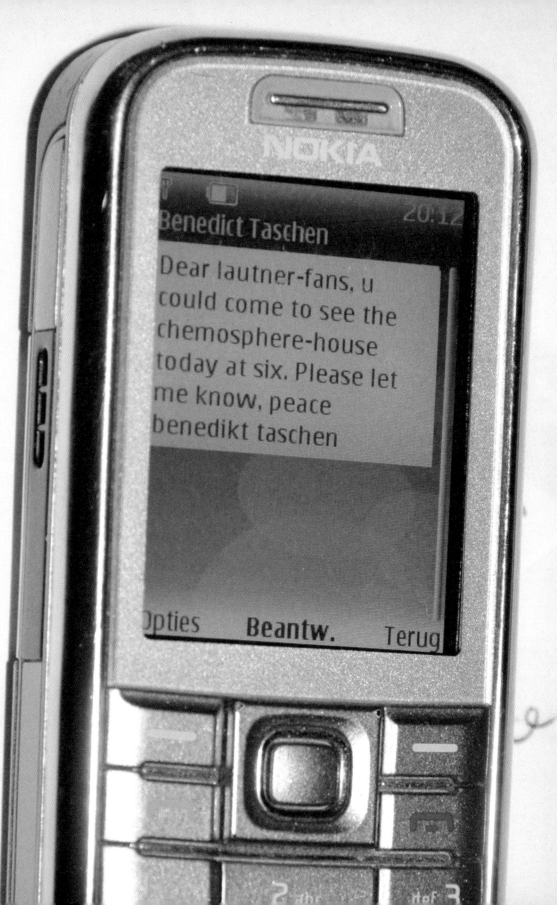

ALDRICH

#123: Swimming pool and addition,
1977-1978, extant
501 N Cahuenga Blvd, Los Angeles, CA 90004

Thursday, 10 July 2008

A project that is mentioned in Lautner's monograph, but without an address or status, is a project for Mr and Mrs Robert Aldrich. The first drawing we find in the Lautner archive shows an attic renovation from 1953, followed by an office pavilion in the garden of a house on Longwood Avenue in L.A. The section shows a volume on stilts, where the walls are conceived as large blocks of stone. It's very possible that it was actually built. While most of the drawings are floor plans and sections, we also find a perspective drawing, in colour, dating from 18 November 1967, for something that looks like a sculptural garden, complete with a gate, a well and a large gargoyle coming out of the side of the box on stilts. Then there is another working drawing for a bar room at the same address. JRK: 'I looked for Robert Aldrich endlessly. Because the history of Hollywood has been well documented by websites such as the International Movie Data Base, we can now trace clients of whom we only have a name and the year of the design. This is how I got in touch with the film director Otto Preminger's children, and I also find a photo of the director Robert Aldrich. There seems to be a relation between winning an important prize and shortly afterwards, commissioning Lautner to build a house.' By now, the container labelled 'Aldrich' has revealed various designs, with addresses, including an 'extension and pool for Mr and Mrs Robert Aldrich' for a different location. The swimming pool is shaped like an athletics track, and the extension is a simple, rectangular volume. Another drawing turns up for yet another extension of an Aldrich house, a simple study and a rectangular pool. And another

design for an extension of a kitchen, striking because of the large arches on the sections. The designs were made in a period of 25 years. If this has really all been built, it would mean we have found three new Lautners.

As soon as we leave the archive, we get to work. Now that we've seen the plans for three different locations, we are burning with curiosity to find out what is left of them. Nothing on Google Earth indicates that the building was ever built at the first address, for which there are no less than four different renovation proposals for the attic. The same goes for the second address. For the third address, Lautner designed a study and a swimming pool. Google Earth unmistakably shows the shape of the swimming pool. We make no attempt to find out who lives there now; instead we just drive there. We find an unimaginative retro-style house on the corner of the street. There is no answer when we ring the doorbell. We walk around the corner, where a ribbon window in an addition clashes with the rest of the house. This could be Lautner's. The long garden wall, which masks the difference in height between the pavement and the garden, is completely covered with ivy, so

the whole city is full of flags with Lautner's name on them, so there's no escaping him. We have made him genuinely happy with our news that he owns a real 'Lautner'. The name Aldrich rings a bell: he produces an old nameplate with the names Bob Aldrich and Al Van Schmuss from the garage. Facing the garden, the addition has a wall of windows with a six-foot roof overhang. We completely forget to ask if we can have a look inside, too. When the house is put up for sale a few years later, Lautner's name is prominently mentioned.

previous: Weinstein
next: Stevens

that we can see very few details. JRK: 'In order to catch a glimpse of what it looks like behind the wall, Tycho aims his camera over the wall with outstretched arms, as it turn out, right in the owner's face, who pops up like a jack-in-the-box to ask what we think we're up to.' When we tell him that he's been swimming in a Lautner design for years, his face lights up. Because of the exhibition,

ALEXANDER

Saturday, 5 May 2007

The Alexander house, from 1951, is situated in Long Beach in a typical suburb. It is a house where we are immediately invited to come by *and* where the original client still lives. Her husband was Lautner's dentist. The house is not very striking from the outside, a one-storey house on level terrain with an overhanging roof on all sides. Judy Lautner accompanies us. Mrs Alexander recognizes her immediately: 'The last time I saw you, you were six years old.'

The front door is in a part of the façade that's slightly recessed; the roof sticks out by about nine feet here. Above the entrance Lautner has made large openings in the roof, so that plants can grow here, covered, almost up to the front of the house. Like in many American houses, the front door leads you straight into the living room. The interior is a surprise, after all. The living area consists of a large open space, divided up into different parts. The sitting room is two steps lower, while the roof goes up gently and asymmetrically (like in the Schaeffer house). A half wall with bookcases separates the entrance from the sitting area. When you walk past the book-cases, you get to the separate master bedroom. The outdoors is subtly linked to the indoors because there is a strip of green between the floor and the wall which starts outside, comes in past the front door and ends after nine feet in a cutaway in the brick floor that serves as a planter trough. Lush plants grow here, illuminated by the skylight above it (like in the Bergren house). Behind this planter trough is the kitchen, where the daylight comes from an internal window. This main part of the house, which is parallel to the street, also contains the garage, the dining room and the den. Connected by the overhanging roof with its large cutaways, a bedroom wing extends from the house at a sixty-degree angle, with two small bedrooms and one large one. Because of all the glass, each room makes

the most of its connection to the garden. The house has barely been changed, apart from a section of the covered terrace next to the dining room, which has been closed up. The old interior photos in Lautner's monograph show the same furniture there is now, and even various knickknacks on the bookshelves are still in the same place. One can spot examples of many themes that were central to Lautner's work during this period in the house. There is, for example, the fitted furniture marking the edge of a difference in level, like in Lautner's own house from 1939, which separates the living room from the entrance when you come in, something he would do again in Harpel 1 six years later; the predominantly flat roof, which subtly increases in height to let in light so the space below is defined, like in the Schaeffer house built two years earlier; and the central, built-in planter trough, which comes back in the Bergren house from 1951. It's good to see that the house still looks perfect after more than fifty years. While one of our students, Loe van den Ven, finds a four-leafed clover in the garden, we get ready to drive on to a house built almost thirty years after the Alexander house and that sparked JRK's decision to immerse himself in Lautner.

previous: Kaynar Factory
next: Rawlins

ASTOR FARM

Lautner is said to have realised a small building for Astor Farm in Indio. Our research in the archives yielded a set of sketches from 1942. In the war, Lautner earned his keep with various odd jobs, including plumbing. The Astor Farm in Indio was one of the few assignments he had then, and it is also one of the first works carried out under his own name. It seems to be an extension of an extant house, referred to as a 'caretaker's cottage'

mystery. Aside from these few sketches, we weren't able to find a trace of it – even after years of searching on the internet, through historic societies or in the archives. Apart from the drawings in the archive, at the time of writing we haven't found any more information about this 'future house'. One of the secondary effects of creating a comprehensive overview of a person's work is that new material tends to turn up after publication of the book. We hope this will also be the case here.

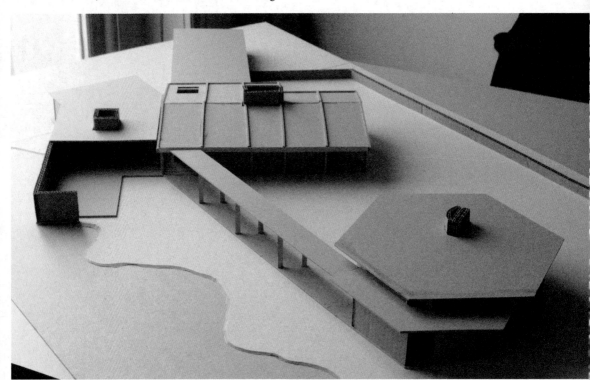

on the drawing, with a 'future guest room' on the north side of the cottage. On the west side, there was also a 'future house', which was connected to the cottage by a 'covered walk'. The floor plan of the cottage consists of circular parts. We find another drawing of the 'future house' with four versions of what is referred to as a 'ranch house' on one sheet of paper. There is a rectangular floor plan, one where part of that floor plan has been rotated by 45 degrees, a round version, and one with angles of 30 and 120 degrees. This gives some insight into Lautner's way of working, although we can only speculate as to whether he showed the drawings to his clients in this form. While we are not certain about the exact location, an informed source tells us that it's a place where there is now an ordinary house. Which of these designs were carried out and which were not sadly remains a

Wednesday, 2 May 2007

The Baldwin house, completed in 1955 and famous from the photo were an enormous tree emerges from the terrace, is occupied by someone who consistently rejects every attempt at a visit from us: Mrs Baldwin, who commissioned the house together with her late husband. JRK: 'In the consecutive years that we went to L.A., I spoke to her every time. Whenever I call her, she knows who I am immediately, and the answer is always a resounding no.' She does tell us that she is about to start with some minor remodels, which set off the alarm bells for us. There is an original, unrestored Mercedes 190 from the fifties parked outside the front door, covered under a thick layer of bird droppings. That does not bode well for the state of the interior. The house is situated on a road that goes up a steep hill, so that you can look down on the roof of the house. The main shape is a polygon with sharp points. It is a small house, but with a number of striking details: the living room is triangular, with a ceiling that hangs down in an inverse pyramid, which makes the space grow higher towards the edges. A large tree sticks straight through the cantilevered terrace. The side of the house has a curious pattern of slit-shaped openings, like the Bergren house, which dates from the same period. Towards the street there is complete privacy: the bedroom corridor, which is on the street side, is lit from above, through a strip of glass louvres, while the rest of the façade is completely closed off. This theme comes back in one of Lautner's last works, the Boykoff Remodel.

previous: Hancock
next: Lautner

Sunday, 5 April 2009

When JRK calls again in 2009, Mrs Baldwin is more accommodating: we should call her as soon as we arrive in L.A. However, our phone calls go un-answered, and because the house is very close to our hotel, we decide to drive past it after all, one early morning. We ring the doorbell, but there is no answer, although we have the feeling someone's home. The house seems to be completely in its original condition, but it is pretty run-down. It is difficult to see from the street whether the tree that was growing through the terrace is still there. It looks as though we're going to have to wait until the owner dies before we can see the house. From this point of view, the house is in the same category as Mauer and Zimmerman: the owners seem to be so embarrassed of the state of their house that they don't want to show it to outsiders.

previous: Turner
next: Fischer

Wednesday, 8 April 2009

We drop by the Baldwin house once more that same week. We don't manage to speak to the occupants then either, so we don't get the chance to see the echo of the peculiar little Bergren windows and the precursor to the expressive ceilings in the Crippled Children's Society and the Marina Fine Arts Store with our own eyes.

previous: Garcia
next: Howe

Saturday 11 November 2017

When we try to get in touch again after eight years, neither our letter nor our phone call is answered. As we are faced with a closed door yet again, it seems like nothing has changed, apart from a few trees that have been cut down. When we look inside, our suspicion that the interior is still fully in its original condition is confirmed: even the furniture we recognize from a photo taken in the fifties is still in the same place.

previous: Salkin
next: Zimmerman

#34: Baxter-Hodiak, Remodel house,
1949-1951, extant
#110: Gefsky, Addition, 1971, extant
8650 Pine Tree Pl, Los Angeles, CA 90069

Tuesday, 1 May 2007

This is the remodel of a house from the twenties, for the actress Anne Baxter, Frank Lloyd Wright's granddaughter. In the extension, Lautner tried to make a bridge between the living room and the garden. A curved, built-in bench with an integrated flower box runs from indoors to outdoors through the façade, according to a small photo in the back of Lautner's monograph. When we ring the bell, a nurse opens the door and lets us know that the master of the house is very ill and can't receive any visitors. Upon further insistence, he goes to ask the owner anyway, and we are invited in. The man, Harold Gefsky, an agent in the film industry, appears more dead than alive, but still seems to take pleasure in receiving us and tells us stories about Hollywood in the fifties. He bought the house in 1966 and now he is lying here, on a bed in the middle of the living room, waiting for the end. Gefsky hired Lautner in 1971 for the addition of an extra room. Lloyd Dysland made the construction calculations. It is likely that this project was carried out, but we were not able to see what exactly was added when we visited in 2007, and besides, the house is so full of stuff that it's hard to find anything of Lautner's here. The smell of approaching death is overwhelming. We search in vain for the only element of this house that seems worthwhile, as far as we know: the bench that goes through the façade. Unfortunately, it is no longer there. An interesting detail is that the house was thought to be haunted, before Harold Gefsky lived in it. A year after our visit in 2007, Gefsky dies at the age of ninety, and the house is put up for sale. On the site where the house is listed, there are a number of interior photos of the empty house, where Lautner's interventions can clearly be seen. In 2009, the house is bought by an Italian company, which hired the architectural firm Johnston Marklee to restore the house and fix up the interior.

Afterwards, the house is listed as for sale again in 2011, with an asking price more than one and a half times as high as the last time.

previous: Shusett
next: Sunset Plaza Gate

Thursday, 3 May 2007

In the heart of the oldest part of Hollywood, there is a square with a shop called Beachwood Market.

In 1950, Lautner was asked to turn a building from the twenties into a corner shop. Lautner's changes were remarkable. He replaced the two arches in the façade with a slanting, double-height glass front that protrudes out from the building. He installed a curved ceiling, which curls upwards towards the façade. As a result, daylight penetrates much further into the building and you can see the Hollywood Hills and the Hollywood sign between the shelves. The raised ceiling is a familiar feature in other projects too, like the Schaeffer house and the Bubbling Wells Resort, but the combination with a curved ceiling is unique. Here we see Lautner break free from the shackles of European Modernism, with its simple, straight form language. Initially, Lautner had imagined this ceiling as a mirrored ceiling, but this was probably never carried out. He wanted to make a mirrored ceiling in the Roven house in 1987, but unfortunately that house was never built. Lautner's remodel of Beachwood Market was later altered again: the shop was expanded to include the adjacent building and Lautner's subtle entrance was moved. This had the effect of completely changing the circulation in the shop. Lautner's original client still owns the supermarket, and he is still in good health. JRK: "'You must be JR" he creaks, as we drive up in our two burgundy Dodge Grand Caravans. Mr Williams, who I spoke to extensively on the phone, welcomes us. Again, we are struck by how full of vitality Lautner's clients still are.' He also takes us to his own house (Williams), which Lautner designed for him in 1948, two years before Beachwood Market.

previous: Midtown School
next: Williams

#4: House, 1940-1941, extant
7714 Woodrow Wilson Dr, Los Angeles, CA 90046

Thursday, 10 July 2008

The 1941 Bell house is one of Lautner's first independent projects. The assignment was passed on to him (just like the Mauer house assignment) by Frank Lloyd Wright, who had got stuck because the costs for his design were getting out of hand. Wright's influence can still be found in the house, in the use of materials and the detailing. Just like Wright often did, Lautner makes the layout dynamic by putting the living room at an angle in relation to the rest of the house. The living room is a kind of island in the garden, reachable through a narrow hallway. There's room to eat both inside and outside. The angle results in a surprising perspective from the glass corner windows, which face the spectacular view diagonally. TS: 'When I visited the house as a student in 1994, it was a treasure, in perfect condition, apart from a modest addition.'

The impression we get of the house now is a completely different one. The house is empty; a complete renovation is drawing to a close. The house has the same owner as fourteen years earlier, but apparently, he decided it was necessary to make changes to the house. The interior seems to be fairly intact, but the diagonal view has closed up. When we get outside, we are shocked to see that the beautiful red brick terrace with steps has been replaced by a brand-new terrace made of large, slightly tinted concrete slabs. It is completely at odds with the refined character of the house. The dark red bricks of the original terrace gave it something earthy, which made it seem as though the house was literally emerging from the ground. It's a mystery to us why someone would change something like that. The brick chimney with a fireplace on the outside wall has not escaped either. There is a beautiful black-and-white photo of this part of the building by Julius Shulman. He must have held the camera at knee height to take it. The original fireplace has

been bricked up carelessly and there is an outdoor grill. What is most upsetting of all is the way the electrical wiring has been screwed onto the wall: apparently, shoddy workmen are an international affliction.

But the house is in a fantastic location, on a huge stretch of land in the middle of the Hollywood Hills. There's a pavilion in the garden, on the edge of Laurel Canyon, which could even have been designed by Lautner, given its detailing. The Bell house is mainly known from photos by Julius Shulman, for instance the aforementioned photo of the exterior with fireplace and pergola, the interior photo taken diagonally across the house with the three square skylights and an exterior photo of the entrance with carport, all taken shortly after the house was completed. Then there are the photos Alan Weintraub took, in *The Architecture of John Lautner* by Alan Hess, including one of the hallway connecting the main building to the extension, which is most likely not by Lautner. Visiting the house melds together all these fragmented images into a balanced house, which stays close to the language of Lautner's mentor in terms of architectural expression. The distinctive features are for example the pyramid-shaped stucco ceiling with horizontal wooden beams in the living room and the glass corner windows. Of course it's a good thing that a house like this is renovated, but some alterations really come at the expense of quality.

suite on top of the house, among other things. JAG further developed the plans, but the renovations were cancelled for budgetary reasons. It's a good thing that the plans weren't carried out. There's a photo of a scale model of the extension floating around on the internet, and it looks like it is on a completely different scale to the original building, which would have led to a disaster, without Lautner's direct influence.

previous: Fischer
next: Flowers That Bloom in the Spring Tra La

In the early nineties, the owner, Larry W., was working with the architecture firm JAG (John Ash Group) to develop a shopping centre. Lautner's former collaborator Guy Zebert was working for the firm at the time. W. also asked John Ash to carry out a series of upgrades on his house. When it looked as though the planned work would exceed a renovation of the bathroom, Zebert put John Ash in touch with Lautner himself, who was appointed as an advisor and made a sketch for a new master

BERGREN

#44: House, 1951-1953, burnt down 1957
#70: Rebuilt and addition, 1957, extant
7316 Caverna Dr, Los Angeles, CA 90068

Tuesday, 1 May 2007

On our journey, we happened to visit the obscure Bergren copy in Whitewater before we visited the original Bergren house, built in 1953. It occupies a specific place in Lautner's oeuvre: the house is small, spatial and inventive, but above all pleasant to live in, witness the fact that the client rebuilt it to be almost exactly the same after it had been completely destroyed by fire a few years after completion. It lies somewhat concealed on a hilltop, where there is no doubt a fantastic view. But at first sight, these surroundings look less inspiring than the boulders near the copy. The entrance is about thirty feet away from the road, reachable via an insanely steep driveway. The first thing you see of the house is a lavishly designed carport. Thanks to our visit to the pirated house, we know more or less what to expect, but even so, the original is surprising, and not only because the view is different. The walls of the living room, which ensure that you look out over the landscape from a different angle, the mini patio in the middle of the space, which originally served to drain the rainwater from the roof, and the oversized planter trough along the side wall of the living room with the peculiar windows: these things do make the house extraordinary. The interior has recently been renovated. Sadly, the owner has tricked the house out with a shiny concrete floor, a top-of-the-line stainless steel kitchen and a large widescreen television, which his girlfriend can't keep her eyes off during our visit. These choices are so clearly in contrast with the fragile balance of a simple fifties house that it almost hurts our eyes. An extra room has been built between the carport and the living room, as a result of which this house has definitively lost its original charm. Still, it is a nice house with a split-level living room, separating the sitting and dining parts. A ten foot square mini patio originally brought nature indoors, but when we look inside, we see that the patio, which was the focal point of

the whole floor plan, the heart of the house, has disappeared. The large triangular planter trough behind the sofa is empty, and part of it has become a pond. The atmosphere that Lautner created is no longer here, while it was preserved in the copy.

previous: Bergren Studio
next: Sheats Apartments

Sunday, 5 April 2009

If you follow Lautner's houses on the internet, you see more and more of them for sale or to let. This also applies to the Bergren house. Even a simple house like this is worth multiple visits, because a different time of day yields different insights, or we can photograph parts that we forgot in 2007. When we visit the house in 2009, there is nobody home, so we can walk around the house at our ease and photograph the outside properly. The façade that looks out over the valley will later give us the key to finding a property that was very difficult to track down: the Seletz Studio. When we re-examine the façades, the house turns out to be more refined than we had originally thought. The floor-to-ceiling glass panes on the rear façade are slightly staggered, for instance, so that there is no need for extra window jambs for more stability.

previous: Carling
next: Coneco Corp

BERGREN STUDIO

#75: Studio, 1957, demolished
7312 Caverna Dr, Los Angeles, CA 90068

Tuesday, 1 May 2007

The Bergren house is no more than a stone's throw away from the Garcia, Eisele, Carling and Deutsch houses. There are rumours that Lautner designed a studio next to this house for the same client. The current owner of the house that was built where the studio used to be confirms that this studio used to belong to Ted Bergren, but also informs us that there is barely anything left of it because of a fire in the eighties, not to be confused with the fire that reduced the Bergren house to ashes. We arrive late for our appointment and no one is there anymore. Sadly, this means we can't carry out our own research on the house. Outside, there is nothing that refers to Lautner. Guy Zebert tells us that the studio was built for Ted and Betty Bergren's son John to live in, who was named after John Lautner. Following Betty Bergren's death in 1968, the studio was subdivided and rented out until Ted Bergren retired and moved to Hawaii. The original Bergren Studio consisted of a large open space with a bathroom. A spiral-shaped concrete slope connected this space to the patio below, complete with a matching roof of curved, laminated wooden joists. There are no photos of it, and Guy adds, 'Interesting how time changes perspective. At the time we were doing this work, it had no significance to anyone. Only personal satisfaction to us and the client.'

In 2017 we visit Guy Zebert and ask him if he can sketch the Bergren Studio. Despite claiming to suffer from a faltering memory, the 88-year-old

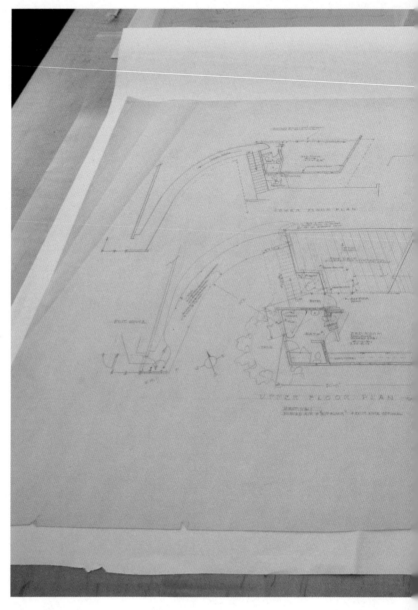

Lautner employee manages to reconstruct the project right down to the dimensions of the joists and columns that were used. The next day we find drawings in the archives that confirm his sketches. But Guy did say that it was a simplified version of the drawings that was built, due to financial reasons. An interesting part of the project was the covered walkway, which curved upwards and connected the Bergren house to the studio. The building that now stands on the same spot no longer has anything in common with Lautner's design, aside from its foundations.

previous: Garcia
next: Bergren

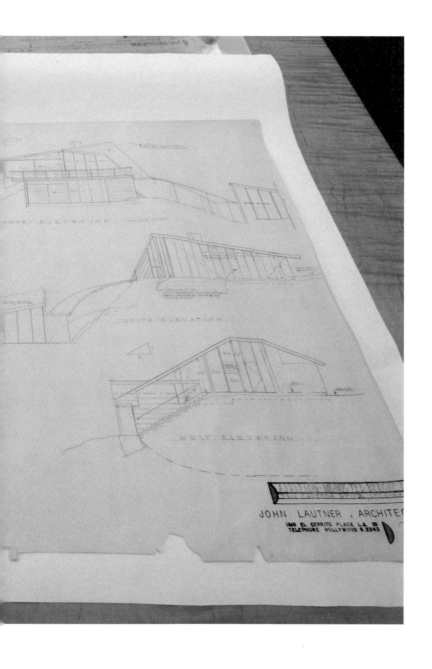

BEVERLY HILLS ATHLETIC CLUB

#12: Remodel, 1946, demolished 1970s
120 S Roxbury Dr, Beverly Hills, CA 90212

We hope to find material on the Beverly Hills Athletic Club in the Lautner archives. In 1945, Lautner began a partnership with Douglas Honnold, a successful commercial architect. Together they designed a number of projects, including Darrow Office Building, Coffee Dan's, and this club. The club is said to have been built in 1946, but we couldn't find anything else on it, including whether it still exists or not. Our hunt led us to Elizabeth Honnold Harris, Douglas Honnold's daughter. She turned out to be an invaluable source of information for our research.

The collaboration between Lautner and Honnold ended abruptly in 1946, when Lautner had an affair with Honnold's wife, Elizabeth. As a result, John and Mary got divorced, and Mary went back to Marquette, Michigan with the four children. In 1949, John and Elizabeth were married and bought a house at 1820 El Cerrito Place, where John converted the garage into a drawing office. Honnold's daughter Elizabeth lived here as a teenager from the late forties to the early fifties. She has an excellent memory for all kinds of information about the firm, the projects and the clients. Her information is especially valuable as the archives from the time of Honnold and Lautner's collaboration has been lost. We did research on this, too: Honnold's firm was taken over by a large commercial firm. When that firm ceased to exist, the archives were stored in a cellar, which was then devastated by a fire. Large parts of the archives were lost. After the remains were moved elsewhere, there was another fire there. Now there's really nothing left of them.

Elizabeth gave a lively description of the interior of the Beverly Hills Athletic Club: 'We always called

it "the Club"... It had a handsome street entrance by John's magical touch with redwood, concrete, elegant lighting and some giant planter areas with giant (what else? John loved BIG STUFF) plants – elephant ears, mega-size floppy tropical thingies, etc. Coming up on it at night was super... and

inside, one stepped down into the dining room and the bar was offset behind some (John's magic again) redwood vertical panels. I remember having dinner there on many occasions.' She couldn't remember the location anymore, only more or less what the street looked like. After years of searching, we found a magazine article about the club, published in *Arts & Architecture* in 1946. Lautner's monograph does mention a club, but it does not say whether this is the Beverly Hills Athletic Club. During the remodel of the club, Lautner made a second construction under an extant roof, which defines the space, but

2010, we saw blurry black-and-white pictures of the club for the first time.

only carries itself. On the drawings, there was also a church/mission station next door. Finally, a clue to help us find the address! The church was well known. However, we were very disappointed when we discovered only a large carpark at the address in question. During our fourth visit to the archive in

#114: House, 1973-1983, extant
#138: Pool and terrace addition, 1988, extant
6515 Point Lechuza Dr, Malibu, CA 90265

Friday, 4 May 2007

Malibu is a 'nice, quiet little beach community' that stretches out along the coast. Lautner built six houses here, including the Beyer house. TS: 'In 1999 I wanted to see as much of Lautner's work as possible after I had gone through everything in his monograph, but where do you start when the addresses are unknown and Google Earth doesn't exist yet? I thought that if you followed the Malibu coastline, you couldn't miss the Beyer house, because it's in an unbelievably beautiful location on a rock jutting into the sea. After combing the coast for hours, we found the house. I'd never seen anything like it: a house where the rocky coast seems to continue inside the house. I would have loved to go inside and have a look, but I was only given that chance years later.'

This is an extreme house for people with an extreme budget. Once we knew who it belonged to, it was easy to make an appointment. In 2007, with the generosity common to people of his calibre, the current owner not only agreed to a visit immediately, but also organized for the project architect Richard Turner to give us a personal tour of the house. The house serves as a holiday home and is kept in a permanent state of readiness in case the owner decides to go and stay there. There's a floor plan in Lautner's book, but it only encompasses part of the house. It seems like a dream job to be allowed to design a capital villa in a place like that, but for Lautner, the project was very frustrating. Because of the spectacular but vulnerable location, there was a long and painful process of obtaining the right permits: it took nearly ten years, from 1975 until 1983, before the house was finished. When the Coastal Commission finally agreed to the plans, costs had to be cut drastically. Lautner envisioned the house having a large concrete shell roof, that sloped down towards the sea. But the

project architect, Richard Turner, suggested making the roof out of wood and stucco. Although this made the house affordable, it also lost its force. Richard Turner: 'In the meantime, Lautner kept losing interest in this project, especially after he had started work on the nearby Pacific Coast house.' Although some elements betray Lautner's involvement, the house lacks the master's finishing touch. There is no relationship whatsoever between the refined organic floor plan and the dumpy roof.

Because the roof is so thick, the cut-out skylights look very unrefined.

Despite all this, it remains a remarkable house. The faint feeling of disappointment at first sight disappears when we walk around the house. As is frequently the case in Lautner's oeuvre, the façade facing the street is not very inviting, but when you enter the front door, you walk into a completely different world. This is something he was already doing forty years earlier, in the Hancock house:

when you come in, you arrive in a courtyard that leads to the heart of the house. The miracle of spatiality and the view is postponed for a long time, however. Because the rooms look out on the next bit of coastline, the view from these rooms is slightly different every time. The route through the house goes via the music room, which is situated on the second floor, in fact, the level you enter the house on. From here you have a beautiful view of the waves crashing on the rocks, while

is mainly concrete, with large boulders here and there, a combination that feels pleasant in this unruly landscape. The cream-coloured, stucco roof should have been made of concrete too, of course: that would have made it a masterpiece. Once you arrive in the living room, you're standing under an enormous curved roof between large rocks, with the sea almost reaching the façade. In the Elrod House, the rocks shape the space as they were found, but here they have been put in place. For some reason the whole design, for a Lautner, makes a rather insincere impression.

The emphatic presence of the ocean, with waves that slap the windows from time to time, goes a long way in making up for this, however. The living room extends to the outermost tip of the rocks. There is a large, concrete fireplace placed pontifically in the wall, comparable to the one in Segel, so that the magnificent view of the ocean turns into a view of a large fire, at night. As we are looking outside, dolphins jump out of the water right in front of us. If Lautner was able to make something like this without giving it his full attention, what must we expect when he pours his heart and soul into it, like he did with the Pacific Coast house?

previous: Garwood
next: Crippled Children's Society

the view of the horizon is obscured by the curved roof. The original plan that Lautner started out with was extended on both sides, with a gym on the south side and a bathroom wing on the north side, with an improbably large private bathroom for each of the two occupants. On the north side, there is a sculptural terrace with a swimming pool that is sheltered by a curved wall. There is a second wall with a jacuzzi behind it, and a terrace, a few steps down. The material used outdoors

#42: House, 1951-1952, demolished 1990
220 N Rockingham Ave, Los Angeles, CA 90049

During our visit to the archives in July 2008, the most important find is the complete set of drawings of the Bick House from 1952; we didn't know what it looked like before. The client, Manny Bick, and Lautner didn't get along. Lautner's step-daughter Elizabeth described Bick as 'a nasty little fellow with a lot of bookkeeping on his mind'. The Bick House seems to have disappeared off the face of the earth. It is said to have been torn down in 1990, but for a long time, we doubt whether it was ever built in the first place. There are no photos and we can find no one who remembers the house. This is remarkable, given the fascinating drawings in the archive. We finally find proof that it did really exist on www.historicaerials. com, which has many aerial photographs, including ones from the fifties. On an aerial photo of the location in question we can clearly see the contours of Lautner's design. Bick didn't live in the house for long, which Lautner himself referred to as 'poorly built'. Even so, it was a remarkable house with a pavilion-like construction, with each room in a separate wing. The living room is a high space in the shape of a semicircle, where the curved side is closed and the straight side is completely made of glass. This is all flanked by various parasol-shaped elements, which don't return in any of Lautner's other work. In 1990, the entire site was bulldozed to make room for a colonial-style villa that was pontifically erected in the middle of the plot.

When we visit the archives again in 2010, we finally find images of the Bick House. Each attempt at finding out more about this project until now has been fruitless. We did find drawings and even an extension design for a different client, 'Dr and Mrs D. Marcus, 9730 Wilshire Blvd'. There are various dates on the drawings, in Lautner's handwriting: 'July 1951', 'Oct 15 1951', 'feb 29 1952' and 'June 28 1957'. Five years after construction was completed, the house already seems to have had a new owner, who asked Lautner to

design a new wall and a pool at the same address. Whether these were ever put in is not clear. JRK: 'When I write to a Dr D. Marcus who has an office on Wilshire Boulevard in 2012, I get a reply saying I have written to the wrong Marcus. Could there be more D. Marcusses with an office at this address?' But now, we have finally found slides. The drawings showed a kind of large umbrellas as a covering for the terrace, which most resembled the

roof of the State Capitol Bank in Oklahoma City by Bailey, Bozalis, Dickinson and Roloff. This means these umbrellas were really built. The fifty-year-old slides are discoloured in that characteristic way: all the green has dis-appeared, and the red has remained. The central column that carries the circular roof is also a jamb. When we get home, we enlarge the photo properly and discover that Lautner himself is sitting inside, on the sofa.

It's strange that nobody seems to remember the house and that Lautner didn't include it in his monograph.

BOSUSTOW

*#69: House remodel, 1956-1958, extant
16154 High Valley Pl, Encino, CA 91436
#113: Cabin, 1972-1976, extant
1263 Lassen View Dr, Westwood (Lake Almanor),
CA 96137*

Thursday, 9 april 2009

In the list of works at the back of Lautner's monograph the Bosustow Cabin was a riddle: we have been searching for years for proof that this cabin was actually built and, if so, whether it still exists. We found drawings of it in the archive, but no address. The Google Earth images of this remote area, Lake Almanor in northern California, are extremely indistinct, nor are any reference points to be found in Street View. Bosustow also commissioned the UPA Studios in 1948. JRK: 'After a long search I managed to get in touch with one of his two sons: Tee Bosustow. We were delighted to hear that the cabin had indeed been built. He wrote that he had helped his father with the building, and even emailed me a photo.' He didn't know if it was still standing, hadn't been there since 1984, nor did he know its exact address. TS: 'In the end I sent the photo to the Almanor Country Club on the off-chance. To my surprise I later received an email from someone who said he was the current owner of the cabin. He was willing to make an appointment with us.'

On the trip that was the reason for our journey to California in April 2009, we are accompanied by Tee Bosustow, the son of Stephen Bosustow, who commissioned the Bosustow Cabin. He works, like his father, in animation. We pick him up in Van Nuys: a lively seventy-one-year-old who settles in on the back seat for two days and is very good company. As we drive out of L.A. our GPS tells us, 'In 466 miles, turn right.' Our journey, which already seemed like a heroic quest, is now a real road movie.

While we're in the car with Tee Bosustow, he remembers that Lautner, in addition to doing the UPA Studios and the Bosustow Cabin for his father,

also did some advisory work for the renovations of a house in Encino. We go to see the outside of the house. The detail of the tree that grows through a hole in the roof of the carport reminds us of Bergren and Silvertop and could certainly be Lautner's.

*previous: Oboler
next: Lautner (Three Rivers)*

Friday, 10 April 2009

After two days' driving, the last hours through snow-covered woods, we reach Lake Almanor. It is a peninsula and a gated community which you cannot enter without an appointment, but we are expected. When we get to the site, we do not recognise the cabin from drawings, but Bosustow manages with some difficulty, despite the various extensions on the street side, to find some features he recognises. On Google Street View, we had gone past the building several times without recognising anything of Lautner in it; we are slightly disappointed and afraid that the interior has been altered unrecognisably. But when the door of the Bosustow Cabin opens our fears prove ungrounded: inside it has hardly changed. Bosustow looks around eagerly, full of memories: the last time he visited the house was on his honeymoon!

The changes are mostly additions, including an

like in Pearlman Cabin and in Harpel 2. Because of the slanting windows, one's gaze is directed towards the lake, below. The roof slopes down with the hill, which further dramatizes one's view of the water. We have never seen anything like it, and certainly not in a simple cabin. All the interior walls are made of pecky cypress, a very exclusive kind of wood that gets strong grain patterns and a structure with holes after 125 years, because of a certain kind of fungus. The doors have been sawed out of the floor-to-ceiling boards in such a way that the patterns in the wood continue. The house has two stone elements: a wall by the entrance and a central chimney.

The owners think their cabin is very beautiful but have never heard of Lautner. They would like to renovate the kitchen, which is made of the same cypress wood as the rest of the house, and we do our very best to talk them out of the idea.

It seems incredible that this work has never been published. Our theory about this is that nobody knew it had really been built, first of all. A number of houses were built without Lautner's involvement, and in the case of the Bosustow Cabin it's not even sure whether Lautner ever saw it himself. Secondly, the location is so remote that nobody took the trouble to go and look, and besides: the exact address was unknown. This house is truly a discovery. We agree to keep it secret until the publishing of this book.

previous: Lautner (Three Rivers)
next: Turner

extra room on the street side and a large wooden terrace on the edge of the water. Luckily, it hasn't been pontifically built right in front of the living room, but on the side, near the kitchen. The house is made of old wooden telephone poles. The living room, with its enormous windows, is fully oriented towards the view. The glass is jammed between the wooden poles. Because the façade tilts forwards strongly and has been built in a large curve, it seems as though there is no glass in the façade, just

BOYKOFF

#136: Remodel, 1986-1989, extant
11499 N Thurston Circle, Los Angeles, CA 90049

Tuesday, 1 May 2007

When you Google Boykoff residence, one of the hits is the website of a former employee of Lautner's: Vaughan Trammell, who only responds – rather economically – to our emails after quite some time. He worked for Lautner for over ten years and left the firm in 1988. He married Lautner's office manager, Christine Tanaka. There are various photos of the house on its site, not just exterior but also interior shots. The Boykoff house was a remodel project, carried out in 1986. After we have scanned Bel Air at least twenty times on Google Earth, we finally manage to localise the house thanks to a tip from Martin Daoust.

On the phone, the elderly Mrs Boykoff tells us that her husband has died and that she doesn't give tours anymore. After we've had a good conversation, she agrees to let us visit after all. Although we thought we had made it clear we would be coming with a group of students, she initially only wants to let one person come in: 'So which one of you should I give the tour?' At that point, we're pretty close as a group, and we put our best foot forward. In the end, she lets us all in anyway.

Mr Boykoff had designed this modernist box himself, but wasn't very pleased with the result. Lautner was called in to make suggestions for improvement. Mrs Boykoff explains that Lautner didn't really want to do the renovations and it took a lot of persuading to get him on board.

Again, this house is completely different from other Lautner houses. The scale of the alterations was much smaller than in other places. The biggest change was the placement of an extra closed façade in front of the house, creating a series of private patios between the street and the bedrooms, which makes for a particularly introverted atmosphere

inside. On the other hand, all the barriers between the living room and the deep ravine on the garden side were removed. Mrs Boykoff tells us that she wasn't immediately enthusiastic about a railing made entirely of glass as she has a fear of heights, but Lautner replied resolutely, 'Let's just build it and if you don't like it you can always replace it!' Now, twenty years later, we see that the glass railing is still there. When you look down from the

balcony, you see that the house stands on giant stilts. Way down below, there's a swimming pool. In order to interrupt the static, rectangular layout, Lautner introduced a diagonal axis right across the house, where the most conspicuous new element is a wide black line that runs diagonally across the floor from indoors to outdoors. This was specially thought up for visitors leaving the parties the Boykoffs frequently hosted. If they could walk along it in a straight line, they could drive themselves home. The rest of the house is decorated with a lot of mirrors, clever cupboards and technical gadgets dating from that time, like a projector with a screen that can be completely concealed in the ceiling. Despite the fact that it seems to have been an assignment that mainly concerned the interior, Lautner's alterations are spatially radical. The view towards the street has been

closed off; the panoramic view has been opened up completely.

previous: Payne
next: Walstrom

BROOKS

#31: Brooks, Remodel, 1949, extant
#58: Lek, Addition, 1954, demolished 1990s
12445 Viewcrest Dr, Studio City, CA 91604

Thursday, May 3 2007

After a long journey over winding back roads we arrive at an obscure Lautner project from the fifties: an extension for the actor Nico Lek de Tachinville and his wife. The current owner is the blockbuster director Penelope Spheeris, who personally gives us our tour, in high platform shoes. She is shadowed by an enormous Native American man who doesn't say a word, but who looks at us as though he'll sever our heads from our bodies if we so much as lay a finger on his boss. In the house we discover that the Lek Addition that Lautner mentions in his book slid off the mountain ten years ago, after a downpour. But then it turns out that Lautner did another remodel for this house five years earlier: the Brooks Remodel. That does still exist, but not in the same state. The entire inside of the house has been painted high-gloss white, and too much has been changed to immediately recognise it as a real Lautner. But there are also recognisable elements present: the fact that you enter the living room on a higher level; the roof that follows the slope of the hill, which focuses one's gaze outside, towards the view; and the low ceiling coving with the hidden lighting. Mrs Spheeris is very candid: when we remark that the house seems made for hosting fantastic parties, she tells us that the success of *Wayne's World*, in 1992, turned her into a millionaire overnight, but she also lost all her friends at the same time. When asked if she uses the swimming pool often, she answers drily: 'I fell in once, when I was drunk…'

previous: Tyler
next: Foster

BUBBLING WELLS RESORT / DESERT HOT SPRINGS MOTEL

#18: Motel, 1947, extant
67710 San Antonio St, Desert Hot Springs, CA 92240

Sunday, 29 April 2007

Desert Hot Springs must have seen better times. After the construction of Interstate 10, this little place ended up off the beaten track. The consequences of this are beautifully portrayed in the Pixar film *Cars*: the village is increasingly deserted because there is no longer a way to make a living there. Desert Hot Springs was once a lively health resort, but nowadays it's a disconsolate place, full of dilapidated trailers and suchlike. Still, there is an early gem in this godforsaken place: a motel designed by Lautner in 1947, which together with the neighbouring bathhouse used to form the Bubbling Wells Resort. The surroundings are boiling hot and bone-dry, and there is a merciless wind. Because the permanent desert wind makes everything rattle and creak, Lautner decided to make the walls and the roof of the hotel out of concrete, with windows that face away from the dominant wind direction. In 2007, the man who had big plans for the hotel died suddenly, and during our 2007 trip, it is for sale again. The estate agent, Crosby Doe, a specialist in selling architectural masterpieces (the first person you call if you win the lottery), is prepared to come to the hotel and open the doors for us, something that Lautner fans probably ask him to do more often than he'd like.

The complex, consisting of four units, is surrounded by standard houses with no architectural value. Lautner has created a motel here where each unit forms a private world. Each unit has two outdoor spaces: an open one towards the street, for parking your car, and a private patio situated three steps higher than the surroundings. Because of this difference in level, you can look out from the patio, but you can't look inside from the road. There was originally a gate in the wooden fence, enabling you to step straight into the desert. Indoors and outdoors are perfectly integrated in the unit. The side wall is made entirely of glass, with large sliding doors that let in fresh air. The unit looks out onto the closed side wall of the next unit across a narrow, shaded garden, where plants form the transition. Because these concrete walls are folded in several directions, they are stable in themselves, and because of the shadow patterning, they are pleasant to look at. The roof, which is carried by angled steel columns, is slightly raised and displaced on one end in order to maximise the amount of light coming in on two

sides. The motel is somewhat run-down, but still in its original state.

previous: Wolff 2 'Wind Song'
next: Bubbling Wells Pool

Sunday, 21 March 2010

In March 2010, we are near Desert Hot Springs again, so we drop by the former Bubbling Wells Resort again. It has new owners, who want to turn it into a hip hotel. The second of the three street-facing units has already been done up. We had heard that it had become very 'slick', but at first sight it isn't too bad. What does catch the eye is the

Now they just have to work up the nerve to tear down the house that was built right behind it at some point, and which disrupts the outline unpleasantly. It would be a lot of fun to stay in this motel for a night, but we'll have to wait some time to be able to do that. In 2011, the renovations are complete and the motel is open again. It occasions a stream of publications, with favourable reviews and incredibly beautiful photos. The hotel is a good example of how a Lautner destined for demolition can successfully be given a new lease of life. The website of the hotel shows another remarkable feature: a wall has been erected on the street side, closing off the front of the units. According to the owner, Tracy Beckmann, this was prompted by a flood: if this were to happen again, it would cause extensive damage. Where the desert previously formed the boundary of the units, a perfect world has now been created behind a wall.

previous: Hope
next: Bubbling Wells Pool

Monday, 13 November 2017

We arrive at the hotel in the dark. The new owner has expanded the walled garden theme to the whole complex, which Lautner had used for all four units here. The addition of a new wall has created a patio, which hides the four units from view from the street. As soon as we pass the gate, we arrive in a completely different world: a rock garden with cactuses and beautifully illuminated semi-detached units. The spatiality of the rooms is still unsurpassed. The roof is not connected to the walls on either side, so that it seems to float. There is an outer wall made of glass under the roof, but the space continues up to a wall that's three feet further away. This means that the garden almost literally becomes part of the interior. Detaching the windows from the actual outer wall is an architectural technique that Lautner continued to use successfully later in his career.

The interior is stylised to a tee, with retro design furniture and a record player with a pile of

varnished red cedar fence, which replaces the old white one. We wonder why the bolts holding the stands in place are so irregularly spaced, but upon closer investigation that turns out to be an original detail. It remains unclear why the gate that used to be in the fence has not been reconstructed. Behind the fence, things look promising after all, although it will take a lot of money, time and insight to restore the building to its former glory.

records, a book about Lautner and even the movie *Infinite Space*. There is a record by Duke Ellington, the jazz hero in whose music Lautner saw an analogy with the way his firm worked: every band member did his own thing, but together they sounded fantastic. In daytime, the space is very different than at night: in the dark it feels intimate and sheltered, but in daytime the relation with daylight and the outdoor space emerges. The owner, Tracy Beckmann, tells us proudly about her plans to ask Lautner's former employee Ken Kellogg to design four more units for her. While the result is beautiful, the question remains of how far you can go in this context to maintain the functionality of a building that is more than sixty years old and keep the integrity of the original design. Either way, we had a wonderful night's sleep at 'The Lautner', as the hotel is currently called.

previous: Sheats-Goldstein
next: Elrod

BUBBLING WELLS POOL

#19: Pool House, 1947, demolished after fire
Yerxa Rd, Desert Hot Springs, CA 92240

Sunday, 29 April 2007

The Bubbling Wells Resort was originally conceived as a much larger project, but only the swimming pool diagonally across the street was ever actually built. But by the time we visit the hotel in 2007, it has been demolished. There is now another swimming pool on the same spot. Nothing remains of Lautner's design, except the few photos taken by Julius Shulman. The photos show two pools surrounded by a wall with glass openings under a pergola.

previous: Bubbling Wells Resort
next: Bergren Copy

Sunday, 21 March 2010

In 2010 we take another look at the place where Lautner's pool house once stood. It's possible that the roof beams, with their striking ends, were re-used, but other than that nothing remains of the building. Initially, the new owners had planned to reconstruct the pool house, but in the end these plans were abandoned. Reconstruction is always open to debate, but on the other hand we would have loved to see the building in real life.

A day later, in the archives, we look at drawings for the pool in Desert Hot Springs, Bubbling Wells Pool for Lucien Hubbard. In 2009, Pnina Avidar invited us to run a Lautner atelier at the Academy for Architecture and Urbanism at Fontys University of Applied Sciences in Tilburg. Our focus was primarily on making models of buildings we couldn't visit or projects that were halted. On this occasion, a student had already tried to make a model of it, based only on Shulman's photo in the large Taschen book. Because of the angle of the photo and the irregular shape of the pools and the roof, it was impossible to make a good

reconstruction. The floor plan we find now finally shows what it was like, and gives insight into the layout of the changing room building. Through individual changing rooms, you come past three toilets: the drain pipes are visible in the outer wall as three bulges, just like in the façades of the adjacent Desert Hot Springs Motel. The last dra wing is a large perspective in pencil on tracing paper. A reconstruction would now be child's play.

We are also sure now that what we found at the location has nothing to do with the original construction.

previous: Bubbling Wells Resort
next: Weinstein

CARLING

#17: Carling, House, 1947-1948, extant
#142: Eicher, Remodel and addition, 1991, extant
7144 Hockey Trail, Los Angeles, CA 90068

Friday, 4 May 2007

The Carling house from 1947 is one of the houses that was later renovated by Lautner himself; it is referred to as such in his monograph. The time between the house's construction in 1947-1948 and its renovation in 1991 spans nearly his whole career. The inventiveness of the house, but also the contrast between the original and the renovation make it one of Lautner's most interesting houses. The finishing of the interior of the original house, built for the musician Foster Carling, adheres closely to what Wright was doing at the time, such as the horizontal bands of redwood, the red concrete floor and the hexagonal base for the placement of the walls. The kitchen lies off the living room like a deejay booth, and offers a view of the whole space. A subtle split-level layout separates the different areas. But Lautner went further by experimenting freely with all kind of elements: a suspended hexagonal roof construction, so that the façade doesn't need any supporting walls; a built-in sofa, which was given the Hawaiian name *hiki e'e*, with hinges and wheels. With the push of a button, the sofa swings outside so that you're suddenly no longer sitting cosily by the fireplace, but on the terrace instead, enjoying the view. The cherry on top of the cake is a swimming pool that extends from outside to inside and is covered by an electrically operated sliding glass wall. He repeated this element in the Elrod house: there too, sliding glass wall cuts right across the swimming pool after the remodel of 1971. The hinged façade comes back in the 1982 Turner house, where a piece of the façade swings out with floor and all.

Foster Carling remained in the house until Jim Curley took over in 1977. He had various restoration works carried out on the house by the original contractor Johnny de la Vaux and Roban Poirier. In 1991, on request of the then owner Bruce

Eicher, Lautner himself also carried out extensive changes on the Carling house, which was already overloaded with ideas and beautifully executed details. The carport was closed up to make a larger master bedroom. This also meant that the original entrance disappeared. The route through the house originally went past the inside of the bedroom wing, under the overhanging roof, and past the swimming pool to the living room. The wing with the kitchen, bathroom and bedroom was shoved under the living room roof like a piece of furniture. All of this changed in the renovations: the front door can now be reached from outdoors, along the outside of the wing. Now you step right into the living room from the street, which, in fact, is not unusual in the United States. The dining room wall has been replaced by new floor-to-ceiling windows, like in the Sheats-Goldstein house. The same sheets of glass have been used to close up the carport.

The contrast between the original house and the addition couldn't be greater, but perhaps this is the only way to do it. The theme of the roof not following the space below is carried through to the extreme where the new glass walls meet the roof, like in Mauer and Polin/Jacobsen, except here it has been done with frameless glass. This creates a composition of vertical slabs and planes. TS: 'In 1999 I discovered the Carling house by coincidence. It is close to many other architecture classics and can be seen clearly from the road as a strange flat cake with an interesting roof construction and glass

lucky 'custodian'. Like many homeowners, Ramser doesn't know that Lautner built as many as twelve houses within a radius of a mile. He is happy to accept our invitation to join us to visit the Eisele Guest House, five hundred yards away.

previous: Crippled Children's Society
next: Eisele

Sunday, 5 April 2009

While we are on our way to the Bergren house in 2009, the Carling house suddenly pops into view again. It peeks over the slope above Mulholland Drive in two places. The striking roof construction and extraordinary glass angles of Lautner's 1991 renovation catch the eye immediately.

The house has been the property of fashion designer Jeremy Scott since 2013. He asked Mark Haddawy, the owner and restorer of Harpel 1, to restore the house to make it period correct. It looks fantastic again now, but a striking addition has been made, of a balustrade in the same style around the terrace.

previous: Deutsch
next: Bergren

details. We ring the doorbell. A lady opens the door and asks us to come back on Sunday. We return on Sunday, but unfortunately there's no lady to be seen and the door stays shut.'

During our trip in May 2007, we do have an appointment, and we are warmly received by the owner, Steve Ramser. The house is suddenly full of people, because apart from the students, both of Lautner's daughters and Frank Escher are there. In the documentary *Infinite Space*, our host remarks that he doesn't 'possess' the house, but is merely a

#46: Remodel and addition, 1952,
altered beyond recognition
233 S Palm Dr, Beverly Hills, CA 90212

Friday, 27 April 2007

After six months' preparation, we land in Los Angeles at the end of the afternoon. We haven't made any appointments for the day of our arrival but on the way to the hotel, behind the Kodak Theatre on Hollywood Boulevard, we pass three Lautner buildings whose owners have not answer-

On 10 July 2008, we pay a second visit to the palm tree lane where Lautner carried out remodels for Fern Carr. In 2007, we weren't sure if we had the right house. The occupants wouldn't let us in. According to the drawings in the archive, we had definitely found the right house, and now we know where to look. There are people working in the garden who don't bat an eyelid as we walk around. Apart from a few small elements, like the spacing of the windows and a skylight, nothing has been preserved of Lautner's changes. According to the

ed our letters: Darrow Office Building, Carr and Lippett. We know little about these, so they seem 'obscure' projects to us, and we are not very interested in them at this stage, but as our programme for the rest of the week is packed full we decide to visit them immediately.

Although Carr has clearly been marked on the map of realised projects, we have no idea what to expect. When we reach the address, we find an unimaginative standard house with a roof like the ones you see all over Los Angeles. Only the triangular dormer window is somewhat unusual. We ring the doorbell, but the occupants pretend not to be home. We take a photo of the beautiful lane of palm trees and continue on our way.

drawings, he had transformed the whole back garden into a greenhouse you could walk straight into from the dining room. But now the house just has a normal back garden.

In 2010, we first find photos in the archive that confirm that this remodel involved much more than a few changes in the interior. The photos show that the dining room runs into a conservatory, which occupies almost the entire lot. When we were there in 2008, there was no sign that this conservatory ever existed.

previous: Embassy Shop
next: Weinstein

previous: Darrow Office Building
next: Lippett

Saturday, 28 April 2007

We heard rumours that Lautner did a remodel for neighbours of the Chemosphere and the Harpel 1 house. During our 2007 trip, we arrive in front of a Swiss chalet, the exterior of which gives no indication that Lautner had anything to do with it. Inside, there turns out to be a curved grand staircase, which makes a new spatial connection between the front door, at street level, and the living area two storeys higher, designed in 1963 for a certain Mr Castagna. The master's signature also seems to be imprinted on the way the staircase ends and flows into the paving of the exterior, which continues deep into the house. The current owner, Mr Richman, was the manager of Marilyn Monroe's estate after her death. He tells us that Lautner dropped by one day in the early nineties to have one more look at the remodels he had carried out thirty years earlier, but Richman himself actually had no idea what Lautner's input had been. He also tells us the story of the 'Mexican handyman' whom he addressed as he was enthusiastically demolishing the second floor of house next door (Harpel 1); he turned out to be the owner. As we walk outside, we see the remains of his relationship with Marilyn lying in a bin.

A year later, we find drawings in the archive that confirm that we were right about the third house between the Chemosphere and Harpel 1: this drawing clearly shows that Lautner drew a remodel for Mr and Mrs Joseph Castagna, where a central staircase sweeps through all the floors in the house, from the entrance to the living room, two storeys higher.

In the summer of 2011 a rental house on a real estate website is advertised as being an unknown but authentic Lautner design. It belongs to Mrs Castagna-Regas, who also commissioned the Castagna Remodel next to Harpel 1. We contact her via email and find out she is a niece of one of Lautner's regular contractors, Johnny de la Vaux. She tells us that Lautner designed this house for her parents and that her uncle Johnny built it in 1953. At first glance, going on the photos, it doesn't look like a real Lautner, but the mezzanine with the undulating stairs made of stacked boulders and the integrated planters do suggest Lautner may have been involved. Later we see drawings that confirm this, although the house wasn't built entirely in accordance with the design. This features connections between columns and beams constructed from large, triangular plywood boards. These elements appear never to have been carried out in this house, but did return in Lautner's work on the Garwood house nearly two decades later. But it still remains unclear whether Lautner was involved in this design himself, or whether he was just doing a friend a favour by putting his signature on the drawings. Attributing further works to Lautner is tricky, because it begs the question why he didn't include them in his list of works. It's also curious that nobody seems to have ever mentioned or even remembered this house.

When we visit the house in 2017, we understand why Lautner doesn't consider it his own work: it is much too generic for that, despite the oversized rock formation situated between the ground floor and the living room, which is higher up.

previous: Harpel
next: Malin

COFFEE DAN'S

#13: Bar, 1946, demolished,
1500 N Vine St, at W Sunset Blvd,
Los Angeles, CA 90028

#14: Bar, 1946, demolished,
452 S Broadway, Los Angeles, CA 90013

#15: Bar, 1946, demolished,
8th St between Olive St and Hill St,
Los Angeles, CA 90013

Honnold Harris, Lautner may have been involved in other designs, which were awarded to Honnold. 'There was a Biff's that may have been a Lautner, unknown where (John hated the client). Tiny Naylor's was named after the owner, a large tubby man nicknamed Tiny. The one in Hollywood (Sunset corner of La Brea) was a Honnold-Lautner with emphasis on Lautner. Daddy caught clients like a master angler and John did the real magic thereafter. They were an ideal duo... alas for human nature taking that away. I am not sure who got the subsequent drive-ins in the Naylor empire,

Together with Douglas Honnold, Lautner designed a number of branches for the Coffee Dan's chain, each of them slightly different. Only a few photos remain, and there are no drawings left at all. That's what happens with coffee shops: they have a high turnover rate, and a new owner wants a new interior that goes with his own identity, of course. In 2010, we finally find photos of three branches of Coffee Dan's in the archives: one at 452 Broadway, with a narrow entrance and a large awning; one in the 1500 block of N Vine street, with large, slanting panes of glass, integrated plants and an awning that continues inside as a space-defining element; and a last, very simple coffee shop on 8th Street, which shows parallels to the design for the Embassy Shop. Branches were also built on Wilshire and Hollywood Boulevards, but they were designed by Honnold, after he broke with Lautner in 1946. In this kind of assignment, Lautner experimented with floor-to-ceiling frameless glass for the first time, which he later went on to use often in his residential designs.

According to Lautner's stepdaughter, Elizabeth

but the Sunset corner one was the pilot triumph.' Although we searched for confirmation from other sources we did not find proof that the famous Tiny Naylor's, which openend in 1949, was in fact a Lautner design, but we would not be surprised.

Wednesday, 2 May 2007

The Concannon house was built in 1960, two years before the Sheats-Goldstein house. When we visit it in May 2007, only the garage is still standing. The neighbour, Mr Goldstein, bought it in the early nineties and after consulting Lautner, decided to sacrifice the house to make way for a tennis court and an extension to his own house. Lautner's drawings never made it past preliminary sketches. But Goldstein persisted with his dream, and after a difficult process of obtaining permits, he was given the green light in 2001. The Concannon house was demolished and work on the tennis court commenced, though by now it had grown to include a theatre, a bar and guest accommodation. It would probably take until 2015 before the spectacular project was finished. But it's still a shame that this extraordinary house was not saved. Would Goldstein not have been better off choosing another neighbouring house to release his passion for construction on?

In October 2009, during the Lautner atelier in Tilburg, one of our students threw himself into making a model of the demolished Concannon house. That model is what really enabled us to appreciate the spatial qualities of the house: when you come in, you walk through a covered walkway that goes past the garden, which is closed off by the cliff face on the other side. Because the walkway is curved, it is not possible to see how long it is. In the living room a beautiful panorama unfolds, which is amplified by the fact that the sitting room is half a level lower. The way in which the space expands and is linked to the view is of an unprecedented cinematic quality.

The Concannon house is one of the houses that museum director Melissa Metuscak chose for her Lautner exhibition in Marquette in 2011. She had seen a web album by JRK with photos of the model of the house, which we had made as part of the Lautner project in Tilburg, and she asked if she could borrow it for her exhibition. Unfortunately, the model hadn't survived. But on the initiative of Ko Jacobs, our former student Hayke Zweede, who had written a thesis on Lautner years ago and was one of the first students to sign up for the US trip in 2007, made a new model, sponsored by the Academy of Architecture in Arnhem. It was a beautiful model, which was shipped to the US in late June. Things threatened to go terribly wrong when the model showed up in Arnhem again, completely broken, a few weeks after it had been sent: American customs had refused the crate because UPS had forgotten to put the right stickers on it, and customs had apparently searched the model for illegal goods. In great haste, the model was patched up again by Ko Jacobs himself, with help from Tycho, and it was sent again, with the right stickers this time, where it arrived just in time for the opening of the exhibition.

previous: Sheats-Goldstein
next: Vine Street Offices

CONECO CORP

#53: Coneco Corp, House, 1953-1954, extant
#87: Thiele, Addition, 1962, extant
3868 Scadlock Ln, Sherman Oaks, CA 91403

Friday, 11 July 2008

Coneco Corp is a nondescript and unknown house in Sherman Oaks. Lautner did include it in his list of projects, but without pictures or drawings. It was named after the developer/contractor who had it designed as an investment in 1953 and had it built a year later: the Coneco Corporation. Pat Hamilton, the owner, lived in it himself and sold it to the Thiele family seven years later: Mrs Thiele still lives there. In both 2007 and 2008, she tells us she cannot receive us for health reasons. From the street side, you can see a large, asymmetrical roof. Next to the entrance, a curved wall turns inwards. Even in these less striking houses, Lautner's signature is immediately recognisable.

previous: Goldsmith 2
next: Tyler

Sunday, 5 April 2009

After three years of emailing, we finally get to see the inside in 2009: the fact that Lautner's daughters join us probably helped. The Coneco Corporation house is the first house we visit together this year. There turns out to be another Lautner project at the same address, the Thiele Extension from 1962. In the monograph, this extra bedroom is listed as never having been constructed, but in fact it has, and what's more, it is of high quality and complexity, complete with an expressive roof and frameless window connections on the corners. Lautner had also designed a terrace with a swimming pool, but that was never constructed due to financial reasons, the elderly Mrs Thiele explains to us. The roof is unattached to the wall on the street side, which curves inwards towards the entrance. A strip of glass forms the link between this wall and the roof. The front door brings you straight into the living

room, which is completely open up to the roof. A curved, brick half wall runs through the space, which begins at the entrance as an outside wall and subsequently serves to separate the living room and the kitchen. On the living room side, the curved wall forms the back of the built-in sofa. The curved wall is a completely unexpected element in this house, which at first sight seems to be right-angled. The large glass windows on the garden side let in so much light that a fixed sunblind has been attached to the outside wall. The bedrooms are half a floor higher up, and at the back of the house, Lautner has added a master bedroom, which is raised above the terrace. The house has been owned by the same owner for nearly fifty years, who has clearly left his mark in the form of an overwhelming amount of stuff: furniture, books and other possessions. There is so much that the quality of the interior has been somewhat snowed under. From this point of view, it is reminiscent of Baxter-Hodiak. In order to comprehend Lautner's development properly, it is crucial to visit his lesser-known and unpublished works, even though Lautner did not consider them worthy of including them in his monograph. But it is definitely the case that he tried out elements in these projects that he later applied more successfully, or that he later left out altogether.

One could see the staircase in the Coneco study, for instance, as a forerunner to the stairs in Walstrom.

previous: Bergren
next: Jacobsen

CONRAD

#92: Addition, 1964-1965, extant
3000 Terraza Pl, Fullerton, CA 92835

Monday, 14 July 2008

devotees in a long time who have seen this work in reality. Although the roof has been carried out in a much simpler way than the designs in the archive suggested, Lautner has managed to turn it into something extraordinary yet again, thanks to all the glass. The ability to turn a simple assignment

Although this project from 1964 was on the list of projects, it had sunk into oblivion, so nobody knew what it looked like. The assignment was simple: an indoor swimming pool behind a standard house in Fullerton, an L.A. suburb. We found all kinds of wildly inventive drawings in the archive. On Google Maps we spot a rectangular extension, which seems to indicate that the project is still in existence. When we ring the doorbell in 2008, we are met with surprise. The owner is an elderly Asian gentleman who barely speaks English. Lacking a common language, we explain as best we can that his pool house was designed by the architect whose name is emblazoned on flags across L.A. Something begins to dawn on him and he lets us come inside. The pool house seems to be completely intact, but it is not quite the same in real life as it is on the drawings. The long Olympic-size pool was undoubtedly meant for swimming laps. It lies under an asymmetric roof, which has a skylight that runs the full length of the building and rests on columns, with frameless glass on one side of implausible proportions. This makes the swimming pool seem like an open pavilion. But apparently, it is rarely used anymore. We walk around fascinated, realising that we are the first Lautner

into something exceptional commands respect and makes us realise that all of Lautner's work is worthy of investigation.

previous: Henry's Pomona site
next: Preminger 2

Friday, 11 July 2008

In July 2008 we visit a number of 'obscure' projects, like this 1981 swimming pool next to an Arts and Crafts type urban villa. For this trip, we sent new letters to the projects where we hadn't been welcome in 2007, keeping in mind that fortune favours the bold. This approach worked for the Crahan Pool. The original client gave the house to an order of nuns. The sisters were sensitive to our perseverance: apparently, we *really* wanted to see the swimming pool. At a carefully chosen time, in order to disturb the peace as little as possible for the residents, we are warmly received by sister Christine M. After talking about our 'mission' for half an hour, we are finally allowed to see the swimming pool. It is a long, narrow pool for swimming laps, with a round, asymmetrical end, set in a terrace of flagstones and bordered by a curved wall. It's a beautiful, clear addition by Lautner, which anchors the house nicely. What is striking is that the long back garden is cut in half lengthways by a wall. The round bulge makes room for a terrace by the swimming pool. On the other side, there are garbage containers and the entrance to the garage. The wall ensures that there is more space wherever it is needed, and that utility is separated from leisure. This project shows that even for small-scale work, Lautner looked for optimal spatial layouts and did not resort to conventional solutions. The project was never publicised and never visited, but as a small assignment it is crucial for the new directions in the development of Lautner's work. One could see the curved wall as a finger exercise for his last masterpiece: the Pacific Coast house in Malibu.

previous: Stevens
next: Goldsmith 2

CRIPPLED CHILDREN'S SOCIETY

#115: Rehabilitation Center, 1973-1979, extant
6530 Winnetka Ave, Woodland Hills, CA 91367

Friday, 4 May 2007

derogatory way when he talked about 'façades and fashion' as being superficial.

previous: Beyer
next: Carling

The Crippled Children's Society building is a rehabilitation centre for disabled children. Built at the same time as the Beyer house, here too the roof stands out against the rest of the building. It is one of the few non-residential buildings that hasn't been torn down throughout the years. The original design consisted of six wings of different sizes, arranged around a garden that extends deep into the building. Not all of these wings were built, in the end, which we only notice when we study the floor plans. The roofs of the wings come together in one central column, from which one can see everything that's happening inside. It's a panopticon, which allows for direct observation from a central post. The ceilings of the wards slope upwards to the fully glass windows, so that the amount of light streaming into the building is maximised. The roofs of the larger wings are more than a storey thick. The construction and installations are located in these closed volumes. In published drawings, there are also windows in the ends of these roofs, but they were never made, which makes the roofs look very heavy from the surrounding garden.

Although Lautner himself was disappointed that he didn't get more assignments for large buildings, this project is not one of his best. This may be a consequence of the many compromises that have to be made for buildings of this scale. Another aspect is that Lautner primarily designed from the inside out, where the façades were the logical consequence of the organisation of the indoor space. That works well for small, residential houses, but for larger, freestanding buildings, the design of the façade is an iconic factor. When compromises are made on this point, the result, in a building like this, is rather peculiar, and in our eyes, less successful. But Lautner never cared much about façades. He even used this word in a

DAHLSTROM

#28: House, 1948-1949, extant
780 Laguna Rd, Pasadena, CA 91105

Thursday, 3 May 2007

We had to make a lot of effort to visit this house. All our letters went unanswered, and it was impossible to find a phone number or an email address. Sometimes death notices or public lists of political party sponsorship can be useful in tracking down owners, but that too had not helped us get in touch with the owners of the Dahlstrom house. Earlier successes had made us overconfident and greedy, so we called the opposite neighbours a few days before our trip and asked them to pass on that we would show up at the house on Thursday 3 May 2007. The owners then called us back, full of enthusiasm. When we arrived at the house, these people turned out to be extremely friendly and hospitable.

This house too, designed in 1948 for a triangular lot, has an independent roof construction, with volumes slotted in underneath. The main shape of the house is rectangular, rounded by the entrance, where the roof forms the carport, with a curved appendage on the garden side, where the kitchen and the formerly covered outdoor space are. Interestingly, the walls consist of parts of a circle, which creates a fascinating route to the living room immediately upon entry. The main bedroom is separated from the living room, for instance, by a freestanding round wooden wall. A large, round sliding door allows one to open the bedroom up to the living room. On the street side, the division between inside and outside is formed by two bookcases, which stand in the glass façade. The round, open fireplace also occupies the division between inside and outside. This makes it seem as though it is in the middle of the room. Behind the floor-to-ceiling, frameless windows there is an area with plants, and slightly further out there is a concrete retaining wall, so that the experience of the space extends outside. This is also the case in the Schaeffer house and the Bubbling Wells Resort, both from the same period. The glass details in the Dahlstrom house are implausibly ingenious, and the high point is a little bookcase that has been hung up as a rotating carrousel in the corner of the pane glass windows. A small, curved side wing protrudes from under the roof, containing the kitchen, which looks out partially over the living room and partially over the garden. The roof is

carried by lightweight steel trusses, the same beams that have been used in the next house we visit, the Hatherell house. The formerly covered outdoor area next to the kitchen has since been turned into a study. The house still looks almost the same as it does in the photos by Julius Shulman in Lautner's book, but the character of the house is not given its due, because the occupants have decorated it with classical furniture and large carpets, which largely hide Lautner's concrete floor from view. Although the house has various fascinating components, like the free floor plan with movable elements, how the glass and built-in furniture together form the façade, the different ways in which the house moves from indoors to outdoors physically and programmatically, as a whole, it makes an artificial impression. The effect of the complicated details is fairly limited, considering how many there are.

Lautner must have realised this himself, because he did not repeat it in later designs.

previous: Mauer
next: Hatherell

DARROW OFFICE BUILDING

#7: Office building, 1945, extant
9885 Charleville Blvd, Beverly Hills, CA 90212

Friday, 27 April 2007

The Darrow Office Building is one of the few projects dating from Lautner's collaboration with Douglas Honnold (1945-1946) that is still standing. In 2007, we had no idea what the building would look like. The two-storey building makes a very defensive impression, with a striking, austere façade. On the first floor, Lautner made horizontal blinds in front of the windows, there is a walled courtyard on the side, and the light on the upper floors mainly comes from the centrally placed patio. The front door can be reached via a staircase that ends behind the blinds. You're standing outside here, but inside the shell of the building, which makes the transition between inside and outside interesting. The building houses a Beverly Hills chapter of the Church of Scientology. We are allowed in without much hassle. Sadly, nothing remains of the original interior. In this early work, Lautner's most important themes are immediately visible, although he didn't seem to have found a way of dealing with Los Angeles's banal ugliness yet, apart from keeping it at bay as much as possible.

This is the first visit of the Lautner expedition.

next: Carr

Sunday 12 November 2017

Ten years later, we visit the Darrow Office Building again. For the final version of this book, we have decided to illustrate all the projects with a photo in landscape rather than portrait orientation. For some projects, we only have portrait-oriented photos that capture the essence of that project; reason enough to go back and photograph a number of projects again.

Now that we've visited Lautner's entire oeuvre, we can't help but see this project in a different light. The building is on the corner of a large main

road, Santa Monica Blvd, and an unsightly side street. As such, the building has two faces: a formal façade on the boulevard, and an informal one, with its aforementioned horizontal blinds, on the side street.

The highlight of the Darrow Office Building is the way in which the entrance is linked to its environment. In order to reach the landing outside the front door, you have to go up a set of steps that are situated at a right angle to the street. The landing can be reached from two sides: from the public pavement and from the private parking place. Because of the angle, it is not only the case that one's progress towards the front door is subtly guided, but it also turns out that the angle follows the bend of the distinctive grid-pattern of the city's streets. Thus Lautner links the large scale of the surroundings to the small scale of the building.

Again we notice how you are taken in by the building when you climb up to the landing. You're inside already even when you're outside, standing on a landing that also functions as a transition from public to private space: brilliant!

previous: Salkin
next: Foster

DEUTSCH

#38: House, 1950-1954, extant
7163 Macapa Dr, Los Angeles, CA 90068

Friday, 4 May 2007

Not far away from the Carling House is the Deutsch house from 1950. Julius Shulman's photo of it in Lautner's monograph shows a side of the house that cannot be seen from the street. In fact, if you only know the house from this photo, it is unrecognisable from the front. Only the window details betray Lautner's involvement. Unfortunately we were unable to establish any form of contact with the owners, so during our 2007 trip we have no choice but to drive past it on the off chance they'll let us in. When we arrive at the house, we see our own envelopes among the mail on the doormat. No wonder our requests went unanswered. The Deutsch house is a relatively small house with a diamond-shaped floor plan. The roof slopes towards the view and peaks on the short axis. On the street side, the house is very closed, so we can see little of the interior. The outside looks fairly intact. The other end of the house lies on top of a steep slope.

previous: Eisele
next: Zahn

Sunday, 5 April 2009

Against our better judgment, we also drop by the Deutsch house in 2009. We published a report of our first trip in the *Foundation News Letter*. We wrote that we had a range of different responses from homeowners to our request to look inside their homes: 'Some of them responded very enthusiastically, but others didn't let us in, like the "non-answering Deutsch residence", where we saw our own letter on the doormat.' Then suddenly we got a letter from the owners: they were unpleasantly surprised by having been described this way, especially because they had made every effort to save the house and restore it to its original state. Because they had doubts about our integrity they would certainly not be letting us in in the future, either.

In the hope that time heals all wounds, we ring the doorbell anyway. This time, too, there is no one home, but we can see that the house has

since been renovated. The original, slim casing has been replaced by a modern version, which makes us hesitate at the thought of the rest of the renovation. Because the house looks very closed from the street, and we were unable to see the back from below the last time, we decide to climb for as long as it takes to catch a glimpse of the edge of the roof. It is remarkable how you can climb all over the place here, totally undisturbed, without anyone asking what you think you're doing. But unfortunately, if we ever want to see the inside of this house, we'll have to get in personal touch with the owners.

previous: Fischer
next: Carling

Tuesday, 7 April 2009

A few days later, we find ourselves outside the Deutsch House for a third time, to no avail. At least this time the sun is on the façade, so we can take a few photos. We hardly count on the idea that we'll ever see the inside of the house.

previous: *Zimmerman*
next: *Malin*

Monday, 22 March 2010

In 2010 we finally manage to make an appointment. The lady of the house is a niece of Harry Williams, who commissioned Beachwood Market and his own

Under the diamond-shaped roof lies an almost symmetrical floor plan, where the axis of symmetry runs from the open study to the tip of the living room. The masonry combined with plain wood under a roof with exposed beams give a bare and plain impression. The high, slanting roof above the living room, together with the drop ceiling above the entrance and the study alcove mean that upon entry, the house opens up to the view spectacularly: a maximum effect with very few means. It is remarkable that the many beautifully finished built-in cupboards are still intact, even in the kitchen.

The current state of the house clearly illustrates the dilemmas one is faced with when trying to renovate a sixty-year-old house faithfully, but also as practically as possible: the original casing is no longer available, and modern-day construction regulations make it impossible to restore the terrace balustrade in its original state. That is a great shame, because now one mainly has a view of the railing from the living room, instead of nature. In order to keep from obstructing the view, Lautner had kept the balustrade open and low. The extra room, which is still included in Shulman's photo in the monograph, but not on the floor plan, has been demolished.

previous: *Speer*
next: *Eisele*

house, two years earlier. The Deutsch House is one of Lautner's more compact designs. It is placed widthwise across the lot, so that it is fully turned away from the street. In the description in his book of this modest house, Lautner wonders despairingly how it could be possible that he had been branded an architect who only works for the ultra-rich. The house was built between 1950 and 1954 by the client himself, who was a furniture maker, on a very modest budget, with help from contractor and former ship interior builder Johnny de la Vaux.

#16: Guest house, 1946, extant
7301 Mulholland Dr, Los Angeles, CA 90046

Friday, 4 May 2007

This 1946 house has to make do with just one small black-and-white photo in the back of Lautner's monograph. Since it was built, no one has ever taken the trouble to visit it, to the immense disappointment of the current owner. When he received our request from the Netherlands, he was delighted: in the last fifty years, nothing like that had ever happened. Finally, in 2007, his gem had been discovered, and from the other side of the world, too! Jamie R. inherited the house from his uncle Lloyd, who had made a fortune with his Adolph's Meat Tenderizer and bought the house ten years after it was completed from the client who had commissioned it. The location is incredibly beautiful. This part of the Hollywood Hills doesn't just have views of downtown L.A. and the San Fernando valley, but also the Pacific Ocean, in clear weather. In order to make sure the view would be safeguarded in the future, Lloyd R. also bought the surrounding lots. An internet search brought us to a worrying website: a local architectural firm showed drawings of a large villa with the same address as the Eisele Guest House. We were very anxious: modest houses in perfect locations are often torn down. Luckily, when we asked around, it turned out that when Lloyd R. died, the construction plans died with him.

The Guest House is a very interesting work from Lautner's early days. It is part of a series that also includes the Mauer house and the Schaeffer house: the room-dividing walls are placed at an angle to the main volume. These 'twisted' grids create a dynamic layout. Actually, this theme wasn't revisited in architecture until deconstructivism became popular in the eighties. Lautner had initially made a different design for this Guest House, consisting of two curved shells that twisted together, with a roof made of lightweight concrete, a form language that only comes back much later in Lautner's oeuvre. In the version that was eventually constructed, he used a wooden rafter construction put together from sheets of plywood, like he had done in the Mauer house. The sawtooth ceiling is made of wooden parts placed at an angle to the main volume, which gives the house an intangible character.

In the Eisele Guest house, Lautner went a step further than in the Mauer house: he did not only introduce two directions in the floor plan, he also made the glass wall of the living room slant forwards. The bedroom at the top of the house has a staggered façade, which creates natural zoning inside. The house has recently been beautifully restored. Our only criticism is that the rafters were not returned to their original state. Lautner combined elements from this Guest house and the Mauer house shortly afterwards, in a house where the complexity has been taken up another notch: the Schaeffer house. Jamie R. was delighted when Frank Escher found original photos in the archive, which must have been taken shortly after construction.

We are surprised to find such unknown work of such high quality. Because we've arrived with more people than expected and the atmosphere soon turns festive, the owner quickly produces extra food and drinks. The swimming pool at the centre of the house also looks very appealing, but because we still have another appointment, we keep our clothes on. From the very top of the hill we make

another interesting discovery: from here you have a direct view of the Chemosphere, across the valley. Too soon, the time comes when we have to say goodbye, but thanks to Jamie's profuse hospitality, we come back here often.

previous: Carling
next: Deutsch

Sunday, 5 April 2009

In 2009, we are invited to a party in the Eisele Guest House, which the owner has thrown specially in honour of our visit. He suggested making it a Lautner party, which gave us the opportunity to invite a number of homeowners and former colleagues, including Alan Hess, Kelly Lynch – owner of the Harvey house –, Lautner's former collaborators Warren Lawson and Julia Strickland, and Lautner's master structural engineer Andrew Nasser, who was the structural engineer for the Pacific Coast house and the Turner house, among others. The host asked us beforehand whether we had now been inside Benedikt Taschen's Malin house (the Chemosphere). No, we're not welcome there anymore after our run-in two years ago. In response to this, he suggests inviting Benedikt Taschen to 'our' party. He thought Taschen would definitely come if Julius Shulman was going to be there, so he was invited first. The 98-year-old photographer immediately promised to come, and subsequently, Taschen was invited. Mr Taschen was very honoured, and his presence could be counted on.

We arrive fashionably late: there is already a Mercedes S class in front of the house. We are warmly received and immediately introduced to Benedikt Taschen. We get talking and Taschen asks us how many Lautner houses we have already seen, and which ones we haven't seen yet. 'Well... almost all of them, over ninety of them, except yours.' 'Okay, if you have already seen so many, I'll show you mine. I'll call you in the next few days.' *Maybe*. We don't feel completely assured. When Taschen is introduced to Lautner's great-grandson Joey, our fortunes change. Taschen generously invites Joey to come and see his house, and tells him he can bring a few friends.

The party is fantastic. Now it is clear what the house was designed for, with its perfect setting without neighbours and a fantastic view all around. Now that we have been here a few times, it feels familiar. It is astounding how a relatively small house can be so complex. When the sun sets, most of the guests leave. JRK: 'Together with Taschen, I lift

Julius Shulman, who has held court all afternoon,
into his wheelchair. After the phone conversation I
had with Shulman in 2007, when I asked him if
we could come by for an hour with our students,
this was a special moment. Shulman had found
an hour much too short, and he called our plan to
focus on 'nothing but Lautner' and also to visit as
many projects as possible on one
day "a very bad idea", only to end
the conversation with a clipped
"goodbye".' (Julius Shulman died
three months later, on 15 July 2009.)

When we're alone with the
owner of the house and Judy and
Karol again, who are staying here,
he asks us if we managed to sort
things out with Taschen. We think
we did, thanks to Joey.

previous: Wolff
next: Seletz

Monday, 22 March 2010

Since we 'discovered' the house, it
has become a pied-à-terre for Judy
and Karol whenever they are in Los
Angeles.

On our trip in March 2010,
Judy and Karol serve dinner for
us and the owners of the Deutsch
house. By night, the view is even
more spectacular than by day.
This is really a unique location,
which Judy aptly described as
'in the middle of nowhere in the
Hollywood Hills'. This relaxed visit
also gave us the opportunity to
photograph the set of drawings of
the house.

previous: Deutsch
next: Gootgeld

ELROD

Monday, 30 April 2007 – Tuesday, 1 May 2007

As an architect, Lautner is much less famous than his buildings are, and the Elrod house may be the best example of this. In the film *Diamonds are Forever*, Sean Connery cautiously enters the house as secret agent 007 before being roughly driven into the pool by two ladies.

Without a doubt, the Elrod house is one of the most re-markable and explicit houses of the twentieth century. It was designed in 1966 for the interior architect Arthur Elrod, who gave Lautner carte blanche. When Lautner visited the location, it was just a stretch of land that had been bulldozed flat, with a view of Palm Springs. He had it carefully dug out to a depth of nine feet, so a few large rock formations emerged. Lautner used the rocks as space-defining elements and composed the house with a heavy, circular concrete roof resting directly on these rocks. This round roof consists of eighteen segments, half of which are folded open to let in light. Three segments are fully open. In the original design, the edge of the roof did not function as the division between inside and outside; instead, this partition ran underneath it in free-form on the valley side. The façades were carried out in frameless glass, which made it look as though they weren't there. Although many consider digging out the plot of land a stroke of genius on Lautner's part, the architectural critic Kenneth Frampton considers it reason to disqualify him, in his book *American Masterpieces*. He saw it as an expression of perversity rather than proof of a highly-developed feel for the possibilities of a place. The picture he paints of Lautner as a nonconformist, who only built extravagant villas for the super-rich is very one-sided.

In the archive we find drawings of a proposed extension for the house commissioned by Mr and Mrs Steven H. Maloney, who bought the house after Arthur Elrod died. The underground guest wing had then already been built, also the 'sliding aircraft hangar doors', as Maloney called them in an email exchange in 2012. To the north of the house a tennis court was to be built and a swimming pool for doing lengths, complete with a pool house with a very unusual roof: a curtain of water was to pour down from it and into the swimming pool. These plans were used again for Dr Djordjevic,

who bought the house in 1978, but he did not have them carried out either.

JRK: 'Because of its distinctive roof, this was one of the first houses I found through Google Earth, but it took a good deal more time to get hold of contact details for the owner, Mike Killroy. Then followed one of the most memorable phone conversations I have ever had. Because we had already made plans for various visits on our 2007 trip, we would be in Palm Springs at the weekend.

Precisely that weekend, there was going to be a big music festival in Palm Springs. The owner of the Elrod house explained that we were welcome to come by, but that he had originally bought the house on the condition that the previous owner could use the house one weekend per year. Of course, it was the weekend we wanted to visit. The disappointment must have been palpable. He asked how many people there were in our group. "Ten people." "'That's perfect, the house sleeps ten!

patio. The patio is circular, with the same diameter as the living room. Just like Bond, we cross under the overhanging roof and enter the living room through the glass door. The housekeeper gives us a brief explanation about the light switches and says, 'You have to be out by 8 AM.' She hands us the keys, urges us not to use the two swimming pool doors simultaneously, and departs, leaving us alone in the living room. As a result of the architectural force of the living room, we don't notice all kinds of details until much later.

The house has been extensively renovated several times, and an entire wing has been added, which is larger than the original house. The first remodel, which had the greatest impact, was carried out by Lautner himself, after a storm had blown off the façade. The glass, which originally followed the eight-step difference in level and ran deep into the round room, was not restored, but replaced by two gigantic electric curved sliding doors, which slide across the pool and follow the line of the roof. The pool was previously fully outdoors, although it used to be half covered by the roof, but now it is bisected by two enormous doors, like he did earlier at the Carling house. In order to make it possible to hang the doors from the edge of the roof, the elegant concrete disc that supported the roof, which previously became broader towards its base, had to be shortened to a column, so that the doors could move behind it.

Above the new terrace that was built behind the swimming pool, there is a skylight dome, with an open staircase leading down. It gives access to a whole new world with guest rooms, bathrooms and a gym. Although the detailing is coarser, it still fits into a series of buildings that we know were built in a late stage of Lautner's career. Elrod himself had the wing built, before he was killed by a 17-year-old in a pick-up truck who drove through a red light in 1974. In the next thirty years, the various owners made a number of changes to the house, none of which are improvements: the extension originally had a beautiful built-in planter on the roof edge that served as a railing, but now

Would it be a solution if you came on Monday?"'

We can hardly believe it, and at the last moment it almost goes wrong: the housekeeper wants to cancel our visit because she hasn't had enough time to clean: 'The house is dirty', she says, with a French accent. Eventually, we manage to convince her to let us come after all. With great excitement, we drive into the gated community at the agreed time.

The French lady opens the copper door that gives access to the private part of the entrance there is a standard fence and there is no sign of the former subtlety. The fine, delicate railing by the pool has been replaced by a heavy wall. During the last remodel, after Lautner's death, the frameless skylights were replaced by windows with heavy frame profiles, which considerably damages the architect's intention.

The sun sets and we're sitting on the terrace with a beautiful view of Palm Springs, protected by the dome. The difference in level halfway under the dome is striking: the higher part is the actual living room, while the lower part directly joins up with the surroundings. We drink champagne in the pool, order pizzas, do cannonballs in the pool, listen to music, climb on the rocks.

Later in the evening, we go on an expedition to the Hope house at the end of the street. When we get back, the Elrod house looks deserted. JRK: 'We quickly make the rounds, ending in the bath-room, where the two person jacuzzi is full of partying students.' While most Lautner houses really seem to come to life at sunset, this house is at its best at night. Two students decide to sleep in the living room, so that the concrete dome is the first thing they see when they wake up the next morning. Because we are spending the night, we get the chance to experience the house as inhabitants, which is completely different than simply visiting. While the attention always goes out to the living room in this house, a study of the other spaces and their relation to the living room yields a much more complete and complex picture. The later addition initially seems like a disruption of the original house, but programmatic-ally, it fits astonishingly well. The height of this more or less under-ground room is majestic. I wonder why Lautner barely mentions this substantial addition in his monograph. The way in which he presented his oeuvre, what he kept quiet and what he placed emphasis on, is worthy of study in itself. The rooms in this house are so strong it doesn't matter that the original furniture has been removed: this does not detract from the quality of the house. We settle down in the master bedroom. Behind this bedroom, where you can enjoy the view in between the boulders, there is a luxurious bathroom with a

power shower, jacuzzi and private terrace. By the time exhaustion hits us, young fathers with a chronic lack of sleep, the party in the living room is still in full swing.

Slowly, daylight fills the Elrod house. Students are sleeping on sofas here and there. They are roughly woken up by Tycho as he jumps into the pool. The splash resounds against the concrete dome: 'Good morning, this is your wake-up call.' We realise that the party is almost over and quickly take some photos in order to capture as many details as possible. Still filled with gratitude towards the owner for the trust he bestowed, we notice to our horror that the large sliding doors won't open anymore: the cable that operate the door has derailed. Although we can hardly imagine that this is the first time it has happened, we don't want to leave the house like this. The cable is held in place by an enormous counterweight, which is impossible to budge by hand. Luckily there's a jack in the car, which solves the problem. We leave the house, relieved, and take one last look at the Hope house, which looks coarsely detailed by daylight. A concrete shell roof would have been beautiful.

In Palm Springs, we visit work by other architects from the golden age of modern American architecture, to better place Lautner's work in its cultural context. Lautner occasionally expressed his surprise at the fame and reputation of his contemporaries; Richard Neutra was one of these: in Lautner's opinion an architect who endlessly

the house in Palm Springs. The circumstances seemed ideal: beautiful location, dedicated client, unlimited budget. The famous photo that Julius Shulman took of the house is, together with the photo of Pierre Koenig's Case Study house #22 for the Stahl family, the iconic face of modern architecture in the United States. After such a photo reality can only disappoint. Beth Harris, the wife of the couple who had the house restored, gives us permission to see the house as long as we don't take any photos. The house looks brand new, not as overwhelming as in Shulman's photo but still breathtaking. The growth of Palm Springs means that the desert, which used to be behind the house, has been completely built up, while in the past there was only the house designed by Raymond Loewe. Wright was offended when he wasn't invited to design the house. Five years later he got a second chance with the commission for a house for Kaufmann's wife Liliane, directly behind the Neutra house. Wright made no bones about his dislike when he wrote to her, 'I will get you out of the nasty nice cliché with a fine sweep.' On the plan he made for the Boulder House, he drew a miserable sketch of the Kaufmann Desert House, a marked contrast with his own generous design. The most remarkable was the circular swimming pool round the living room. Wright made this on special request for the client, who loved swimming but hated doing lengths. Liliane Kaufmann died in 1952, and consequently Wright's Boulder house was never built. It is not clear if Lautner knew about this design when he designed something similar for the Marbrisa house in 1971.

previous: Bergren Copy
next: Hope

Tuesday, 14 November 2017

repeated himself, a one-trick pony. If this is so then the best example of his 'trick' is in Palm Springs: the Kaufmann Desert House, built for the same clients as Frank Lloyd Wright's Fallingwater, designed when Lautner was working for Wright. A project that Lautner did not approve of, incidentally, because of the lack of spatiality. Edgar Kaufmann Jr, the son of businessman and philanthropist Edgar J. Kaufmann Sr., thought it was time for the next generation of architects and suggested to his father that Richard Neutra design

Jeremy Scott, who managed to buy the house for a relatively small sum of money in 2016, has asked Mark Haddawy to restore this house, too. Through him, we've been invited to have a look at the latest progress. The entire interior is being redone, the skylights are being returned to their original condition, and the 1971 guest house is also being restored, including the planter troughs on the edge of the roof. There is a set of copies of the original drawings in the house. We discover that Lautner had also designed another guest house on the other side of the house, under the master bedroom, but it was never built. The dilemmas one faces during a renovation/restoration of this kind are considerable. Personally, we would have chosen to go a step further back in time and would have removed the large, curved doors Lautner himself once came up with. The subtle, inward-folding façade would have been reinstated, just like the foot of the column that curled towards the view so beautifully: this was what it looked like when Leland Lee photographed it.

In July 2018, Adele Cygelman, who is doing research on the works of Arthur Elrod, sends us the following message: 'So I found an intriguing press release (with no date) in the Elrod archive about a "Gentleman's Retreat room" at the annual AID show at the Hollywood Palladium, sponsored by Stockwell Wallpaper.' She shows us some pictures that we had seen ourselves in the archive, but were never able to identify. It turns out that Lautner and Elrod already worked together before they created this masterpiece.

previous: Bubbling Wells Resort

This was the final visit of the Lautner expedition.

EMBASSY SHOP

Thursday, 10 July 2008

During our search, we got in touch with Carolyn Gootgeld Levine, daughter of Nouard Gootgeld, who had Lautner build him a house in Beverly Hills in 1952. Carolyn told us that her father has asked Lautner and his partner at the time, Honnold, to design the façade and interior of a liquor store and delicatessen, the Embassy Shop. When we asked for more information, Carolyn found a few photos of the shop in a shoe box. Eventually we managed to find the right location; the property was still there, amazingly. In 2008, it housed a luxury bread shop. Nervously, we go inside, looking for traces of Lautner. We stare around in disbelief: the entire interior has been stripped and the shop has been made 'hip' with exposed walls, plain wood floors and furniture. They have never heard of Lautner here. We buy some sandwiches, but although they are quite good, by American standards, our disappointment makes them taste like nothing.

previous: Sheats Apartments
next: Carr

During our first visit to the archive in July 2008, we find sketches and drawings of a stand for Evans & Reeves for the California international flower show, which took place in Inglewood from 3 to 11 March 1951. The design was characterised by a central lantern-shaped pergola, which we also find in Bick, from the same year. We are not sure whether the design was ever carried out or not; we have never managed to find photos, but Lautner did list it as having been carried out in his monograph.

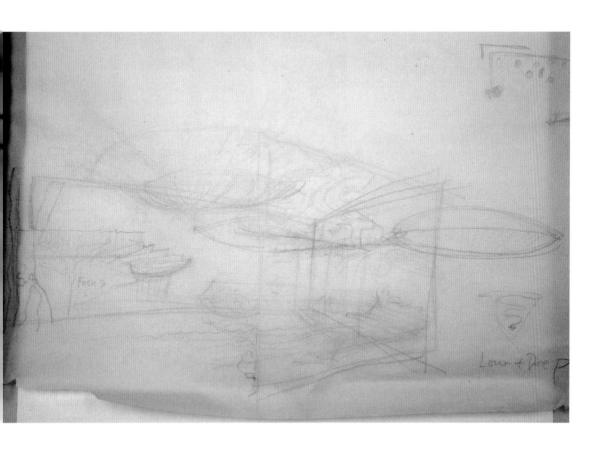

FAMILIAN

#105: Familian, House, 1969-1972, extant
#137: Nicholas, Addition, 1987, extant
1011 Cove Way, Beverly Hills, CA 90210

Tuesday, 1 May 2007

This gigantic house, designed in 1969, is situated on a posh street in Beverly Hills, fully withdrawn from the street itself. A peculiar triangular pyramid covered with flagstones dominates the view from the street. The triangle accompanies the stairs to the entrance. At the front door, we notice that the lush planter troughs under the large roof continue inside. During our 2007 trip, we ring the doorbell, but Mr and Mrs K themselves are not home, and we aren't allowed in.

previous: Walstrom
next: Shusett

Tuesday, 8 July 2008

In 2008, we do have an appointment. The house was completed in 1972 and is rather remarkable within Lautner's oeuvre, with an L-shaped floor plan. At the same time, it is one of Lautner's largest houses, although that's not immediately clear from the street. From there, the only thing you notice is the pyramid covered with flagstones. The house belongs to a man who made its fortune in the dotcom boom. Once we knew his name, finding his email address wasn't so difficult. We soon made an appointment. We are kindly, but also somewhat suspiciously received by the lady of the house, who gives us a tour. Inside, it turns out that you see the short side of the L from the street, and that the house extends far back and up. It was restored and renovated in 2001. Initially, they approached Lautner's former colleague Helena Arahuete for this, but eventually, society architect Mark Rios was hired to adapt the house to fit the family's lifestyle. Some changes are successful, such as the skylight over the stairs. Others are more questionable, like the renovation of the facilities, where the lowered bar, formerly in the kitchen, was removed. It is also regrettable that the swimming pool was moved. Mrs K thought Lautner had put the pool in the wrong place, and so she had it moved to the back

of the garden, by the sitting room. Initially it was situated along the side, by the rocks, where it was nicely integrated in the landscape and had a link to the public part of the house. No trouble or expense was spared during the renovation and it is not noticeable straight away that the house has been interfered with.

When you enter through the enormous front door, you are immediately in the most spectacular part of the house, where the long and short wings meet. On the subject of the front door, Mrs K tells us that Lautner didn't want to make an ordinary front door, so he chose a cathedral door. We are shown some fancy technical features, like a projection screen that disappears in the sloping roof at a push of a button. But what is truly sensational is the spatiality. Various rooms flow into one another. The sequence of the living room – under a high gable roof –, dining room and staircase is phenomenal. It is remarkable that despite the scale, the house still has a comfortable, homey atmosphere. The use of materials, with dark wood, flagstones and white walls bathed in sunlight, makes it a very pleasant place to stay. Because of the type of architecture, with exposed beams and an overhanging roof, this house is often referred to as a city ranch. In 1987 Lautner carried out a commission known as the Nicholas Addition. This project was on our 'mystery list' for a long time, but we now know it was just a minor alteration to the garage.

When we leave again, the owner asks us if we know why the flagstone pyramid was built and whether it's possible to get into it somehow. She suggests flippantly that it would make a perfect final resting place for her mother-in-law.

previous: Lautner, Ernest
next: Fischer

#56: House, 1954-1955, extant
2487 Canyon Oak Dr, Los Angeles, CA 90068

Thursday, 10 July 2008

On July 10, 2008, on the way to our appointment at the Bell house[4] we drive past the 1954 Fischer house[55], which is only mentioned in passing in Lautner's monograph. JRK: 'For a long time, we didn't know what it looked like, until I got hold of a copy of *John Lautner, Architect, Los Angeles: Eine Ausstellung zum 80. Geburtstag*, the book that was published in 1991 by Ludolf von Alvensleben to accompany the exhibition in Vienna for the occasion of Lautner's eightieth birthday. In the back, there is a list of works, with a tiny photo of each of the projects mentioned. The Fischer house was photographed from below, with a large terrace that sticks out over the garden below. And to our astonishment, all the addresses were listed! These were addresses that we'd spent a year's worth of evenings scouring Google Earth for. But luckily, the list was far from complete and full of mistakes, so all our work hadn't been for nothing.'

   Although we have managed to get in touch with the owner of the Fischer house, she spends a few months of every year out of state, so we won't get to meet her now. The house turns out to be in perfect condition. It is situated on a large intersection of three roads, with a long, low façade that follows the bend in the road. When you stand at the centre of this bend, you see yourself reflected seven times in the vertical windows. By the front door, the wall separates from the house and encircles a patio. To the left of the house, where the street takes a sharp drop, a staircase goes down. While we don't like trespassing, we can't resist the temptation to see the floating terrace. From below, it still looks the same as it does on the photo in the Austrian book. One thing is certain: we really need to make an appointment to further explore the house.

previous: Familian
next: Bell

Again in 2009, the owners aren't in L.A. when we are. By now, we have seen the drawings in the archive: this, too, is a very interesting house. It still looks to be in mint condition. This time we go a step further in exploring the house: we point our camera over the wall that protrudes from under the volume, next to the entrance. There is an intimate patio behind it. A curious visitor couldn't look over the wall and into the patio, but because the patiofloor is a few steps higher, you do look over it from the patio. The same principle was applied earlier at the Bubbling Wells Resort in Desert Hot Springs. We drive on to a lower street to see the large, protruding terrace that floats about thirty feet above the slope.

   In the archive, we also found drawings from

1983 for a drastic expansion of the Fischer house, commissioned by Mr and Mrs Levenstein. The house stands on tall stilts against a steep slope. In this proposal, an entirely new storey has been added under the extant house, with two children's bedrooms and a master bedroom suite, where the bathroom is designed in such a way that you can enjoy the view while having a shower. Because the drawings are fairly detailed, we suspect that the

decision not to build this addition was taken at a very late stage.

previous: Baldwin
next: Deutsch

Sunday, 21 March 2010

By now, the Fischer house is the place where we have most often stood outside, unable to get in. In 2010, it is still inhabited by Mr and Mrs Levenstein. This time, Judy and Karol accompany us. After years of lobbying, we are finally met with an open door. A short tour of the house quickly raises the same question we were left with after our visit to the Stanley Johnson house: why did Lautner not include this beautiful house in his monograph? In his notes for the monograph, Lautner wrote about this house: 'marginal, omit'. What could have inspired such a thought? Was he confused with another project, or did he have a disagreement with the client, were his ideas compromised? Maybe he was disappointed that the plans for the extension were cancelled. It may not be Lautner's most spectacular house, but it is unmistakably a house that was designed and built lovingly and carefully.

From the street, you walk down a set of steps to the front door, which lies a few yards back from the street; this means you enter right in the middle of the house. The living area is five steps up from the front door. Behind the front door, you are led in spectacularly, towards the light. This effect is created by the volume in the middle, which is intersected by a patio on the street side and the terrace on the valley side. The space flows like a yo-yo from the kitchen side into the other side, where the living room is.

The street in front of the house slopes down, which inspired Lautner to have the house slightly dug in, creating a spatial dynamic. All the rooms lie under a large, lightly sloping gable roof, which you look up against from below. In the living room, a corner of the façade sticks out, towards the view. Because the land slopes down sharply, you look into the tree tops from the living room. In the living room, the roof reaches its highest point, and light streams in from two sides: from the façade, where there are built-in bookcases under the windows, and via the patio, which extends to below the roof, just like the terrace, which is situated between the kitchen and the living room. The owners have maintained the house perfectly in its original state since the day they bought it, around forty years ago. In fact, they almost bought the Sheats house, which was also for sale at the time, but they eventually decided this house suited them better. (And it's lucky they did, because without Goldstein, Lautner's career would have been quite different.) Mrs Levenstein also tells us that she initially found the extension Lautner had designed fantastic, but that she was worried that it would affect the character of the house too much. When we say goodbye, she gives us a few magazines with articles about Lautner, including a *Los Angeles Times* 'Home' supplement from 3 November 1968, with a fantastic photo of the Elrod house taken by Leland Y. Lee on the cover.

Once again it is clear that the Elrod house, although it was renovated and extended by Lautner himself in the seventies, looked more elegant in its first incarnation and that Julius Shulman was definitely not the best photographer of Lautner's work.

previous: Stevens
next: Speer

FLOWER SHOP FOR MR. SAMUEL MORHAIME

#61: Shop, 1955-1956, extant,
demolition pending 2018
921 W Olive Avenue, Burbank, CA 91506

Saturday, 11 November 2017

In 2017, the Los Angeles Conservancy informs us that a flower shop called Samuel's Florist has been scheduled for demolition. They say it's a design from 1955 by a famous architect. The drawings in the city archive list John Lautner's name. However, Lautner never recorded this project in his own monograph. We manage to find some photos through Facebook and Google Street View clearly shows a typical fifties design, in almost original condition. Naturally, we don't want to miss a single Lautner building, so we immediately plan a new visit to L.A. We had seen the drawings for the flower shop before, but because it didn't look very elaborate, we couldn't have suspected that the design had actually been built. It is one of Lautner's three 'flowers' projects, between Evans & Reeves's stand for the California International Flower Show and the flower shop called Flowers that Bloom in the Spring Tra La.

So after six years, here we are in L.A. again, which gives us the opportunity to tie up a few loose ends for this book, visit a few people in the Lautner network, and retake a number of photos we weren't completely happy with. The flower shop in Burbank is no longer in use when we arrive. The building looks fairly run down, and only when we look closer do we see a few unusual details. The construction is made of standard prefab concrete parts, for example, that can be slotted together with tongue and groove joints and have been used as freestanding columns in the façade. These columns

have been decorated with mirrors, which must have had a spectacular effect. We haven't seen this kind of features in any other work of Lautner's, but the fact that the project is unlisted does provide food for thought. When we see other drawings in the archives, a day later, we understand why this project can't be considered a 'real' Lautner after all. The layout is different than it is in the drawing, and that also applies to the position of the façade. The glass is positioned in front of the columns, while on the drawings it is situated on the inside of the columns, with the result that the columns would have been a more prominent part of the façade. The entrance also isn't set back, unlike in the drawing. The rectangular roof would have served as an awning, in that case. The hinged shutters in the drawing are absent from the building we see before us, if they were ever present at all. When is a Lautner still a Lautner? This project, which was the reason we decided to undertake another pilgrimage to California in 2017, is a doubtful case. Or maybe it's not.

previous: Harpel 2
next: Salkin

#130: Shop remodel, 1982,
altered beyond recognition
11710 Barrington Ct, Los Angeles, CA 90049

Thursday, 10 July 2008

In 1982, Dan Stevens, of the wonderful Stevens house from 1966, asked Lautner to design the interior of a flower shop. This shop, with the curious name 'The Flowers That Bloom in the Spring Tra La' (how do you answer the phone in a shop with a name like this?), was for Stevens's third wife. The couple had bought a rose nursery and sold the flowers in this shop. Nothing of the interior of this shop in an ordinary mini-mall was preserved, although you could recognise something of Lautner in the way in which the shop window ends in a horizontal element. When we visit it during our 2008 trip, there is a Health & Beauty shop in the space. Later, we hear from the project architect, Vaughan Trammell, that the concept for the shop never worked the way Lautner had imagined it. His idea was to display the flowers in the open space on stacked display racks. That way the flowers would be clearly visible from outside. Lautner had an invisible cooling system installed, which was meant to cool the flower displays only. Unfortunately, the cold air turned out to circulate through the whole shop, causing the windows to fog up. In the end, the flowers were placed in separate fridges. Another former colleague of Lautner's, Warren Lawson, tells us, 'I also wasn't very impressed, I'm sorry to say, with the architecture. A lot of Bouquet Canyon flagstone and glass is all that comes back to mind.' In 2012 we finally manage to lay our hands on a photo of what the shop looked like at the time, through Dan Stevens's daughter, Gwen Neidlinger.

previous: Bell
next: Preminger

#35: House, 1950, extant
4235 Las Cruces Dr, Sherman Oaks, CA 91403

Thursday, 3 May 2007

In 2007, we visit the Foster house from 1950, the photos of which have always intrigued us. They show a straight volume that ends in a round shape, ornamented by strange, narrow strips of windows at different heights. It is made of silver-grey wooden planks and stands on stilts on a slope in the armpit of a hairpin bend. Our letters went unanswered, so we drive past it on the off chance there's someone home. We ring the doorbell, and a vaguely familiar-looking man in a bathrobe opens the door and stares at us, surprised, but lets us in anyway. It's inspector Frank Tripp from *CSI Miami*. While we fan out through his private property, he sits back down in front of his computer in his bathrobe, apparently unruffled.

The straight volume is covered by a lightly sloping roof, which flows into a roof covering the round balcony on the living room side. The roof is positioned around a central concrete column. Because the balcony floor has a different centre than the roof, a dynamic unity is created. The façade between the living room and the terrace lies halfway across the circle, a returning theme in Lautner's work. The actual surface area is minimal, but because the space continues as it curves outside, it doesn't feel small. When you step onto the balcony, you step out of the volume, as it were, so that you can look back at the house. The silvery grey wood visible in the original photos has unfortunately been painted brown.

previous: Brooks
next: Iwerks

In 2017, the Foster house, still owned by the Foster family, is being done up for sale. The renovations are being supervised by Helena Arahuete and carried out by Roban Poirier, who we have arranged to meet at the house. As a starting carpenter, Poirier did jobs for Lautner regularly since 1972, from installing a new door in the Baldwin House to a great deal of complicated jobs on many of

Lautner's projects. This culminated in the construction of the interior of the Goldstein office, a photo of which graced the cover of Lautner's monograph in 1998. He is full of stories about the man himself. He tells us about Lautner's cheerful reply after he proudly informed him that he had received his contractor's diploma: 'Congratulations, you just joined the fraternity of assholes!' Poirier tells us that Lautner also made a design for a house across the street, the Lindenberg House from 1958, which was never carried out. This statement is confirmed the next day, when we stumble upon the drawings for the house in the archives.

previous: Segel
next: Rawlins

GANTVOORT

#20: House, 1947-1949, extant
3778 Hampstead Rd, La Cañada Flintridge, CA 91011

Thursday, 3 May 2007

The Gantvoort house was designed in 1947 for a Dutchman who came from the former Dutch East Indies with a collection of teak furniture. The house was first sold in 2007, after the clients lived in it until they died in 2004. Unlike many other houses from this period, this house seems to be in excellent condition and practically unchanged. Unfortunately, despite the appointment we made with them, the occupants aren't home, so we can only see the house from outside. Thanks to the large expanses of glass, we still manage to get a good impression of it. The house has an independent, free-standing roof, which is supported by a slim steel structure of open lenticular trusses and slanting, standing columns. It lies parallel to the hill and is anchored to its surroundings by the pool, the carport, and various terraces. The interior walls have their own logic: sometimes they follow the joists, sometimes they follow the spaces they enclose, independent of the construction. A lowered strip in the ceiling, formed by parallel wooden rails running the length of the house, marks the organisation of the house, with bedrooms on one side, and utility rooms on the other. It is a pity that the door stays shut, because the independent supporting structure calls for further investigation. Lautner had previously tried out the idea of a roof that is completely independent from the rest of the design, in the Mauer house, which we will be driving past later that day.

previous: Iwerks
next: Schaeffer

Saturday, 12 July 2008

For our trip in 2008, we have managed to make an appointment with the new owner of the Gantvoort house. From outside, it looks like a simple hangar,

and when you look at the floor plan, you could hardly think this house has more to offer than an interesting steel structure. However, it turns out that nothing could be further from the truth: inside, this is in fact a very spatial house. There is a high level of transparency: on the one hand, this is because the façades have been carried out in frameless glass, and on the other hand, because they are located in unexpected places. That is to say: not where the roof ends, or where there are structural elements. As a result, they become part of the background, and the attention is drawn only to the supporting structure, the floor and the roof. Another interesting aspect is that various different places are defined in the open space, because there is a ceiling of wooden slats at the bottom of the steel structure, while the actual ceiling continues above the steel trusses. We came across another remarkable detail in the bathroom, where there is a slanted column next to the bath. Between the column, the wall and the edge of the bath, a sheet of glass acts as a shower screen. There is a semi-circular cut-out in the sheet of glass, so that you can operate the shower from outside, without getting wet.

When we visit, the house is completely empty: it is for sale again. The owner bought the house less than a year ago on a whim, but can't afford to keep it because of the credit crisis. By now, his wife, for whom he had actually bought it, has left him.

number of bedrooms and bathrooms, there is little hope.

next: Schaeffer
previous: Henry's Glendale site

Although it is of course wonderful to be standing inside the house, the absence of furniture is also an omen of an uncertain future. But this does showcase the materials the house is made of, like the ochre-coloured concrete floor, which was laid in diagonal strips and runs on to the covered terrace. The estate agent is also present, but we don't trust him much: he may recommend the house as a teardown. As long as the recommended price for an architectural gem like this is only based on the

#76: House, 1958-1962, extant
7436 Mulholland Dr, Los Angeles, CA 90046

Tuesday, 1 May 2007

During our many drives through the Hollywood Hills in 2007, we inevitably pass the Garcia house (also known as the Rainbow house) on Mulholland Drive. It was built for the jazz musician Russell Garcia and his wife Gina Mauriello Garcia, both followers of the Bahá'i faith. One of the rules of this faith is that you must not sleep in the same room as where you eat. This inspired Lautner to create two distinct volumes, separated by a large staircase, covered by an enormous arched roof. The space beneath the curved roof, on top of the bedroom wing, used to double as a carport. The arch also framed the view. Behind the front door, you descend to the terrace that connects the two parts of the house: a living, cooking and dining wing to the right of the stairs, and a bedroom wing to the left. There are photos on the internet of a very extensive renovation, for which the house was almost completely dismantled and rebuilt with utmost precision. We aren't welcome yet, because apparently, it is not completely finished, although that isn't noticeable when we arrive in front of the house.

We walk to the front door and discover that the house is suspended in mid-air, only supported by four very thin stilts. The stairs between the street and the front door hang over a steep abyss. Apparently, as you descend the staircase, a spectacular panorama of L.A. unfolds, but we'll have to wait until a next time to see that. There is another set of stairs leading to the right end of the arch. At the top of these stairs, you can look into the living room at almost the same angle as in Shulman's famous photo, where Lautner himself is sitting on the sofa. It's almost a disappointment that he's not sitting there anymore.

previous: Sunset Plaza Gate
next: Bergren

A few days later, the Garcia house from 1962 is the last Lautner we visit on this trip, but now from a lower street. From here you can clearly see that it is a detached house at the top of a very steep hill, and it immediately becomes clear why the house is nicknamed the 'Rainbow house'. We are standing in the exact spot where Mel Gibson yanks the stilts out from under the house with his pickup truck in *Lethal Weapon 2*, sending it crashing down the hill,

on fire. As a result, the original client, who had by then emigrated to New Zealand, got on the phone in tears, convinced that the house had really been destroyed for the film.

previous: Polin
next: Lautner, Ernest

In 2009, after years of renovations, the house looks like it was completed yesterday. It falls into that category of houses that is acquired by a collector or devotee after years of neglect, someone who goes on to restore every last detail, making adjustments here and there to update it for contemporary use. While this kind of house was originally relatively cheap to build thanks to clever techniques and the fact that many owners helped build it themselves,

the upkeep now costs a fortune. Lautner was able to build this kind of houses thanks to a young, creative class of clients; the preservation of his work, however, depends on dotcom and Hollywood millionaires. After years of emailing the owner, we have now built up enough trust to merit an invitation to visit the house. It is wonderful to be able to go inside when we didn't make it past the front door on our last visit.

This house has one of the most spectacular entrances ever built: behind the front door, which is actually a gate, you arrive underneath the roof, where you turn right and descend a generously curved staircase. The stairs float freely in the air. As you walk down, the panorama of L.A. unfolds step by step. Downstairs, you stand on a terrace, still outside, under the curved roof. On the one side, there is the real front door, and on the other side there's the entrance to the bedroom wing. Living and sleeping areas are strictly separate: you can only cross between the two areas by going outside. At the bottom of the staircase, the door on the right gives access to the living room, which is as high as the arch here. From here you look out over the living room, which lies three steps down from the entrance landing. Marking this difference in level is a built-in piece of furniture that acts as a counter-top for the kitchen on one side and as a cupboard on the other; on the living room side, there is a large, built-in corner sofa next to it: the sofa where Lautner was sitting on the aforementioned photo by Shulman. Today, his great-grandson is sitting on it. In order to emphasise the character of this wide-spanning arch, it has been kept from touching the floor on both ends with a strip of glass. On the photos, the living room looks like a somewhat strange room with hangar-like proportions, but in reality, that is absolutely not the case. The room has a pleasant scale and the small differences in level between the kitchen and the sitting room create sub-spaces, which give one a remarkable feeling of protection. JRK: 'In 2011, I got in touch with the original client Russ Garcia, who was still making records at age 95. While they were very pleased with Lautner's design, by their own account, they live in an ordinary house in New Zealand.'

The current owners had the house restored by Marmol & Radziner, who also restored Neutra's Kaufmann Desert House. During the renovation of the Garcia house, they did not only completely reconstruct the house, but especially in the finishing, they went to great lengths to recreate a real sixties feel. There isn't a tap, light switch or swathe of wallpaper that isn't period-correct. It is fantastic that there are people who will go this far, but there are also critics who say this verges on kitsch. But the most important thing is that the spatiality, as the curved roof, which gave the house a lightness it no longer has.

previous: Malin
next: Baldwin

Lautner intended it, has been retained, and that the house is protected for many years to come. In the bedroom wing, the restoration architects allowed themselves a number of liberties. One of the extra bedrooms, for instance, has been turned into a bathroom with a bath by the window, so that you can enjoy the view as you soak. This is a purely functional change, which we suspect would have been acceptable to Lautner because it does not substantially affect the house. In the original

situation, there was an open carport above the bedrooms, under the curved roof. This carport, which was directly on Mulholland Drive, with a view of L.A., was closed a few years after the house was completed, because it was such a beautiful spot that loads of passers-by would boldly step into the house to enjoy the view on Sundays. Sadly, the original situation wasn't restored during the renovations.

The owner shows us a Lautner sketch that shows a swimming pool halfway down the slope of the mountain, on the lower right side of the house, which was never executed. During the renovations, they decided to construct this swimming pool after all, but now on the left side of the house, because another house had since been built in the original spot. While we take a few more snapshots, the sun sets, and the brightly lit L.A. grid emerges in the distance.

When we look at all the photos in the Lautner archive in 2010, we find a folder of spectacular, stylised photos of the Garcia house, which must have been taken just after it was completed. In the images, the house still has the open carport under

Saturday, 28 April 2007

When we first stand outside this house from the early seventies, we actually know nothing at all about it, apart from the fact that its construction was a difficult process with many changes. In 2007, all we can see from the street is a carport. We haven't managed to get in touch with the owner, despite phoning him dozens of times. The house is in a beautiful spot on a cliff at Point Dume, with many celebrities as neighbours, such as Chad Smith (drummer for the Red Hot Chili Peppers), Bob Dylan and Julia Roberts.

previous: Pacific Coast House
next: Stevens

Friday, 4 May 2007

When we are in Malibu again a few days later, we drive past the mysterious Garwood House at Point Dume again, but again in vain. The house is directly next to the 2005 Lever / Morgenthaler House by architect Bart Prince (in 2012, someone applied for a demolition permit [!] for this house). With Google Earth or Bing Maps we only manage to get a general impression of the house, but on the floor plan, which we later find in the archive, we notice an enormous outdoor workshop, which folds around the garden.

previous: Segel
next: Beyer

Sunday, 13 July 2008

In 2008, we drive to Malibu for a third time to try to get inside the Garwood house. Seeing the drawings in the archive a few days earlier has made us very curious. The only thing we can see through the fence is a carport with striking columns. Again, no one answers the door. We hope to be able to see the house from below, but all the paths to the beach are private and under surveillance. In 2012, the house is suddenly put on the market with an asking price of sixteen million dollars. That has nothing to do with the house, but only with its fantastic location on a cliff, and all the famous Hollywood actors it has for neighbours. For the first time, we see photos of the interior on the estate agent's website. It doesn't look very Lautner-esque; in several places, there is a shiny natural stone finish. The way in which the columns meet the beams and the various angle rotations in the floor plan do betray Lautner's input. The fact that it's for sale gets our hopes up that we'll be able to visit it someday. That hope is instantly crushed when we find out that the people who bought the house are the singer Chris Martin (Coldplay) and actress Gwyneth Paltrow.

revious: Springer
next: Lippett

GOLDSMITH 2

#118: House, 1975-1978, extant
15300 Rayneta Dr, Sherman Oaks, CA 91403

Friday, 11 July 2008

For Mr and Mrs Goldsmith, Lautner designed two houses for two different locations. While only the second house was built, Lautner refers to it as the first in his monograph, illustrating it with floor plans and a cross-section. We discover that there is an error in the book: the cross-section shown is not of the Goldsmith house, but of the later Lucy house in Horseshoe Bay. Both houses have a curved volume with an enormous clerestory

to sell it a few years after it was finished. Of course we want to see the house with our own eyes. We didn't manage to get in touch with the occupant, so we drive there on the off chance we can get in. We find a recently renovated house, painted completely white. This would have been the first time that Lautner painted wooden elements white, and later it turns out that this feature is not original. The interior has been spruced up too; perhaps the renovations are the reason that no one ever answered the phone when we called. Despite its laborious inception, the house looks very interesting from the outside. The entrance and central stairwell lie in the place where the two main volumes of the house meet. The stairwell connects the volumes, which have a height difference of half

in the roof, opposite a reflective ceiling, which makes the space as light inside as it is outside. The first house was positioned on the edge of a steep slope. The Goldsmiths were very pleased with the design, but they were worried about the cost. So in 1968, they decided to build a catalogue home, which they would then be able to sell at a profit. In 1975 they got in touch with Lautner again to ask him to design a house for them after all, for a different location. At the time, Lautner was very busy with the design for the Hope house, so he himself was not closely involved with this project. Project architect Helena Arahuete: 'It was a difficult location, where a mudflow regularly came down in the middle. The house was designed as a bridge over it.' Lautner wasn't happy with the way the design was carried out and called it a 'lousy building job', and the clients themselves didn't get much pleasure from it either: they described the project as a 'financial nightmare' and were forced

a storey. The lower volume has three storeys; the higher one is V-shaped. The sharp shape of the volumes comes back in the shape of the windows and the front door. The outside makes us very curious about how the house looks inside. Years later we manage to get in touch with the original clients and we receive photos of what the house looked like at the time, with a subtle finish and warm materials.

previous: Crahan
next: Coneco Corp

In 1989 Jim Goldstein asked Lautner to not only redesign his house, but also his office, which was situated on the twentieth floor of a standard sixties office building. Here Lautner worked with mirrors and crooked walls in order to bring in as much as possible of the surrounding landscape. The ceiling was fully included in the design as a fifth façade, so that the room in no way seems like a standard office space anymore. The design stood out for its beautiful details, drawn by staff member Andrew Nolan and built by contractor Roban Poirier, who consistently refers to Lautner as 'the Chief'. After the rental contract ended the company located on the two floors above and below Goldstein wanted to expand, and made it impossible for Goldstein to renew his rental contract; he was forced to leave the building. Luckily, Nolan had designed the interior in such a way that it could be dismantled completely, and it has since been stored in eighty wooden crates in the cellar of the Los Angeles County Museum of Art.

GOOGIE'S

#32: Restaurant, 1949, demolished 1989
8100 Sunset Blvd (at N Crescent Heights Blvd),
Los Angeles, CA 90046

Sunday, 13 July 2008

Almost every day in July 2008, we drive past the location on Sunset Boulevard where Lautner's Googie's Restaurant stood, which brought him both prosperity and adversity. While 'Googie's' used to be a name that could be worn like a badge of honour, it was turned into a swearword by faultfinders from the East Coast. Architecture critics compared the strikingly cheerful design with the architecture of garish fast-food restaurants. After a while, the style of these restaurants, with their wild shapes, exuberant typography and cheap materials, was referred to as *Googie architecture*. According to these critics, it was nothing more, intellectually speaking, than flimsy, disposable road-side architecture, a paragon of our reprehensible consumer culture. The building that Lautner made for Googie's became famous for its location on the intersection of Laurel Canyon Boulevard and Sunset Boulevard, which were very hip at the time. People like James Dean would go and eat there. Lautner condemned the way in which his subtle design, conceived with the location firmly in mind, was exploited as a style icon. The extraordinarily scathing critique this project received was a factor in Lautner's decision to turn his back on what he saw as the absurd architectural press, which in turn never forgave him for it. That certainly contributed to the fact that Lautner was long considered a footnote in architectural history.

After the restaurant had changed hands a number of times and undergone a great deal of remodels, the whole block was bought up by a project developer in the late eighties, and a large shopping mall was built there instead. In our search for information about the history of the restaurant, we came into contact with Steve Hayes, who worked as a doorman at Googie's for years. He tells wonderful stories about Hollywood's heyday. One of the highlights for him was receiving a kiss from Marilyn Monroe there. Since there are only a few known photographs of the restaurant, we were curious what it had been like. Hayes sketched the interior for us and gave a detailed description of the space and the finishing. One of our students in Tilburg, Barry van Ham, made a very detailed model of it.

previous: Lippett
next: Wolfe

GOOTGELD

#40: Gootgeld, House, 1950-1952,
altered beyond recognition
#94: Rothschild, Kitchen remodel, 1964-1965, demolished
1167 Summit Dr, Beverly Hills, CA 90210

Tuesday, 23 March 2010

The Gootgeld house, completed in 1952, was a mystery for a long time. It is only mentioned in passing in Lautner's monograph, without photos or drawings, while it is a large villa with a generous budget. It's striking that the design was made together with his former partner Douglas Honnold, whom he had broken with in 1946. The client, Nouard Gootgeld, was good friends with both Lautner and Honnold, however, and managed to bring the men closer together, breathing new life into the productive collaboration.

TS: 'For some time, I have been in email contact with Carolyn Gootgeld Levine, Nouard Gootgeld's daughter. She sends me childhood photos where part of the house is visible. She has very clear memories of the house where she grew up in, and at my request, she has written them down in as much detail as possible:

The entire west side of the house was totally faced with floor-to-ceiling plate glass. The den also faced west, opening onto a common area between the den and the living room, therefore receiving much light from the living room. A row of square amber opaque windows ran along the top of the back wall, presenting a dramatic design element, and allowing light in.

John and Doug just loved to sit roosting on the ultra-modern orange sofas watching how the ambiance of the den, living room, and adjoining patios affected people. Just being in that house could make a person high. The adjacent living room had a completely different feel. Like so many of Lautner's rooms, it was a dizzying, mostly glass-enclosed space ship of a room, that floated above the world. At night, the dramatic angle of the roof overhang, with its ceiling spots, was particularly breathtaking.

Patios here and there were landscaped and backlit just as elegantly and paved with a smooth surface warmed from underneath by radiant heating. The patio just outside the common area between the den, living room, and dining room even had a waterfall with a black light trained on both the falling and pooling water. Of course, when my parents had guests, all sliding glass doors were left open, creating an impression that one was deep in a rain forest, sheltered only by a wood-beamed ceiling that had no walls to hold it up.

The entire house was heated by radiant heating, which meant the floor was never cold, and the air halfway to the ceiling was never too hot or cold. Indoor plants – even huge indoor trees – were a must. To round it all out, John insisted on an audio system that reached every corner of the house and grounds (very, very cutting-edge for the time).

Shortly after the house was finished, Gootgeld died suddenly, and the house was sold. The second owner painted the whole house white, and put in kitschy ornaments in the garden. In 1974, the house was bought by a famous lady who was very fond of her privacy. Carolyn Gootgeld also told us that when she drove past the house once, it was completely covered in scaffolding and it looked as though only the load-bearing structure was being spared. Since then, she has not managed to get a closer look at it.

So we don't know what it looked like after that. Using Google Earth, Carolyn Levine was able to ascertain that the base structure and two chimneys must still be intact. To our delight, we did find drawings of the project in the archive in 2010. The material we find is very detailed, with various versions of floor plan studies. Lautner was clearly looking for a sharp volume that follows the contour of the mountain slope in a zigzag shape. But we also find a version based on a circle segment. There

did some work on that extant house before, but a new house at that location was never built.

There are also drawings from 7 December 1964 for a renovation of the house on Summit Drive for Harry Rothschild, Jr., with minor changes, such as a built-in wine rack and a different ceiling in the toilet. Large sheets of paper show the work plan of the house on Summit Drive as it was built. Photos of the construction works also emerge, which show the shape of the roof; it looks like a tangram. The main volume has three angles of 120 degrees. An extended slanted roof doubles in the middle. At one end, the roof accommodates two storeys underneath it. The first thing you see when you come onto the lot is the carport for two cars. Next to that is the starting point for the route through the house, underneath the overhanging roof, where one can enjoy the view. The front door is situated halfway down the stretched-out house, where the volume doubles in height. The house stretches out on either side of the route, with the living room on the left and the dining room on the right, off an enclosed garden. After a last angle in the volume, the route continues on the mountain side and gives access to three bedrooms. There don't seem to be any photos of the original situation, but now we have a clear idea of what it must have been like.

JRK: 'During the research, we both followed leads of our own. We keep each other up to date on our progress, but we don't really get involved in each other's research, unless a certain tactical insight or an intersection of lines of information demands it. One of the projects where we were each following a different line of inquiry is the Gootgeld house. Tycho established contact with the daughter of the clients who commissioned the house, while I focused on organising a meeting with the current occupant. There was an extraordinary detail in this case, because the owner is the ex-wife of America's most famous rock 'n' roll singer. She bought the house after their divorce to allow their daughter to grow up there outside the public eye. There are wild rumours going round on the internet about how the house has been renovated; only the drains are said to be still intact. I sent a message to the email address listed on her fan

is some confusion, until it becomes clear that there are drawings for two different locations in the roll. The second design is for a house in Benedict Canyon, including wall sections and very detailed drawings of built-in furniture. It is a house with three stories, where the third floor is a mezzanine level for the living room on the second floor. When we ask Carolyn, it turns out to be a proposed replacement for the house where the family lived before they decided to move. Apparently, Lautner page: I explained who we were and why we really wanted to visit the house. That was on 23 March 2008. I didn't actually expect that my request would be answered via this route. To my surprise I received an answer from Mrs P's personal assistant on 2 May 2008. Although she answered all the questions I had asked, she immediately told me that visiting the house was out of the question. In the run-up to our trip in April 2009, I tried again, more successfully this time. We agreed on a time and could hardly believe it was really going to happen. At the time we had not seen the drawings yet, so we had no idea what the house looked like, either before the remodels or after them. While we were in L.A., we checked our email every day, and to our great dismay, we received an email from the PA: an important meeting was going to take place at the same time, so our appointment had to be moved. This happened a few times in a row, until we weren't in L.A. anymore. It had been too good to be true, anyway. When we knew that we were going to be in L.A. again for the party at the Hope house in 2010, we tried again. Initially, Mrs P would only communicate with us on the phone, but we managed to talk her into meeting us in person. The appointment was moved one more time. At a certain point, we were afraid to check our email for fear of finding another cancellation.'

At the agreed time, we are standing in front of the gate in the tall hedge, which blocks any view of the house or even the garden. Because we saw the drawings the day before, we know more or less what the layout of the house is, but not what it looks like now. The gate opens automatically when we have registered our presence. We are welcomed by the PA we had been in touch with via email. Her name suggested a Finnish background, which is confirmed by her appearance. She also looks like she could be Mrs P's bodyguard. Because of the lush garden, and because the house has been transformed from an austere fifties style of architecture to a Mediterranean villa, complete with arched windows and decorative fences, it feels as though we've suddenly arrived in Italy. An extra storey has also been added to the house. The house, which was built between Howe and Harpel chronologically, has been unrecognisably transformed.

We are brought to a table in the garden, where we are spoiled with fresh fruit juices and divine strawberries. The PA sits with us for a while to judge whether we are a security risk. Apparently we seem innocent enough, because she goes to get Mrs P. She comes outside wearing a large pair of dark glasses. She looks to be in her mid-thirties, while she's actually just turned sixty-five. Of all the people who own Lautner houses, she is definitely the most famous. We know her, of course, as a dazzling beauty from her time with the 'King' and as mother-in-law to the 'King of Pop'. This is American royalty.

We promised ourselves to speak only of architecture, which visibly relaxes her, creating a pleasant conversation. She tells us how she was looking for a nice place to raise her daughter, and how she transformed the house and garden into what it is now. It is fascinating to see how someone for whom money is no object shapes the appearance of her existence. Her humour and sparkling personality are contagious. She guides us through the house and shows us the whole ground floor. At any point, she is able to tell us exactly what the house looked like when she bought it and what changes she made. In all our visits, we have never come across anyone with such a well-developed spatial memory. What's more, a good deal of Lautner has been preserved. The renovated house is actually a study of the essence of Lautner's architecture. The main shape and the relation between the indoor spaces and the surrounding garden have

still be considered a Lautner. At the end of the conversation we want to take a photo with her to document this extraordinary meeting. She takes this as a matter of course and gives us tips on how best to pose in order to look good in the photo. We understand perfectly well that we've let ourselves be taken in, but we drive back through the gate with a big smile on our faces. In due course, this house simply needs a Mark Haddawy (see Harpel 1) to restore order here.

When we email her assistant to thank her, after we're back from our trip, she writes back that it was the first time, in the 23 years that she has been a personal assistant to Mrs P, that someone outside her personal circle of family and friends was invited into the house.

previous: Eisele
next: Hinerfeld

stayed the same. The zigzag shape of the floor plan still fits in beautifully with the topography of the location, with the enclosed patio on the one side and the panoramic view on the other side. The patio still floods when it rains, like Carolyn told us it already did fifty years ago. The superstar status has disappeared, and instead we are faced with a committed owner. She fell in love with the location and Lautner's interpretation of it. Only the exterior has been adapted to her own tastes and preferences. We ask ourselves how many of its defining characteristics a Lautner can lose and

HANCOCK

#11: Hancock, House, 1945-1946, extant
#141: Todd, Remodel and addition, 1989, extant
2107 W Silver Lake Dr, Los Angeles, CA 90039

Wednesday, 2 May 2007

We visit the Hancock house, an early work from 1945 that Lautner designed in collaboration with Douglas Honnold. He remodelled and extended the house for the current owners, Mr and Mrs Todd, towards the end of his life. We can still remember the excitement when we first came across a picture of the house on the internet, in a 1948 issue of *Arts & Architecture*.

This is one of the few Lautner buildings that is situated on a flat stretch of land, on a street. We ring the front doorbell, but once we get inside, it turns out this door simply lead to a triangular patio behind it, with the house folded around it. As a result, the real front door is at the centre of the house, which offers a direct view of the back garden. If you take a U-turn on your left here, you will find yourself in the living room, which is two steps higher up. The living room faces the street and has double height windows that look out over Silver Lake, across from the house. It looks as though Lautner, lacking context and differences in level, looked for other ways to create an interesting space. The glass façade ends in a bed of rocks, a detail that comes back later, in the Schaeffer house. The bedroom hangs over the living room like a balcony, which is reminiscent of Le Corbusier's work. The house shows certain similarities with Lautner's last house, the Shearing house, especially in the way in which the various spaces are joined together. The house is clearly one of his first designs, with specific details like the louvered panels between the staircase and the hallway that turn into windows on the kitchen. The space between the louvres is filled with mirrors and glass, so that you can see the front door from the kitchen.

The current owners used to live on the other side of Silver Lake, in a house by Rudolf Schindler, but when they bought this house, they asked Lautner to do it up and extend it, 44 years after it was built. In the spot where there used to be a large sundeck, Lautner made an extra room. He managed to create unity between old and new with the modest construction: if you didn't know that the remodels were carried out more than forty years later, you wouldn't guess. Lautner renovated a number of his own houses. Some of these are listed in his monograph, but others are left out, some of which are sizable extensions, like an entirely new wing in the Elrod house.

While we are warmly being welcomed, the doorbell rings: Lautner's oldest daughter, Karol

Peterson Lautner, has arrived. We meet her here for the first time. She has come to L.A. specially from Michigan to spend a few days with us. Because we only had limited contact via email, we have no idea what kind of person she is. The only things we know about her are the year she was born and the fact that she's Lautner's oldest daughter. We gather in the garden, which also has a back entrance at the spot where the garden wall is set back, so that one can put the garbage out without being run over.

The hostess serves a heavenly unoaked Chardonnay from the Napa Valley. Everyone is very impressed by the hospitality and by the hostess's daughter, who turns out to be an internationally known singer-songwriter who was on stage at Paradiso in Amsterdam just a month earlier.

previous: Harvey
next: Baldwin

#57: House, 1954-1956, extant
7764 Torreyson Dr, Los Angeles, CA 90046

Saturday, 28 April 2007

For Harpel 1, on Mulholland Drive, the heartlands of Lautner country, we have an appointment in 2007. The owner, Mark Haddawy, welcomes us. The house is in mint condition: after years of neglect, it has recently been restored to its original state. Harpel 1, from 1954, is the first in a series of neighbouring projects. This commission lead to the next two: Malin, in 1958, and Castagna, in 1963. Willis Harpel was a radio DJ who more than once commissioned Lautner to design a house for him. Harpel 1 consists of a diamond-shaped grid of twenty-three overdimensioned, full-storey, grey concrete columns. Beams rest on these columns, which form a pergola, then a covering, then an actual roof, and finally a pergola again. The space that is defined by the grid of columns is more than twice as big as the actual house. The house is embedded in the landscape in several ways. It is built up against a rock face, which runs into the living room from outside; the three steps that bridge the difference in level between the living room and dining room extend far into the garden and mark the transition between the grass and the pool. There is a skylight above the central column in the living room,

which lets light into the heart of the house. In order to reach the front door, you walk past the slope of the mountain, parallel to the bedroom wing under the pergola. Behind the front door, the built-in furniture forms the transition from entrance to living room, which does not immediately reveal itself. The route from the front door to the living room and terrace is a real *promenade architecturale*:

every step reveals slightly more of the house, culminating in the swimming pool, with its fantastic view of the San Fernando Valley. The room is both opened up towards the landscape and anchored to the rock face. The large fireplace in the wall underscores the earthy character of the room. The house itself was not only restored down to the last detail to its 1957 state, the interior is also completely 'vintage'. Only the kitchen and the hi-fi system are state of the art.

Haddawy tells us about the renovations he carried out. The house had been neglected for a long time, and 'enriched' with additions like a large terrace and even an extra storey. The dismantling of this extra storey caused conflict between Haddawy and his neighbour, who – unbeknownst to him – also lives in a Lautner design. Because he owns a boutique selling vintage clothes, Haddawy has no choice but to work on his house at the weekends. One day his neighbour had had enough of the noise. While Haddawy was working on the extra storey with a pneumatic drill, a middle-aged man suddenly appeared and started screaming at him in Spanish. Because of Haddawy's tanned

finished, he sold it with everything inside it. He bought the Harpel House without having seen it, because he suspected this house would better suit his personality. Impressed by this level of dedication and skill, *and* by his Ferrari 250GT Lusso, we leave for our next appointment. With the neighbour in question.

previous: Stevens
next: Castagna

appearance, the angry neighbour had assumed he was a Mexican handyman. It took a while to explain the situation, but their relationship is still difficult today.

Everything in the house is perfect: you'd wish this fate on all architectural classics. Haddawy had once before bought and restored an 'archi classic': Pierre Koenig's Case Study House #21. When it was

#78: Guest house, 1958, under construction 2017
7762 Torreyson Dr, Los Angeles, CA 90046

When we go through the rolls of drawings in the office of structural engineer Andrew Nasser in 2009, we find something unexpected: drawings dated 23 December 1958 for a guest house in the garden of Harpel 1. This is the real Harpel 2, in other words. What has become known as Harpel 2, from 1966, in Anchorage, Alaska, is actually the third Harpel house. The guest house is situated on a slope of about 15 degrees. The floor plan consists of two overlapping circles. The house most resembles the house for Ernest Lautner in Pensacola, complete with a curved brick wall that follows the contour of the mountain, and the characteristic bevelled roof beams. The house in Pensacola was designed in 1957 and completed in 1959, so it was conceived of around the same time. The drawings were recently found by the owner of Harpel 1, who is now looking into whether he can still have the house built. When we check with Haddawy later to see if he is really planning on having the house built, he replies that it's difficult because no detailed drawings have been found yet. Haddawy persists, however, and architects Escher and Gunewardena are commissioned to resume the project. In October 2016, we receive a photo of the building site from Frank Escher, where construction has finally begun after years spent acquiring the right permits.

Saturday, 11 November 2017

When we drive to Harpel 1 in 2017, we're curious to find out whether the guest house has been completed yet. It turns out that it hasn't, but the foundations and the frame of the retaining wall are finished. Haddawy tells us that they found a complete set of drawings by Lautner after all, even including a beautiful perspective drawing. Because the project is very complex, the construction process is slow but steady. It is fascinating to see how Lautner fitted the concept for the house to the site. The two-storey, cylindrical volume is drawn in on the side of the lot, its back to the traditional neighbouring house where Lautner carried out the Castagna Remodel five years later. It is situated on a lower part of the steep lot, where the view only emerges when you go upstairs, while the building's height has been carefully chosen so that you look over its roof from Harpel 1.

previous: Wolf
next: Flower Shop for Mr. Samuel Morhaime

#96: House, 1966-1967, extant
1900 Stanford Dr, Anchorage, AK 99508

Friday-Saturday, 26-27 November 2010

Willis Harpel moved from L.A. to Anchorage in 1964 and was so satisfied with Lautner's work that he asked him to design another house for him. The important thing was that in the dark winter months there should be enough daylight in the house to create a comfortable environment. In order to visit this house, there was just one condition: we had to see it in the winter. As this makes our third trip in one year we have to keep it short: a weekend trip to Alaska, unusual, to say the least. There are no direct flights to Anchorage from the Netherlands, and we choose to fly via Seattle as there are buildings there that we would like to see. Thus, we end up with a mini-trip of a day and a half in Seattle, a day and a half in Anchorage and two flights of twenty hours each.

After a flight with a wonderful view over mountains and glaciers we land in Anchorage, where the temperature is -10 degrees Celcius and there is at least three feet of snow. The sun gives a beautiful warm light, not rising far above the horizon in daytime and disappearing again at about three in the afternoon. Although our appointment is not until the following day we cannot resist driving straight out to Harpel 2 to take advantage of this lovely weather and take the first photos.

We park opposite the lake. It is completely frozen, and covered by a layer of snow. We see some footsteps, so we venture onto the ice. Carefully we cross the lake, until we are so close to the house that we can see it properly. From this side, what stands out is the clerestory that rises up behind the circular living room, of a size that you rarely see in a residential building. For Lautner, bringing in daylight was the most important task. When we find ourselves on the street side shortly afterwards, the house does not immediately attract attention. The actual visit to the house is not scheduled until the next day. We spend the rest of the afternoon exploring Anchorage.

The next day is cloudy, and we are glad we already took a few photos yesterday. In the run-up to our appointment, we lost touch with the owners and thought they changed their minds about our visit or that our emails had ended up in their junk mail folder. But the master of the house ran for governor of Alaska as a Republican, which made him easy to find. Through him, we managed to re-establish contact with them, which previously went through his wife. We were welcome to visit in November. Because we had to travel so far, we asked if we could spend a whole day in the house, so we could experience the changes in the light.

We are warmly received by the lady of the house, who tells us all about the history of the house. Willis Harpel commissioned Lautner to design the house after he was given the opportunity to run a radio station in Alaska. Soon after the house was finished, Harpel died in an accident with a snowmobile. After that, the house was owned for a long time by two brothers, who took turns living in it. They used it as a bachelor pad and let it get run-down. When the current owners bought it, they did it up, but also changed things here and there. The slanting wall that reflects the light from behind the

near the large clerestory, four steps down, in the circular living room, which is truly magnificent. The straight hallway intersects the round wall, which follows the curve of the space. Because the hallway hits the circle asymmetrically, you enter the round space from the side. The living room is an unbelievable space: a sea of light. Because the light comes from behind the sofa, it directs your gaze

towards the view across the lake. The enormous clerestory is supported by columns that are shaped like totem poles. Mrs C tells us that a connoisseur pointed out that they are fantasy totem poles, a cheerful addition by the contractor.

Because Lautner designed three houses for the same client, it is interesting to see how far the client's influence extended. Harpel 1 is completely unique in Lautner's oeuvre; the grid of heavy columns was something he would never repeat in any way. The guest house in the garden of Harpel 1, which is in fact the second Harpel house, was not built in Lautner's lifetime, but the ideas for this house were realised shortly afterwards in the house Lautner designed for his cousin in Pensacola. The zigzag façade in the Pearlman Cabin, where the glass disappears invisibly into round tree trunks, returns in the third Harpel house (known as Harpel 2), now combined with the never-built clerestories from Goldsmith 1 and the Lucy house, also never built. The diagonal boards of unplaned wood is another element that was applied more than once. The triangular windows are new. The layout

living room, for instance, has been painted light-grey, while it was originally yellow, allowing warm light to flood into the house.

The set-up of the floor plan is simple. From the front door, you come into a central hallway, with three bedrooms and the kitchen and dining room on the left, and on the right a double garage and guest room. The light immediately beckons you into the long, wide hallway. The hallway ends

of the bedrooms is nothing special, but the living room is unparalleled. The way in which the circular form joins the hallway, the clerestory, the view and the dining room: everything has a maximum effect. From the kitchen you have a view of the living room and the dining room, but you can't see the kitchen from there; the kitchen functions as a deejay booth just like the kitchen in the Carling house. Under the clerestory, behind the built-in sofa, there are giant ficuses that are around twenty feet tall. This gives you the sense that you are in a tropical garden, while you have an obstacle-free view of the snow-covered lake. There are few houses that offer an experience like this. What you experience when you stand in this room cannot be captured in a photograph. The relation between the house and nature is perfect, while you remain sheltered from the weather.

Although the house rests on stilts, the stone floor emphasises the connection with the earth. We are brought downstairs, where a lot of extra space was added later by putting outer walls under the house. Clearly it wasn't Lautner who did this: it has a white modular ceiling with strip lighting. If you didn't know better, you'd think you were in a standard office building. The living room is supported by four large columns that are cross braced, limiting how the space can be used. When asked whether the shores can be removed, we advise them not to saw them off, as this will put the stability at risk. The character of the house changes drastically when dusk begins to fall. We walk out onto the ice to take a few more shots.

previous: Marbrisa
next: Midgaard

#36: Harvey, House, 1950-1958, extant
#120: Barnes, Remodel, 1976-1979, extant
2180 Live Oak Dr, Los Angeles, CA 90068

Wednesday, 2 May 2007

Operating on the assumption that it is necessary to speak to Lautner's former employers in order to gain deeper insight into his oeuvre, we approach Helena Arahuete, who worked for him for 23 years. She is the architect who designed and supervised the meticulous restoration of the Harvey house. Lautner's relation with the original client, the owner of Harvey Aluminium, was intense. Lautner's step-daughter Elizabeth Honnold Harris describes this man as follows: 'Leo Harvey stepped into the office at "a thin time"… i.e., only about half a job on the boards and nothing coming in whatsoever. He wanted the best, he wanted a house that nobody else could have or imagine, and he was exacting, picky, firm and totally committed right from the first. He paid the various increments of the fee as they came due without protest or second-guessing, he pored over materials catalogues and took John's judgements on everything as The Way It Ought To Be. He was, in sum, a Perfect Client.' It is interesting that to Lautner he turned out not a perfect client at all. He was a difficult and de-manding client, a wealthy man used to getting his way. Elizabeth remembers Lautner's dinner table rages about the unreason-ableness of the guy. Also Helena, who came into the office much later never heard any positive words about him. This might

explain that the only mention of the house in Lautner's monograph is a postage stamp of a photo in the back. Maybe there were no good photos of its original state, and in the nineties, it was impossible to photograph the house again due to the appalling state it was in.

In 2007, the owners of the house are Hollywood stars Mitch Glaser and Kelly Lynch. They have restored it to its former glory with an unbelievable level of precision. The house has an enormous round roof, carried by circular, concentric beams. The edge of this roof shows strong similarities to that of the 1949 UPA Studios, now torn down, which were designed for Stephen Bosustow. The interior exudes the atmosphere of a thirties house, with a shiny wooden wall finish and pink marble. Originally, the central space was half indoors, half outdoors, but like many of Lautner's covered indoor-outdoor spaces, such as Tyler, Elrod and Hatherell, the desire for more indoor space triumphed over aesthetics and the practicality of having a covered outdoor space. As such, the whole space was transformed into a large ballroom over the years, and the subtle transition between indoors and outdoors was lost. It is possible that the introduction of air conditioning had something to do with this: there was no longer any need for a shady outdoor space.

During the renovations, the clients decided to leave the central space exactly as they found it, based on the fact that Lautner had made these alterations himself, and that the history of the house is embedded in this. No trouble or expense was spared during the renovations. Every light switch was remade exactly in line with 1950s style. Everyone always waxes lyrical about this renovation, but still something seems off balance in the Harvey house. The space with the central column is too large compared to the rest of the house. When the outdoor area was closed up in

the seventies, the character of the house changed drastically. We can hardly imagine that Lautner himself was responsible for this, but both Arahuete and the owners insist that it's true. Years later we come to a different conclusion after visiting the archives.

It's fun to finally meet a Hollywood actress we've seen in a movie, and especially one with such an incredible passion for modern architecture and its preservation: from the point of view of an

architecture enthusiastic, it's the best role for every Hollywood star. The spectacular location means this house is much sought after by property developers, who wouldn't hesitate to tear it down. Leonardo DiCaprio was one of the others interested in buying the house, but luckily Kelly Lynch outbid him. There couldn't have been a better buyer for the house. She is a real patron of modern architecture in general and of Lautner in particular. To meet Helena Arahuete in the flesh on top of this was unbelievable. This is the woman who worked on all the important projects since the early seventies, longer than anyone else: 'A legend in herself.' In the years following our first meeting, we have become friends, and we have also visited houses that she designed on her own. We wanted to see how her own work related to the projects she worked on for Lautner. Helena is a priceless mine of information.

The Harvey house is especially interesting because it marks a turning point in Lautner's career. An important reason for visiting the lesser known works in addition to the famous ones is to see how certain ideas developed, how they were carried out and tested, and how they subsequently found their way into the masterpieces.

In 2009, we find fascinating drawings for a 1978 remodel of the Harvey house, commissioned by Dr Chester Barnes, the second owner of the house, who asked Lautner to carry out a number of alterations between 1976 and 1979. This means Lautner did make the drawings for closing up the outdoor area. But there is an important difference between the version in the drawings and the version that was built: Lautner's drawings don't close off the circle completely – only by about three quarters, creating a so-called screen porch: an indoor-outdoor space, with sliding glass panels and a large fireplace. In addition, we come across a detailed proposal for a new entrance, where the central column is situated in a cylindrical space with a double bronze front door. Like this, one would enter the house through its heart.

It looks as though only the main features of the

design were carried out. It may be the case that the contractor suggested that it would be much cheaper and also more spacious if the circle was closed completely, and the front door was placed on the outer edge of the circle. It's unclear to us why these drawings weren't used as a starting point during the renovations. It's possible that no one knew of their existence or that the changes were considered too radical after all.

previous: Vine Street Offices
next: Hancock

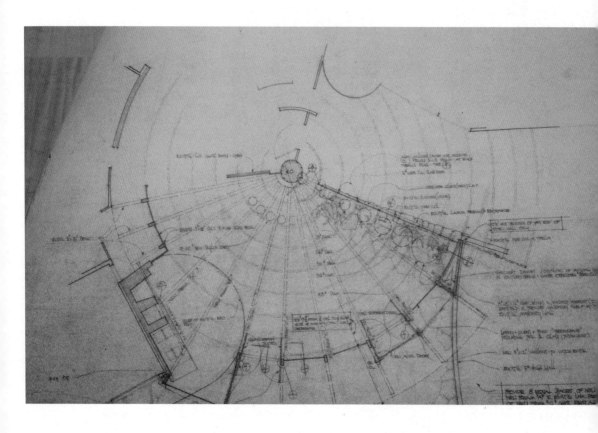

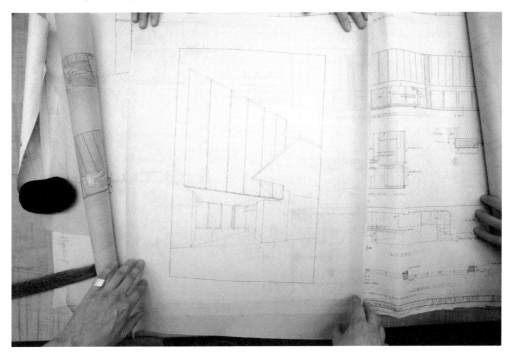

Tuesday, 7 April 2009

Visiting the archive gave us many new leads for further research. We find another design in the archive for the client who commissioned the Harvey house: the entrance and reception hall for Harvlan (Harvey Aluminium Company), his office at 911 S Broadway in Downtown L.A. When we check it out we find a deserted building. The outside still looks the same as the perspective drawing in the archive, but inside it looks like the work was halted halfway through, a long time ago. It remains unclear whether Lautner's remodel was ever carried out.

previous: Eisele
next: Mauer

HATHERELL

#68: House, 1956-1958, extant
10160 Maude Ave, Sunland, CA 91040

Thursday, 3 May 2007

Although the Hatherell house is included on the map in the back of Barbara-Ann Campbell-Lange's book, there's nothing more than an arrow that points to a location off the map. As a result, we spent a lot of time trying to find the house in the foothills of the Verdugo Mountains. When we started our research, the re-appreciation of Lautner's work was still in its early stages. The level of interest hasn't yet reached the stage that we're not welcome for a visit. The owner of this house, too, responded positively when we approached him.

It's the end of a very intensive day when we have an appointment at the Hatherell House in Sunland, just before sunset, the best time of day for all Lautner houses: the time when the diffuse boundary between outdoors and indoors dissolves, as the lights go on indoors. At the end of the road, from where it's impossible to see the house, we come to a paved parking lot. On the west side, there is a single-storey, rectangular box, built from the same simple concrete blocks that many of Albert Frey's designs are made of. Details betray that this is a Lautner after all, like the bay window in the kitchen that protrudes from the closed wall. We are warmly received with a glass of wine, but when we step into the living room we immediately see that something is wrong: we're standing in a large, round room, where the outer wall follows the edge of the roof. The owner tells us enthusiastically that he loves this large room so much because it's big enough to house his whole chair collection. In other words, the house has been remodeled, and in the process, its most important characteristic has been lost.

The house is constructed around a circular space, the construction of the roof of which looks like an enormous bicycle wheel. The living room under the roof was originally half the size, because

the boundary between indoors and outdoors used to be about halfway into the circle. Back then, the other half was a large, covered outdoor area next to the pool. The transition between indoors and outdoors was very subtle, because the walls could be opened up completely. The original position of the wall can only be seen in the extra fortification of the gossamer-thin steel joists. This outdoor area was an express wish of the original clients, who were in the habit of sleeping outside. At night they'd roll their beds outside and leave the dog inside. They would jokingly refer to their house as the largest dog house in the world. They enjoyed their sheltered outdoor area for more than thirty years. But like in many of Lautner's houses, the next owner closed up the space and installed air conditioning in the house.

This is not the only element that is no longer original. On the left side, the house was extended by six feet, while a room was added on the opposite side, using the same concrete blocks and detailing of round walls and roof edge. A slight difference in colour betrays that this wasn't always there. The layout of the windows was changed in the outer wall, while the wooden ceiling in the living room has been painted white. Because of the materials used, it looks remarkably modern. And while the large living room looks fantastic, certainly when the lights are on, it's still a shame that the enjoyment of a covered terrace has been sacrificed in favour of more indoor space. Despite our disappointment, we gaze at the beautiful sunset over L.A. and fantasize about a Lautner enthusiast buying the

house one day, and restoring it to its original state. But because this house isn't located in a desirable area, that seems unlikely. Three years after our visit, the house has changed hands again, after the estate agent had praised it as the 'Lautner with the Grand Room'.

previous: Dahlstrom
next: Segel

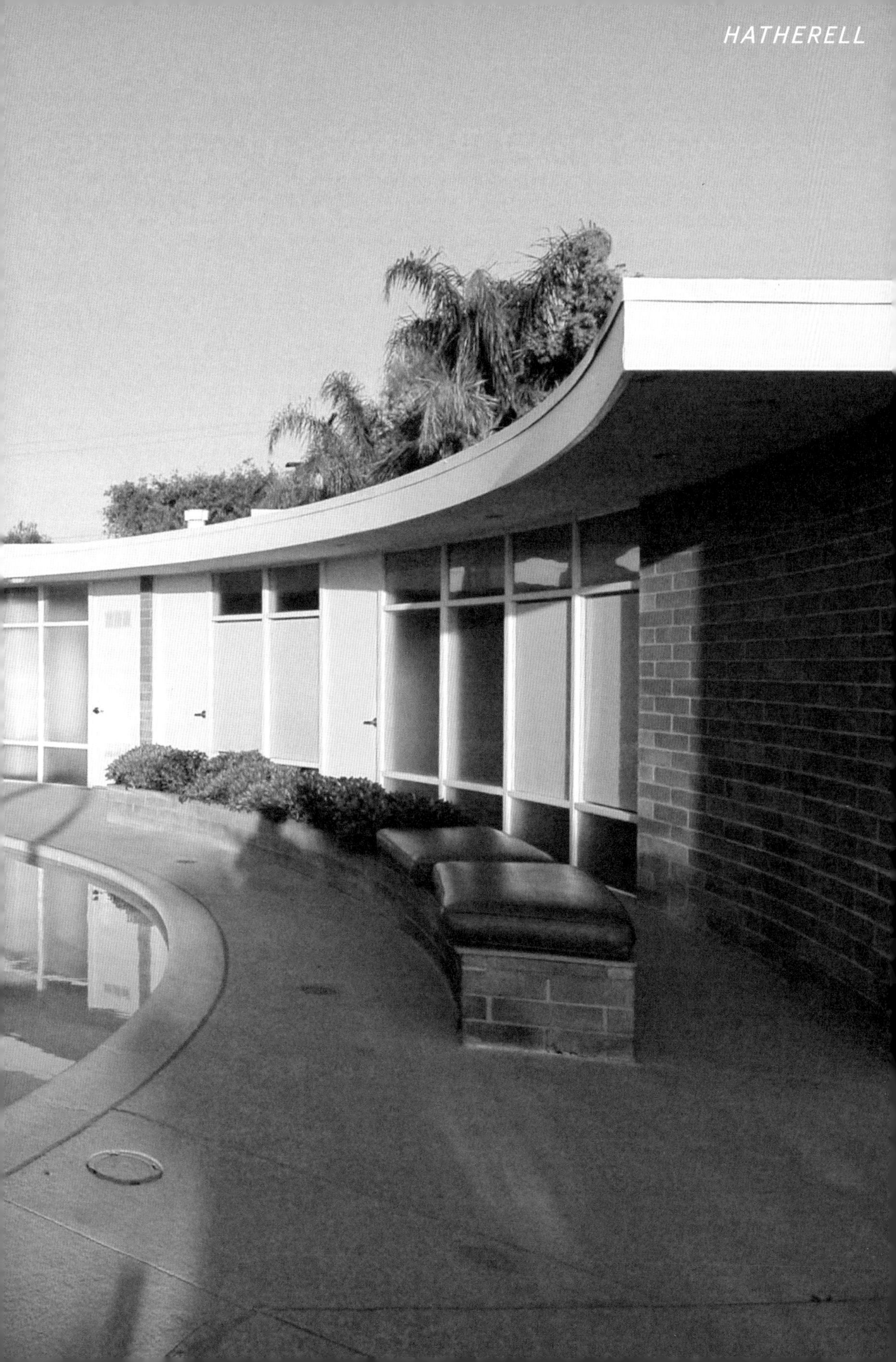

Henry's Restaurants: Because our schedule is less busy in April 2009 than it was a year earlier, we also have time to steer our research towards demolished works. Early on in his career, Lautner worked with Glen Amundson, who asked him to design several restaurants for his drive-in chain, Henry's Restaurant. For twenty years, there was always something to do for one of the Henrys at Lautner's firm. The relationship between Lautner and Amundson was one of mutual admiration. Guy Zebert, a former collaborator, said about Amundson: 'At the conclusion of the Pomona projectI was sitting in a booth with Glen having a cup of coffee and finally had to ask him: Glen, is there anything that ever bothers you? His response was: You know, after surviving the battle of Guadalcanal in the Solomon's Islands in 1943, I could no longer find anything that could be defined as a problem. That said it all for me.' In the end, Lautner built five Henrys, but not one of them is still standing. They all fell victim to demolition. We decide to visit the locations to get a feel for the surroundings of the buildings and see what has replaced them.

HENRY'S ALHAMBRA

#49: Bar / restaurant remodel, 1952-1959, demolished
#93: Addition, 1964, demolished
203 W Valley Blvd, Alhambra, CA 91801

Tuesday, 7 April 2009

One of the five Henry's Restaurants was situated in Alhambra. Now there is only a parking place there, with a remarkably large number of Mercedesses. At

from 1964, where the sketch has been worked up as a large round cantilevered roof, attached in the middle to the outer corner of the simple rectangular volume of the restaurant. There is an earlier design for this location, of a large, triangular canopy, carried by two slanted trusses that meet at an angle, supporting a sign that reads 'Chicken Rough'. The photos and drawings for the different branches of Henry's are all jumbled together, which doesn't always make it easy to see which photo belongs with which location. It's only at the end of the next

the end of the parking lot there is a beigey-brown stucco box with a postmodern entrance. We look at it with disbelief. We go inside; there are around a hundred Chinese people having dinner. We decide to do the same. It turns out that no one speaks English, so we order something at random. When we are served a kind of porridge with frogs' legs in it, we are overcome by a feeling of melancholy: we would rather have tried a 'Chicken in the Rough', the speciality at Henry's: a fried chicken dish that could be eaten without a knife and fork; post-war prosperity came in many forms.

A year later, in the Lautner archive, we find a few photos of the original situation of the Henry's in Alhambra, with a vague pencil sketch of a large round awning on top of it. Also, there are photos

day that we make a unique discovery when we find a photo in a folder labelled 'miscellaneous'. It shows a large, protruding round canopy. This must be the canopy we saw on the drawings for Henry's Alhambra. We thought this design had been binned, but it was actually carried out, and Lautner's earlier design with its characteristic pointy construction probably wasn't.

previous: Mauer
next: Henry's Arcadia site

Tuesday, 7 April 2009

In the location where Henry's Arcadia used to
be, we only find a modern bank, and nothing that
reminds of Lautner's building. Or do we? A little
further on, we spot a fifties diner – from a distance
it looks like something Lautner could have had
something to do with. But when we get closer,
it turns out to be an uninteresting building, and
they've never heard of Henry's. We visit the local
history museum, where we find two blurry aerial
photos of Henry's in better times. Strangely enough
we don't find anything about Henry's Arcadia in
the Lautner archives, so we still have no idea what
it looked like.

previous: Henry's Alhambra site
next: Zimmerman

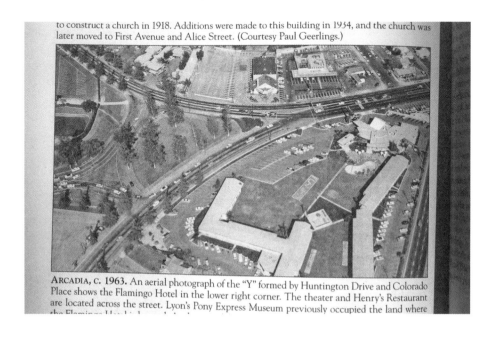

to construct a church in 1918. Additions were made to this building in 1934, and the church was later moved to First Avenue and Alice Street. (Courtesy Paul Geerlings.)

ARCADIA, C. 1963. An aerial photograph of the "Y" formed by Huntington Drive and Colorado Place shows the Flamingo Hotel in the lower right corner. The theater and Henry's Restaurant are located across the street. Lyon's Pony Express Museum previously occupied the land where

HENRY'S GLENDALE

#21: Restaurant building, 1947-1948, demolished 1980
#88: Remodel, 1962, demolished 1980
#103: Remodel, 1968, demolished 1980
520 E Colorado St, Glendale, CA 91205

Saturday, 12 July 2008

As part of our research into demolished Lautner buildings, we visit Glendale in 2008. At the intersection of Colorado Street and S. Glendale Avenue there were two Lautner buildings: the Tower Motors Lincoln Mercury Showroom and Henry's Restaurant, both designed in 1947. In the spot where Henry's used to be, there's now a concrete bank building with a lot of mirror glass. Henry's Glendale was the first of five Henry's Restaurants that Lautner designed. One of the striking features of the design was the outdoor terrace, fully integrated in the architecture.

Later, when we search for plans of this Henry's in the archives, we stumble on a perspective drawing and various photos. Unfortunately, there is no address on the sketches for Henry's in Santa Ana. It looks as though it is only a modest renovation. Whether it was ever carried out remains uncertain.

previous: Gantvoort
next: Tower Motors / Parkway Motors

In the archives there are very detailed floor plans and perspectives of the remodel of Henry's Pasadena, coloured in with tropical colours. This Henry's also didn't survive the test of time, and sadly no pictures have been found yet of the building. The last drawing in the roll is a perspective of the waiting area for take-away food. It's a covered outdoor space where you could wait for your order on a sofa with big cushions: the ideal indoor-outdoor space in the form of a take-away counter of a fast-food restaurant.

HENRY'S POMONA

#67: Restaurant building, 1956-1957, demolished 1986
101 E Foothill Blvd, Pomona, CA 91767

Monday, 14 July 2008

On 14 July 2008, we visit the site of Henry's Pomona. The drive-in restaurant that Lautner designed here was the most striking of the five he built. The leaf-shaped roof was constructed as an enormous upside-down boat, built of large, laminated wooden beams. Under this roof, there was an indoor area and an outdoor area with room for cars. The building was in a prominent spot along the famous Route 66 and attracted customers simply because of its design. It is sad when things are demolished, but sometimes it is unavoidable. However, what has happened here is simply criminal: we find an ordinary mini-mall with a completely nondescript, beige stucco branch of Wendy's, an expanse of asphalt surrounding it. Only a crooked, wooden pylon harks back to days long gone. We wonder how it's possible that such a fantastic building should fall victim to demolition and be replaced by such a nondescript box. All that remains is a handful of black-and-white photos. Because we can't imagine that those magnificent laminated beams were simply thrown away, we drive around for a while, hoping to spot them somewhere. But this is in vain, because if they *have* been reused, it's not here.

In October 2009, our Tilburg student Gijs Hoeijmans builds an enormous 1:50 model of this restaurant, which sets off an interesting series of events. The model gives a good impression of how the building used to function and how it worked, spatially. Through a blog, we get in touch with a journalist from Pomona, who is looking for the story behind the restaurant. We send him photos of the model, which in turn end up in the local paper, *Inland Valley Daily Bulletin*. This leads to the discovery of new sources. One of the readers is an acquaintance of the demolition contractor Brian Hill, who was asked to demolish the building in 1986. Just as we suspected, the laminated beams were not thrown

away. He used the largest ones to build a house himself, which looked like a kind of eclectic cathedral. Unfortunately, not everyone in the neighbourhood appreciated the building, and in 1994, someone started a fire, and the house burned down to the ground. Still, it turns out that a few joists were preserved, because the contractor also sold several of

them. Seven of them have been in a back garden in Claremont for about twenty years, and two others now adorn the entrance to the parking place of a coffee shop in San Bernardino. The owner probably has no inkling of the legacy he drives through every day.

When we visit the archive in 2010, we find various previously unknown photos of Henry's Pomona that we stare at in disbelief. How is it possible that such a fantastic building didn't survive?

previous: Tolstoy
next: Conrad

HILO CAMPUS LIFE SCIENCE BUILDING

#102: Laboratory building, 1967-1972?, extant
Life Science, building 344, University of Hawai'i
Campus, Nowelo St, Hilo, HI 96720

From the second half of the sixties, Lautner started focusing more on acquiring larger commissions such as the one he got in 1970 to build the Hilo Campus in Hawaii, an interesting project comprising a number of pavilions. Our extensive research never produced any evidence that any part of it was realised. It was thought the project had been halted, just like the other large projects Lautner was commissioned to carry out. But while going through the archives in 2010 we discover something interesting in a folder of drawings and photographs: photos of drawings of the Life Science Classroom Facility at the Hilo Campus. In Lautner's monograph the project is categorised as built and is illustrated by two floor plans and a fantastic cross section showing an ingenious ventilation system. We find five versions of the same building: one with a roof spanning two earth embankments; two with a series of classrooms behind an entrance building; one in the shape of a tent and another with an inflated roof. Finally there is a version in which everything is visualised within a large triangular building and one in which four straight volumes are grouped around a courtyard.

In the next folder we finally found our proof: a handful of photographs of a building in a tropical setting, which closely resembled the simplest design version with the straight boxes. So it seems that the rumours were wrong and the project was in fact built, but it is unclear what the extent was of Lautner's influence. The contours of a follow-up trip are slowly beginning to take shape.

Tuesday, 23 March 2010

We visit a remodel that is not included in Lautner's monograph. It concerns the extension of a house belonging to Mr and Mrs Hinerfeld that we found in the archive. Only a small part of it was carried out. The only significant detail that makes it likely that this is a Lautner is the way the carport roofbeam is joined to the masonry. The ceiling is also distinctive: it runs from the low front door into the living room, which is one and a half storeys high. The owner, who didn't know that Lautner had done work on the house, shows us around. In the middle of the living room, there is a doll's house-sized model of an ecological house designed by the owner, which will soon replace the current house. In our eyes, every Lautner lost is one too many, and this remodel is no exception. In 2017, the house is listed for sale, advertised as a 'lot with enormous potential.'

previous: Gootgeld
next: Marbrisa

#106: House, 1969-1980, extant
2466 Southridge Dr, Palm Springs, CA 92264

Monday, 30 April 2007

At the end of the road, not even half a mile from the Elrod house, there is another Lautner house: the Bob and Dolores Hope house, a house of monstrous proportions. Bob Hope was a famous comedian with friends in presidential circles. He died in 2003, aged a hundred. Now his wife Dolores lives in the house, who is nearly a hundred years old herself by now.

It was to be a comfortable house for two people, with enough room to entertain five hundred. The construction of the house was a torturous process that took almost ten years. The idea behind the design was that the house would seamlessly blend into the hilly landscape: the roof would get a rough finish to match the surrounding hills. The volume was imagined as a kind of artificial volcano: a flattened cone with arches that opened out towards the landscape. After Lautner received the commission in 1969, he designed a beautiful concrete shell roof for the house, together with master engineer Felix Candela. But the Hopes were afraid that the costs would spiral out of control, and this idea was abandoned. The construction was then redesigned with a steel construction and wooden sheathing. On Lautner's recommendation, Wally Niewiadomski, the contractor who had previously built the Elrod house down the street, began construction in 1973. To Lautner's displeasure, Dolores Hope insisted on swapping Niewiadomski for Peter Kiewit Construction once the founda-tions had been laid. Kiewit was an enormous contractor for mines and motorways, among other things, and a friend of the family. Then fate struck: on a hot summer's day, the wooden roof caught fire during the joining, and within fifteen minutes, all the wooden sheathing was reduced to ashes. Because of how quickly it all happened,

the steel construction remained intact, however. This lead to a legal battle and the construction was delayed by years. By now, the costs had completely spiralled out of control, with the result that many compromises had to be made in the completion of the house, for which Wally Niewiadomski, the original contractor, was rehired. The relationship between Lautner and Dolores Hope remained

strained and reached a low point when she hired interior designer Laura Mako, the 'decorator of the movie stars', to design the interior in some kind of misplaced Louis style. Photos of the interior of the house were never published.

No matter how many emails we send and how many arguments we trot out, the owner won't budge: no is no. Mrs Hope lives in Palm Springs during the winter months and doesn't want anyone prying around in her house. During our stay at the Elrod house, we go for an evening walk past this strange construction of inhuman proportions. In the dark, the overhang looms towards us threateningly. The roof has a large round hole in the middle, like a kind of impluvium. The detailing

retreat, disappointed. We've reached the limits of our powers of persuasion and perseverance. On the way back down, we come past one beautiful house after another, with the lit-up grid of Palm Springs surrounded by dark mountains as a backdrop.

previous: Elrod
next: Elrod

Saturday, 20 March 2010

In March 2010, this house is still owned by the Hope family, who almost never let in visitors anymore, except for charity reasons, like today. At the end of the afternoon we meet Judy and Karol at the shopping mall at the bottom of the hill; they have also come to Palm Springs for the event and will accompany us to several appointments. Shuttle buses bring the visitors up the hill, and the gated community is opened again for us. We drive past the Elrod house to the end of Southridge Drive and where last time our path was blocked by a big gate, this time we walk along the red carpet to the entrance of the Hope house.

When we arrive in front of the gate, it's almost impossible to imagine that this house is a private home, because of its enormous size. At the entrance, we are received by the director of the Palm Springs Art Museum, who welcomes us as if she knows us. There are around 350 people at this party, which is in fact the kind of society event the house was made for. Helena Arahuete is here too, for the first time since the house was completed in 1980. Because of our part in Murray Grigor's film (*Infinite Space: The Architecture of John Lautner*), everyone seems to know us and want to talk to us. This is very flattering, but of course

doesn't look very subtle: the roofing is made out of segmented strips of copper, the façades are stucco: it's all turned out slightly differently than how it was intended. So there we are, standing by the gate. The security guards aren't swayed by the amounts we offer them in the middle of the night, prompted by too much champagne, and we

we're mainly here to see the house that was the source of so many problems. But on a night like tonight, the house does exactly what it was supposed to do. Because of the materials used, the detailing and the form language, this house shows its kinship to Beyer, and the rocks that continue from outdoors to indoors with the glass placed between them remind of Elrod. As soon as you enter the house, you are led into the patio, an enormous covered terrace with a hole in the middle of the roof, as if you're in the Pantheon. The cave parallels are fully developed here, and the roof is an enlarged version of the scale of the Turner house. Around the patio, which operates as the actual house on a day like this, there are a number of secondary rooms. On one side, the patio seamlessly turns into a spectacular view of Palm Springs, framed by the enormous arch of the roof, and on the other side, it is bordered by a huge fireplace, where an entire band is playing today.

Lautner's goal was to have the house blend into the hill and be shaped like a kind of volcano, complete with rocks and a waterfall. The rocks and waterfall stayed, but the roof was carried out in brownish-pink bitumen, against Lautner's desires; it has since been replaced by the buyer, so that the effect of blending into the hill has been lost. This evening, no one is allowed upstairs; security refused to be mollified. When we take a closer look, the house turns out to be very different from the drawings, and even different from the photos in Lautner's monograph. Nobody can tell us which architect did this. The most important change is that you initially entered the patio directly through a gate, without passing a door first. Now you arrive in a space that has been closed off with glass on two sides, forming a foyer, but one that is sufficiently transparent towards the patio. Here, the reception room, bar and toilets also have deep-pile carpet and baroque wallpaper in bright pink, which hurts our eyes. In the end Dolores Hope got the house how she wanted it anyway. For Lautner, who was interested in making 'real architecture', this was pure effrontery. When it gets dark, one can see the lit-up living area on the top floor very well. After designs that used part of a circle as a floor plan, like the Goldsmith and Lucy houses, which were never built, Lautner finally managed to make a curved skylight in this house, which ensures indirect light. The party is a happening; everyone we speak to says they have never been in the house before. For us, time goes by too fast, even though we were the first to arrive and the last to leave.

After Dolores Hope passed away at the age of

102 in 2011, the house came onto the market for $50 million. It wasn't until 2016 that the house was sold for a quarter of the original asking price. The new owner seems to have good intentions for the house: he has hired Helena Arahuete to transform it into what Lautner originally had in mind.

In 2017 we spend another whole day at the archives, where we make an amazing discovery. A competition design from 1962, titled 'A mansion for the Governor of California', seems to be a direct fore-

runner of the design for the Hope house. Here too, there is an enormous open cone shape, with an overhanging roof on three sides. For an architect who only very rarely repeated himself, the similarities between these two designs are really striking. Very occasionally, a good idea was recycled if it wasn't carried out immediately. This must have been one of those occasions. Guy Zebert says: 'This project was a last-minute charette produced in one weekend by the whole office to meet the deadline. Yes! John thought that the solution for the Governor was suitable for Bob Hope.' The lack of a commissioning client led to a pure and un-diluted idea, which was impossible to realise in the Hope house.

previous: Seletz
next: Bubbling Wells Resort

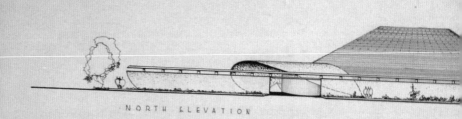

NORTH ELEVATION

A MANSION

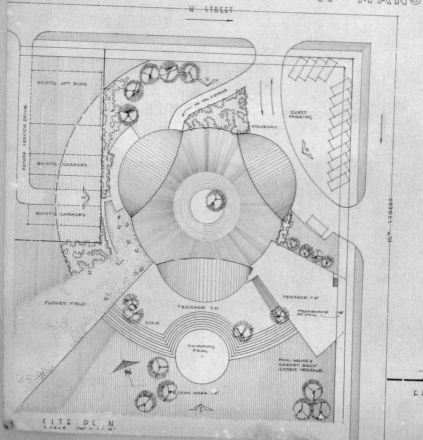

N STREET

SITE PLAN
SCALE 1/32" = 1'-0"

EAST EL

THE GOVERNOR OF CALIFORNIA

...SIGHT PRESTRESSED CONCRETE CONE AND
...WITH THREE INTEGRAL ARCHES CUTTING AT
...POINTS. CURVED CONCRETE WALL WITH WALK
...EETS.

...TE CONE TO BE ROOFED WITH DARK GREEN

...S NATURAL GRAY
...S GOLD AND/OR BLUE CERAMIC OR GLAZE.

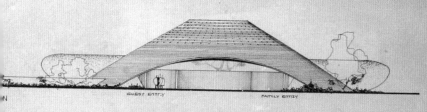

GUEST ENTRY   FAMILY ENTRY

155

#47: House, 1952-1953, extant
1655 Rotary Dr, Los Angeles, CA 90026

Saturday, 28 April 2007

Wednesday, 8 April 2009

We know nothing about the Howe house other than the year it was built. At first glance, it is a nondescript house in an ordinary neighbourhood. Only when we take a closer look in April 2007 do we recognise Lautner's signature. It took some convincing to get the owners to agree to a visit. When we arrive, we are invited in suspiciously. It's clear that they don't understand why we want to nose around. However, Mr and Mrs P., the elderly couple, are very friendly. We are the first Lautner fans who have tracked down their house. It is intensively lived-in and is so full of personal belongings that it's difficult to distinguish recognisable features. This house doesn't seem very special from outside, but inside it turns out that the whole rectangular roof is suspended from one central, wooden column. This remarkable support structure doesn't occur anywhere else in Lautner's projects. The outdoors is brought inside through the inward-facing, frameless glass bay windows. Another striking feature is the presence of ventilation panels next to the fixed windows. Copies of the original floor plans are kept in the house. Apparently that's common practice here. Lautner never publicised this house anywhere, which usually means that there were problems in the design process.

previous: Zimmerman
next: Pearlman

Because we are in the neighbourhood again in April 2009, we drive past to take a photo of the outside, which is still missing from our collection.

previous: Baldwin
next: Yokeno site

156

House, 1958, extant,
designed by James Charlton
4024 Murietta Avenue, Sherman Oaks, CA 91423

Thursday, 3 May 2007

Although we have planned an appointment at the Iwerks house, we have serious doubts about going there as the only people who are convinced that it is a real Lautner are the inhabitants themselves. Lautner did in fact made a sketch for this house, but when his former colleague James Charlton left Lautner's practice he took the commission with him and continued the design himself. The resemblance to Lautner's first sketch is not obvious, although it is certainly a nice house. One recognisable element is the beam beneath the lower terrace, which swings out from the façade in a different direction from the volume above. The whole is covered by a roof whose curved shape reminds of that of Henry's Pomona. The slatted façade of one of the rooms is also a recognisable element, which could have come from Silvertop. The house was recently remodelled by architect Tracy Stone, who also remodelled the Tyler house. It has been well done, particularly through strategically placed skylights. Like several other owners of Lautner houses Page Wood has a music studio with various instruments in the cellar. He also has a theremin, an early electronic instrument played by moving the hands between two antennas. The house is filled with 'spacy' sounds as he and Tycho, who gave up a potential career as professional musician to be an architect, jam together.

The genesis of a Lautner house is not always crystal clear; this is not the only house we visit which was finally built by one of Lautner's collaborators. The Beyer and Goldsmith 2 houses are other examples. In this case it is not known whether the work was done with Lautner's knowledge or consent. Was the collaborator still part of the practice? Did Lautner supervise the development of the project? These are all questions that remain unanswered.

previous: Foster
next: Gantvoort

#22: House, 1947, extant
3540 Multiview Dr, Los Angeles, CA 90068

Sunday, 6 May 2007

In May 2007 we travel to Jacobsen and Polin, two neighbouring houses built at the same time. They show great similarities, not least because of the remarkable support structure of the roof. The main volume of both houses is a regular hexagon, carried by three composite steel columns. Each column is attached to the roof with expressive braces, so that a real table-construction is created. This means that none of the walls below need to be load-bearing. We also saw this in the Carling house from the same year, but that was less visible because of the bedroom wing attached to it. Here, Lautner made even more use of this principle, because the roof is smaller and doesn't completely correspond to the underlying floor plan, which is shaped like a rectangular box. This has the effect of creating interesting spaces in the places where the rectangle sticks out from under the hexagon of the roof: part of the house needs a glass roof, creating a glass bay window. The result is a magnificent dining room. On the other side, the terrace is created in this way. Unfortunately, one of the former owners had the terrace covered over, which counteracts the spatial play between the hexagon and the rectangle and negates the subtle transition between inside and outside. The outer walls slope gently outwards, which dramatises the relation with the surroundings and prevents furniture from being placed against the outer walls. Architect Bill Childers now lives in the Jacobsen house. Despite the terrible condition it was in when it was for sale, he was able to see its quality. He tells us about his renovation plans, which always give us a fright. To keep a house up to date, some adjustments are unavoidable: Lautner himself did this several times, but a good design is easy to ruin if you're not careful.

previous: Speer
next: Polin

In 2009, Bill Childers has finished the renovation that he was planning. At the time, the house was marred by the ugly terrace covering, which had been tacked on. Since then, the owner, who works for Frank Gehry, did work on the house and perfected it, in his own words. The terrace covering has been removed and the terrace has been restored to its original state. This has ensured a much better relation between inside and outside, because it has made visible again that the living room emerges from under the hexagonal roof like a rectangular box. The kitchen has been opened up and the bathroom has been modernised. Maybe he got a bit carried away during the renovation: the dining room, one of the most beautiful ones Lautner ever designed, is now less clearly defined because the kitchen is no longer closed, but open, which weakens the spatial effect of the glass corner in the roof. Another change he made was fully

opening up the ensuite bedroom towards the hill,
where he placed a concrete water sculpture. Even
though the house wasn't restored to its original
state completely, Bill Childers deserves high praise:
he has updated the house for modern living with
minimal damage to the original design.

previous: Coneco Corp
next: Wolff

#66: House, 1956-1965, extant
789 Pearl St, Laguna Beach, CA 92651

Saturday, 5 May 2007

The Stanley Johnson house is one of the lesser-known Lautner projects. It is only mentioned in the back of his monograph, in the list of projects, with the wrong date, and without drawings or photos. Through Judith Lautner, we manage to get in touch with a daughter of Johnson's. She emails us a detailed description of the construction process from 1956 on, and even a few photos. It takes a while before we find the right house on Google Earth, because the street names and house numbers have changed since then. First, we target the wrong house, but then we find an unmistakable Lautner in the shape of an aeroplane wing. We easily manage to get in touch with the current owner, but making an appointment is less easy, because he's a famous photographer who travels the world from assignment to assignment and isn't at home the week we're there. But because we're in the neighbourhood in 2007 and actually have no idea what the house looks like close up, we drive past anyway. We brazenly drive up the long, steep driveway, which curves under the house and leads to a carport, where we park our two red vans. A spectacular sloping roof follows the hill. Other than that, we see an addition that looks like it doesn't belong. Before we've had a chance to walk around the house, we are pounced on by a boy who is all worked up and not open to reason. To avoid accidents, we decide to leave quickly.

previous: Rawlins
next: Jordan

This morning, together with the Lautner family, we visit the house where we found a closed door a year earlier. We drive up the long driveway, pass under the house and park under the pergola. After the unfortunate encounter with a tenant on our last trip, we now have an appointment with the owner and are warmly received. Our expectations are not very high because of the remodels that are already visible from outside, and because of the fact that the house is mentioned in Lautner's monograph without pictures or drawings. When we come in, we are astonished: it's truly beautiful. The roof is shaped like an aeroplane wing and runs down parallel to the slope, towards the sea. The front door is situated at the top of the house. The interior goes down by steps, where each function in the floor plan has its own level, which are connected to one another under the large, sloping roof. It is actually a bit like Lautner's own 1939 house, but then much bigger. From each level, one's gaze is directed down towards the beach. Carefully placed vertical elements touch the roof and subtly define various areas. Skylights further enhance the spatial dynamic. In fact, the house is both the *plan libre* (Le Corbusier) and the *Raumplan* (Adolf Loos) at the

The guest wing, where the tenant lived who strong-armed us off the property in 2007, is also a later addition. The difference in detailing, with large expanses of frameless glass, makes this clear immediately. Later, photos emerge from an earlier time: the house was originally made of plain redwood, which was later painted standard siding green.

previous: Wolfe
next: Tolstoy

same time. The original drawings are in the house, including the early sketches. The bedroom is also very remarkable: you enter it from above and go down a few steps, next to a planter trough, to get to the bed, which is placed diagonally in the room, towards the view. A few years ago, the dining room was extended; it actually looks like Lautner came up with it. The extension was in fact designed by Lautner's former collaborator, Vaughan Trammell.

JORDAN

#*112: House, 1971-1973, extant*
1617 Emerald Bay, Laguna Beach, CA 92651

Saturday, 5 May 2007

The Jordan house, built in 1973 for William and Johanna Jordan, was maybe the most difficult to find. The problem was that the shape of the roof was not very conspicuous and that the Google Earth images of this area aren't very sharp. TS: 'Finally, after at least twelve hours of searching, I find three potential houses. When I look at the orientation of the houses, only one remains: bingo!' Because the house is in a gated community, you can't just drive by and check. The design started in 1971, the same year in which the Marbrisa house in Acapulco was designed. The difference between the two houses couldn't be greater.

The Jordan house consists of two main volumes, both of which have a slanted roof. The volumes lie eight feet apart. The entrance hall and the stairwell are situated in the space in between. The living room on the first floor rests on a concrete table construction, so that the garden runs under the house. The materials used were kept simple: wood, glass and concrete. Wood for the living room, concrete for the garage and the bedroom. Johanna Jordan was a sculptor, and she had her studio in an extension of this space. The actual living area has been raised to the first floor, so one gets maximum enjoyment from the fantastic view. In addition, this creates a shady spot in the garden. Because the two volumes are separate from each other, the living room has glass walls on three sides. On the outer wall of the sleeping/working wing, there is a large sculpture. Because the living room is made of glass, the space between the glass and the concrete wall with the sculpture is spatially drawn into the room: this way, the outer wall of the bedroom wing, which here

operates as the inside wall of the living room, is perfectly illuminated. The sloping roof also contributes to this: the view of the artwork is maximised, while the view of the ocean is framed. Frameless sheets of glass, placed in a sawtooth shape, create a fantastic and unobstructed view of the ocean. Even the parts that can be opened are fully made of glass, with a glass rebate that forms by gluing together two sheets of glass with a difference in size of under an inch. The walls and ceilings are made of identical tropical hardwood. Because the fixed glass has no window frames, the roof seems to run from indoors to out–doors without interruption. This effect is increased because the grain of the planks continues. This makes it seem as though the roof is floating above the living room. Because of the angle of rotation between the volumes and the fact that the bedroom floor lies five steps lower, there are various views through the house. The toilet, which has a surprisingly expressive design in each Lautner project, is a world of its own here too. Where you expect to see a ceiling, there's a clerestory extending upwards, made of the same wood as the walls.

In May 2007, we are kindly shown around by the relatively young couple that bought the house from the original clients. We are expressly asked

which was carried out by a local architect with a German name.

The house looks like it was just completed. The contractor at that time did an excellent job, but he never got to enjoy the benefits since he died three months after the house was finished. Neither the construction nor the architecture seem dated at all. The lightness of the design, its location and the simple materials give the house a timeless character. Nothing indicates that it's over thirty years old. Either the development of architecture has stood still, or this house was far ahead of its time. What we don't know then is that we would end the day in a house of comparable quality. When we ask what they do, as they are in their forties, they answer that they are retired.

previous: Johnson
next: Marina View Heights Headquarters

not to look in the cupboards, because 'there is nothing architectural in the cupboards'. The owners commissioned Lautner to adapt the house to their wishes just before he died, but as he wasn't able to do it, another architect was asked to renovate the former studio space. We don't get to see that space, however, on the grounds that it is a remodel and so can't be very interesting for us. They do say that they aren't pleased with the result of the remodel,

KAYNAR FACTORY

#63: Factory building, 1956-1959, extant
7875 Telegraph Rd, Pico Rivera, CA 90660

Saturday, 5 May 2007

On our 2007 trip, we drive more than 125 miles south from Los Angeles, to San Diego. On the way, we visit a largely unknown project. While it was never publicised anywhere, we managed to track it down, after vague references by Martin Daoust, who carried out a lot of research years earlier. The Kaynar Factory from 1958, Lautner's only factory building, is the last of three projects we visit that Kenneth Reiner built with Lautner, the others being Silvertop and the Midtown School. It is a production hall of 375 by 262 feet for Kaynar, Reiner's company. Nowadays, MK Tools and Abrasives Inc. is located here, completely forgotten in an industrial wasteland close to less popular neighbourhoods in Los Angeles. We drive past on the off chance. What is immediately striking is the concrete roof construction. A system of seven large girders supports a layer of smaller beams, which rest on it perpendicularly. On top of that, a thin, flat roof, poured on-site, sticks out by at least four and a half feet. We walk into the hall, but inside nothing remarkable strikes us. We have no idea what it originally looked like and whether the current interior still has any original elements.

previous: Zahn
next: Alexander

#131: House, 1982-1983, extant
2444 Malibu Rd, Malibu, CA 90265

Saturday, 28 April 2007

Our very first appointment to visit a Lautner house with the Arnhem students is at the Krause House in Malibu. A month earlier, an enormous forest fire reduced a considerable number of luxury villas to ashes, but this house escaped unscathed. It was originally built as a spec house, but the client was so pleased with it that he decided to live in it himself. We have no idea what the house looks like from the street and even have to check the house number to see if we're at the right place. From the street, the house looks like an interplay of volumes with an expressive, ornamental roof edge, which is more reminiscent of the work of Lloyd Wright, Jr., Frank Lloyd Wright's son, than of Lautner. Later we discover that this was added by the previous owner. The house has a so-called 'delayed' entry, like elsewhere in Lautner's work. In other words, when you enter the front door, you are inside the domain of the house, but you are still standing outdoors. A bridge leads to the second front door. There, it turns out that the house has a lower floor, too. In the heart of the house, there is a central open space with a round staircase around it, which ends in a window at both the top and the bottom. The various parts of the house have been grouped around this central axis. The spectacular view is still hidden when you come in. The entrance level is on a mezzanine floor with a view of the dining room and living room. As we descend to the living room, a beautiful panorama over the ocean is revealed. The contrast between the anonymous, closed façade and the openness towards the ocean, after passing through the two doors, is astonishing. In order to maximise the effect of the panorama, the wall facing the beach bends inwards. This way, it is not possible to see into the house from the neighbouring properties, while a mirror on the side wall makes it seem as though the house and the view go on

forever. Because the mirrored wall is sharply angled, you never see yourself in it.

A comparable trick was previously carried out by Adolf Loos in the Kärtnerbar in Vienna, where the mirrors are placed above eye level. In order to prevent interference with the horizon, all the window mullions have been placed at an angle. The skylight can be opened with the push of a button, and the glass floor at the bottom of the stairs allows natural light to fall on the beach, which runs under the house here. What looks like a modest, two-storey house at first sight is in reality a four-storey house standing on high stilts at the edge of the ocean. The spatiality of the house is achieved through the fact that each space has both its own character and its own view of the water. Even from the shower, a narrow slit gives a view of the ocean, through the main bedroom. The current occupant is representative of a specific group of residents. Cultured, refined and hospitable, she graciously oversees a group of Dutch people who are immersed in the experience of the full glory of their first Lautner building: the true beginning of our journey.

previous: Segel
next: Pacific Coast House

#2: House, 1939-1940, extant
2007 Micheltorena St, Los Angeles, CA 90039

Wednesday, 2 May 2007

led architecture critic Henry-Russell Hitchcock to pronounce it 'the best house in the United States by an architect under thirty' in 1940.

previous: Baldwin
next: Reiner (Silvertop)

A few doors along from the Baldwin house stands the home Lautner made for himself in 1939. He had just settled in L.A. and built the house for his young family. He didn't get to enjoy it for very long, as it was sold when he got divorced a few years later, in 1947. We drive past the house with Karol Lautner, and it's the first time she has seen the home she lived in until she was eight. She can still remember the day her father left, carrying a suitcase, and how she didn't understand why he was going, or what was happening. After the divorce, Lautner's ex-wife took the four children back with her to her home town of Marquette, Michigan.

The Lautner house is situated on a slope, slightly lower than the road. From the street, little more than a carport can be seen. We have spoken to the owner on the phone a number of times, but she leads a busy life and unfortunately, she isn't home when we arrive. In fact, she's never around when we're in the neighbourhood, which can't be a coincidence.

The influence of Frank Lloyd Wright is still clearly visible in this house. One nice feature is the downward sloping roof, which draws the eye towards the view. Thanks to the split-level design, a clearly defined dining room and sitting room have been created under this large roof, each with its own character. Originally, the bedrooms were accessed via an outdoor deck. It appears this lack of comfort was a bit too much for later inhabitants, as the balcony is now enclosed, changing the look of the building considerably. The house has undergone so many alterations through the years that little remains of the straightforward simplicity of the original design. As luscious vegetation has also transformed the house's direct surroundings, it only vaguely resembles the house in the rugged photographs that

LAUTNER, ERNEST

#72: House, 1957-1959, extant
539 El Cerrito Pl, Pensacola, FL 32503

Saturday, 17 November 2007

Following the success of the first trip, our passion for Lautner has now really caught fire. After everything we have seen and experienced, we have become even more excited about our ambition to see all his work. The most important source of information is still Lautner's 1994 monograph, but we have discovered that Lautner's decision to treat some of his works more summarily does not at all mean that they are not of high quality.

Lautner built only five buildings outside California. The first one we considered after the ArtEZ journey in spring 2007 was of course the Marbrisa House in Acapulco, but besides the Hilo Campus there are also houses in Aspen and Anchorage and a house for his cousin Ernest Lautner in Pensacola in Florida. The three other houses are well documented but Pensacola is in the middle of nowhere and this is probably why so little attention has been paid to this house. In the summer of 2007 we heard through Lautner's daughters that the house still belonged to the family of the cousin for whom it was built in 1958. We got in touch with Ernest Lautner's grandson, who told us that after fifty years his parents were about to sell the house, as it was becoming too much for them. We found its location through Google Earth; as its roof is a perfect circle it was not difficult to spot. What struck us immediately was that the house is on a large lot, directly on Bayou Texar. You see the danger straightaway: a wooden house on a beautiful big lot can be ruthlessly replaced by a new owner with a 'McMansion'. We decided that we should fly straight to the US to see the house before it was too late.

For our trip to Pensacola in November 2007 we again invited Karol and Judy Lautner to accompany us, and this time Martin Daoust as well. It isn't easy to get to Pensacola: you fly to Atlanta, then drive at least 300 miles through the impoverished state of Alabama before you reach the coast of Florida's Panhandle. A road trip through the US is always interesting, and neither of us had ever been in this part of the country before.

It's exactly ten o'clock in the morning when we arrive at the house. It doesn't look particularly spectacular from the road. A drive leads up to a circular, one-storey house, with a gently sloping roof and a skylight in the middle. The façade is set back under the roof to make room for a carport and a covered entrance. It's made of dark-brown bricks with a light-coloured mortar.

In the living room we are welcomed by Max and

Stephen, Ernest Lautner's son and grandson. Also present is Max's cousin, David Lautner, who built the house nearly fifty years ago. None other than Wernher von Braun, whom he'd been introduced to during his military service, had once told him that Lautner should be pronounced with a German [au] instead of an American [ô]. This is why this branch of the family still pronounces the name the German way, unlike the Californian Lautners.

differences in height. At the entrance, the space under the roof is low: you can only just stand up straight. After you pass the front door you can either continue on the same level to the bedrooms or descend the eight steps leading down on your left to the level of the living room and kitchen. The exterior wall of the living room slopes inwards and the top edge of the masonry follows the slope downward. The exterior wall first follows the circular edge of the roof and then curves inwards like a spiral. A ramp leads down between the inward curving wall and the inner circle formed by the kitchen. Halfway down this ramp is a door that gives access to a two-storey-high space at the garden level, a porch screened off from the outside world by mosquito netting. This wonderful space connects the interior and exterior in a subtle way. Although the roof plan is round, the brick façade under it curves inward at a stronger angle, creating a terrace sheltered by the roof. Standing there you have a view of the water through the mosquito netting between a ring of wooden columns. The porch is an ideal place to spend time until the sun goes down. The office space at the level of the entrance looks out over this area. David tells us they couldn't find a bricklayer who was able to make a wall that inclined inward and curved round at the same time, following the contour of the terrain, so he ended up doing it himself. The roof is supported by a concrete column in the

Sitting on a chair in the middle of the house, David uses his stick to point out how he built the house. He describes it all so vividly we see it happening in front of our eyes. It's a wonderful meeting: at the end of the day we have the feeling we've known everyone for years.

But it's the house itself, above all, that makes this visit one of the most memorable ones of all. Full advantage has been taken of the site's

centre, topped by a steel ring where the 68 wooden roof beams meet. Inside the steel ring is a dome-shaped skylight. The roof's edge detailing has been created by sawing off the bottom edge of the ends of the beams at a thirty-degree angle and applying cladding between the beams, starting from the edge beam up to where the sawn-off beams form a point. This gives the roof a decorative edge, which makes it look very thin from the outside. The underside of the edge beam has been painted blue, a rare example of Lautner applying colour.

The living room contains two stone elements: the central column, with a built-in planter at its base, and the fireplace. For the latter, a concrete parabola on a raised surface serves as the opening of the hearth. A brick chimney protrudes through the roof. An ingenious panel has been fitted next to the fireplace, which you can use to push firewood through. Because we want to see every last detail of the house, we also venture out onto the roof. There we can clearly see how big the house actually is. On the side facing the water, the house is twice as high, and the door of the boat garage can be seen. You used to be able to pull a small boat up inside via the rails. The house was built without Lautner's supervision. After visiting the location, he simply put his plans in the post. He didn't see the house until 1991, when he went there to see how a dressing room could be added and how various other modifications could be made. The idea was for the carport to be converted into an office and for the netting to be replaced with glass. Fortunately this was not carried out, as it would have done irreparable damage to the house, which is now in perfect balance. The only two alterations that were made through the years are the insertion of an extra floor above the kitchen and the excavation of a bomb shelter under the carport – this was the Cold War era, after all. The shelter is now used for storage.

After we've shared a meal together that day, we go back to the house so we can see it after dark. The dark, cylindrical mass we saw during the day now looks like a magic lantern: the shifting perspective adds a great sense of depth.

Once we're inside, the fire is lit, creating a fantastic effect: if you stand in the focal point of the circular row of windows, you see the fireplace reflected around you in seventeen windows, like a ring of fire. Because we have been able to focus on one house all day, we are experiencing it much more intensely, and we feel ourselves connecting to the house in a different way than we would have during a short visit. This time we are really using the house.

The next day we have to get up at 4 AM, so we go back to our hotel in good time. Shortly after we fall asleep, we're woken up by a group of drunk guys staying in the room next to ours, one of whom shouts 'Yeah do it baby' all night. It remains unclear whether this is live encouragement or whether it's directed at something on TV. The same loud voice then repeats over and over, 'Where is my wallet?' – after the 459th time we fall asleep again.

On the way back to Atlanta, we buy a *Pensacola News Journal* and find a whole article about our visit to the house. This is the first media attention the house has received in fifty years. That's great: the more attention there is for Lautner's work, the greater the chance it will be preserved. We've been driving for quite some time when Martin Daoust pipes up from the back seat: 'Do you think he ever found his wallet?'

previous: Garcia
next: Familian

LAUTNER (THREE RIVERS)

*#119: Mountain refuge, 1976,
demolished 2009, 42640 Sierra Dr,
Three Rivers (Tulare County), CA 93271*

Thursday, 9 April 2009

On our journey in 2009, on the way to Lake Almanor, we pass Three Rivers, which lies on the route to Sequoia National Park. This is where, in the early seventies, Lautner bought a plot of land to build a holiday home, the Lautner Mountain Cabin. Thanks to its inclusion in the large-format Taschen book by Barbara-Ann Campbell-Lange, it's one of the few unbuilt projects that is known to a wider audience. The drawings show an elongated, bridge-like volume on high stilts covered by a curved plastic roof. His wife Elizabeth's illness prevented the design being carried out, but it appears that something was nonetheless built here. Lautner was so crazy about the location that, awaiting construction of the house, he went ahead and had a temporary pavilion [119] built, consisting of two prefab domes on a wooden platform. The site is still owned by the Lautner family, who have happy memories of it. After some urging on our part, we are allowed to go see it, even though the sisters don't understand why we want to see the domes: after all, they weren't designed by Lautner himself. Despite the fact that they are prefab elements, we feel that their position and lay-out in relation to the road and river do constitute design decisions, which is why we want to see the site.

It's been around 35 years since the dome and platform were built, and they are in a very poor condition; the family don't see any other option than to pull them down before anyone gets hurt. We are the last visitors to see the domes: less than two months later the whole thing is demolished. It strikes us that the domes are not situated in the most obvious spot: relatively close to the road and along the river with the platform in between the two domes, one of them shielding the platform from the road. It seems to have been a conscious decision not to

place them in the spot intended for the cabin, as this meant Lautner could stay here while the other building was being constructed a little further along. With the book in hand, we scan the surroundings in search of the exact location where the long cabin on stilts was planned. Suddenly we spot some rocks with the same shape as those in the drawing. We can virtually see the house standing there in front of our eyes, at right angles to the road and river. The fact that it was never realised makes it easier for us to follow the thought process that led from the location to the design. A natural path leads up, among the rocks, and would have provided access to the cabin, which you would have entered on the long side. Withholding the spectacular view of the small river at this point, the landscape would have revealed it only after you entered the house. Never before has Lautner's thought process been so easy to follow. It is fascinating to see how he chooses the most difficult spot, posing the greatest construction challenges. He places the building right next to the highest rock and puts the entrance at the spot where the two meet. One end of the building is shaded by the tall trees and the other cantilevers out freely over the river. Just by visiting the locations we are starting to fathom Lautner's way of thinking step by step. It has sometimes been said that, with locations like these, it's not that difficult to design such beautiful houses. Every time, though, the

opposite appears to be the case: Lautner manages to get the most out of locations, using his designs to transform them like no one else.

previous: Bosustow Remodel
next: Bosustow Cabin

LAUTNER (THREE RIVERS)

*#45: Remodel, 1951-1957, altered
10234 Monte Mar Dr, West Hollywood,
Los Angeles, CA 90064*

Friday, 27 April 2007

On our first afternoon in Los Angeles in 2007, we drive straight from the airport past a number of Lautner projects that are located close together, including the Lippett Remodel. We arrive at a traditional house, comparable to Carr, only in this case we see nothing that points to the influence of any architect whatsoever. We ring the bell, and although we see two eyes staring at us through the letter box, the door remains closed. For the group we've been infecting with our enthusiasm for Lautner over the past few months, this isn't a very promising start. As we leave, we notice the neighbouring house has a striking roof extension that could be Lautner's work.

Back home we discover we were standing in front of the wrong house; the remodel was carried out on the house next door. JRK: 'When I emailed the owner of that house, he was overjoyed. In the run-up to the exhibition Lautner had been introduced to a wider audience. The man even asked us what he could offer us when we stopped by. He was sorely disappointed when I had to inform him, a few weeks later, that we'd made another mistake: the Lippet house was actually a hundred and fifty yards down the road.' We made this discovery in the archives in July 2008. Looking back, we realise that our student Loe van der Ven had already pointed it out to us as a special house when we drove through the street in 2007.

previous: Carr
next: Segel

When we called the phone number for the correct address, we were immediately invited to come round; clearly the fact that they lived in a real Lautner house wasn't news to the owners. A couple of years earlier, a certain Frank Escher had already been round to see the house. They also had copies of photographs that were taken when the renovation had just been finished.

The Lippett house is a traditional wooden house that Lautner remodelled a number of times over a longer period. In the living room he played around with height differences and the colours of the ceilings and light coves. Although the alterations he made remain largely unchanged in terms of their form, the dark ceiling has been painted a lighter colour. The natural wood boards that used to extend from inside outdoors like the ones in Bell, Carling and Tyler, have been removed inside and painted white outside. The floor is now covered by a light blue carpet. These adjustments have undone most of the spatial effect of Lautner's modest alterations. There is a built-in planter that seems to have extended outside at an angle, but only the inside section is left, and the container is empty. Something resembling a terrarium was used here of paint it would be easy enough to restore the space's original impact. Happy with our find, but disappointed by its current state, we take our leave.

previous: Garwood
next: Googie's site

to bring nature inside, blurring the transition between the inside and outside. The characteristic bay window in the study is still in place. As in the Pearlman Cabin and Harpel 2, the window is fitted with as special kind of glass with a zigzag structure instead of a flat surface; this means there is no flat surface reflection, creating the impression that the window doesn't contain any glass at all. Using just a few boards, different flooring and a couple of pots

185

MALIN (CHEMOSPHERE)

#77: House, 1958-1960, extant
7776 Torreyson Dr, Los Angeles, CA 90046

Saturday, 28 April 2007

The third house in the row on Torreyson Drive is Lautner's most famous work. The Chemosphere, designed in 1958, is thought to epitomise the space-age era the world had entered at the beginning of the sixties. It was an icon for the future, 'the most modern home built in the world'. Cinephiles know it from its appearance in a number of films, including Brian de Palma's *Body Double*, where it serves as the home of the bad guy. The house was designed for a young aerospace engineer called Leonard Malin, who had taken a year off to help build the house. The builder was once again Johnny de la Vaux, a former builder of ships' interiors who had made the switch to buildings and had worked on previous Lautner projects including the Carling and Harpel houses. Malin was able to buy the land relatively cheaply because the site was so steep it was virtually unbuildable. After a few variations, Lautner came up with the idea of constructing the house high up on a column, with a small funicular leading up to it along the slope of the mountain. TS: 'During my trip to Los Angeles in 1994 people living in the area tell us about a special house on a pole. Because our schedule is jam-packed and the house isn't included in the books, we give it a pass. A stupid decision, as we later find out this must have been Lautner's Chemosphere. In 1999 I saw the house for the first time. Although Lautner did not intend it to be that way, it was a very imposing, futuristic looking house. It was in a terrible condition, though: the windows were boarded shut and it was virtually falling apart. Rumours were going round that a famous person had bought it and they were planning to restore it. This was a happy prospect that would make it worth coming back some day.' All our attempts to make an appointment

with the owner, a famous publisher, failed. After sending letters to the address and the offices of the publisher in L.A. and Cologne, all of them in vain, JRK got one of the people at his office who was fluent in German to call the publisher's assistant. The answer remained the same: '*Tut uns leid, aber ein Besuch ist nicht möglich.*' (We're sorry, but a visit is not possible.) The restoration of the Chemosphere [76] has by now been completed. Admiration for the house has soared in recent years. Having sunk into

complete obscurity in the 1980s and following decades, it is now seen as L.A.'s hippest and most modern house. A fence has been put up at the bottom of the street and all the surrounding sites have been bought up by the publisher. This means there is no way of getting anywhere close to the building these days. When, in 2007, we are finally standing in front of the fence surrounding this magnificent house, the students, unable to resist temptation, press the buzzer. To our surprise, an answering voice asks us, 'Have you spoken to my father?' We confirm, truthfully, that we've been in contact with the publisher's office. The gate opens and we start the steep uphill climb. A narrow staircase initially follows the track of the funicular, before turning into a path. This makes a wide bend through the landscape, passing right under the house and ending at the bridge leading to the front door. Apart from the bridge's modern railings,

the house looks exactly like it did when it was completed in 1960. While we make our way up, the boy who buzzed us in is on the phone to his father. The moment we have literally set one foot inside the place, the truth comes to light and we are told to get out. We see our chances of ever seeing the inside of this house evaporate for good. It seems our identity was immediately clear, because when we get back to the hotel and check our email that

evening, there's already a message waiting for us from the publisher's assistant, telling us how outrageous our behaviour was. If we ever try anything like that again we'll be charged with trespassing. After a whole year of careful preparations, our adventure suddenly takes a wrong turning owing to a naive, impulsive act. Bad, not good.

When we tell Escher about our failed attempt to visit the Chemosphere he restored, he has a surprise up his sleeve. It turns out Current TV made a replica of the Chemosphere, to serve as a backdrop for their TV programmes. Our expectations aren't very high as we ring the bell of a dark warehouse at 1136 N Highland Avenue in an otherwise nondescript area. Once we're inside though, a miracle occurs: we're standing in the middle of the Chemosphere after all. The living room has been recreated down to the smallest detail – apart from the stone floor that is, because the surface needs to be completely level for the rolling cameras. The view has been recreated as well, printed on a huge panoramic screen. With the flick of a switch, the daytime view turns into night. The effect is amazing. Through the lens of the camera, it really is very difficult to tell the difference. Welcome to Hollywood! This goes some way towards lightening our disappointment at being turned away from the original.

previous: Castagna
next: Zimmerman

Tuesday, 7 April 2009

After we are introduced to the owner of the Chemosphere at a party at the Eisele Guest House on 5 April 2009 and he promises us we can come around, we look forward to hearing from him anxiously, hardly daring to believe it is really going to happen this time. On 7 April, we suddenly get a text message: 'Dear Lautner fans, you can come to see my house at 6pm, peace Benedikt'. By then, it's 16:30 and we're on the other side of L.A., so we turn around immediately; it would be tragic if we missed out on

MALIN (CHEMOSPHERE)

this unique opportunity as a result of getting stuck in traffic. We're pretty nervous. When we get there, the gate opens and we get another text message asking us to wait at the bottom. The Lautner sisters Judy and Karol and grandson Joey are already there. They decide to go on ahead and take the funicular up. After waiting for a while, we go up too, but when it turns out Taschen isn't there, we get in again and go back down quickly. The appointment nearly turns into a disaster after all, when we find an irritated Herr Taschen waiting for us at the bottom: 'I told you to wait downstairs!' He has bought up a number of houses at the foot of the hill, where he lives and works. He uses the Chemosphere to receive visitors. Thanks to our visit to the replica at the Current TV studio, one half of the house holds few surprises for us. Now we get to see the other half too. Having visited three-quarters of Lautner's oeuvre at this point, it seems strange that this house is the one that has become the most famous. It is probably due to it being one of his most straightforward designs, conceptually speaking.

The house has been restored to a museum-quality state: it looks like it was built yesterday. This also makes it look more clinical than the other houses we've seen. When visiting a house featured in so many publications, it's often the parts that haven't appeared in print that are most interesting. Compared to the floor plan in the monograph, a number of minimal adjustments have been made, such as the position of the beds in bedrooms #1, #2 and #4, a missing folding wall between bedrooms #2 and #3 and a few more details. Another striking feature are the skylights in the hallway, which provide views of the inside of the roof construction above the wall surrounding the fireplace. The relaxed atmosphere inside the house forms a marked contrast with its phenomenal reputation as an impenetrable fortress and icon of modern architecture.

The house has an eventful history. Leonard

Malin was only 27 years old when he had it built. Construction of the central concrete column took up most of his initial budget. Malin then signed a sponsorship deal with the ChemSeal Company, who acquired the right to use the house for advertising purposes in the first few months after completion. About a decade after the house was built, a steep rise in property taxes forced Malin to sell the house. In 1979, the second owner was brutally killed in the house during a robbery. After that the house had a sequence of owners, none of them staying for long. It was gradually starting to fall apart when Taschen, seeing its potential, bought it in 1999 and had it restored.

No expense or effort was spared during the restoration by Frank Escher and Ravi Gunewardena. Despite this, something isn't quite right. The house was designed for a client with a limited budget.

The choice of materials and finishings reflected this: they were functional and no-nonsense. Now, the bridge is fitted with railings made of extremely pricy tempered glass. We can't imagine this was the idea of the Swiss purist Frank Escher. Later on we hear things did indeed take a different turn: Escher and Gunewardena weren't able to finish the job. Former Lautner colleague Duncan Nicholson stepped in at the end of the renovation process

work in terms of spatial design when you compare it to other projects from the same period. Taking the infamous funicular, we slowly make our way back down to earth.

previous: Deutsch
next: Garcia

and added a finishing touch reminiscent of the Goldstein remodel. And suddenly, the place has something of the feel of a bachelor pad, instead of a family home for an aerospace engineer. But everything has been done to such a high standard that the house has now been preserved as a landmark, and we definitely have Taschen to thank for that. The Chemosphere may be Lautner's most famous house, but it isn't Lautner's most striking

#124: Remodel, 1978, extant
4400 The Strand, Manhattan Beach, CA 90266

Friday, 19 March 2010

In the archives we found drawings for a remodel for a 'Roy Maloney 4400.02 The Strand, Manhattan Beach'. Together with the drawings from 6 and 25 April 1978 there is also a fax that was sent on 19 December 1977, 5.41 pm, with, beside a photo of the extant house, the client's wishes: a new window and a new terrace. On the fax are notes like 'improve looks' and 'look at Leisure' in Lautner's hand-writing. After huge houses like Elrod and Marbrisa, Lautner was apparently still prepared to think about minor commissions of this kind. In three different per-spective drawings, he worked out how to create access to the roof and how the desired windows could be inserted in the façade. He also looked into how the space could be transformed by a 'louvered privacy screen'.

We can't find anything on Roy Maloney himself, how-ever, apart from a mention of someone of this name wait-ing on death row in some prison. The woman who owns the house Lautner remodeled for Roy Maloney lives in San Francisco. Although she doesn't deny knowing the client, she tells us she never heard anything about the remodel. The house is close to the airport, and the first thing we do on the evening of our arrival in 2010 is to drive past. Darkness has fallen by the time we're standing in front of the house. It's clearly the house pictured on the fax and there's a round window in the façade. So it appears Lautner's proposed plan was carried out, at least partially. It turns out the current occupants are a group of German students. They seem a little suspicious of our story, but let us take a look around anyway. Our main impression is that Lautner's proposal for this simple remodel would

have been very effective if it had been carried out completely. The atmosphere isn't very welcoming so we don't stick around for long. Nonetheless, we are pleased to have discovered a new Lautner.

previous: Turner
next: Seletz

MARBRISA

#108: Weekend retreat, 1971-1973, extant
Cerrada de Vientos, Acapulco Guerrero, Mexico

Tuesday, 10 August 2010

JRK: 'As my Lautner adventure began with my wife, I want to share its conclusion, a visit to Acapulco, with her. We drive to our hotel, which lies below the mountain on which the Marbrisa house is built. It was the presence of this hotel that dictated the contours of the edge of the living room of the house: no lights from the hotel should be visible in the living room. The hotel is 'spread out' over the hill, the lift consists of jeeps that speed up and down the mountain.'

TS: 'We have long fantasised over a visit to Lautner's greatest statement, the Marbrisa house in Acapulco, designed in 1971, the year I was born. When we succeeded in making an appointment, we again invited the Lautner family to accompany us. Jan-Richard brought his wife Christine and I was accompanied by Martin Daoust and Daan Zandbelt, architecture lover *pur sang*. We meet Karol Lautner with her granddaughter Jessica and Judy with her daughter Mary in the Resort Las Brisas Hotel, where Lautner himself always stayed. The restaurant has a fine transition between inside and outside and utilises the location perfectly, so much so that one wonders whether Lautner had anything to do with it.'

The house, which used to carry the name of its owners but is nowadays called Casa Marbrisa, is visible from our hotel. To our surprise, it is by far not the only house on the hill; it is completely surrounded by other houses. The size of the saucer-shaped roof does give it a striking appearance. From a distance, we see people in the garden, cleaning the pool. The weekend home is still owned by the client and his family. There was a simple condition for our visit: you can come, but not during the weekend.

The Marbrisa house is without a doubt one

of the most remarkable houses ever built. It is very strange that this house is barely mentioned in architectural history books. Where Lautner already tried, not entirely successfully, to leave out the façade on the Sheats house in 1962, he did manage here: because of the climate, the living room could be turned into a large, covered terrace. Only the bedrooms and utility rooms are really indoor spaces. From the street, you can't see how the house works; you can only see a large concrete saucer in the sky.

After a communal breakfast, all of us drive up the hill together. A fence at the top of the hill leads to the gated community the house is part of. A little further on, a gate in a curved concrete wall, with a sculptural niche for a guard, gives access to a concrete slope, which takes a wide bend to the left under the roof and leads to the actual front door. As is the case with many projects, many photographs of the Marbrisa house have been published that were taken from a certain viewpoint, while photos from other viewpoints are never published, which makes an on-site visit very important. This entrance wall is one of these points. The outer side of it is the only part of the house that has not been covered with a thick layer of grey paint. This layer of paint means that the tactility of the material has disappeared, so that we have to make do with the shape of the house. The side walls of the slope are

high enough to keep the view hidden for a while. In this wall, there are only three small windows, which give a view of the visitors from the kitchen. With a graceful twist, the wall ends underneath the enormous roof, which here acts as a porch over the front door. In front of the door, the concrete paving turns into marble floor tiles with a herringbone pattern, which form an indication of what lies behind the square, steel front door. The front door

fills the hole between the end of the wall and one of the five concrete piers that carry the roof. The door itself is a sculpture by the German/Mexican artist Mathias Goeritz. We are received by staff who subsequently become invisible, except when they supply us with food and drink from time to time, which gives us plenty of time and space to experience how this house works.

Although we know what to expect, it is still a magical moment when we enter the house. Behind the wall lies a perfect world, where the mountains and the sea come together. The angle of the roof has been chosen so that when you come in you look right along it, so that its gigantic dimensions are kept hidden a little longer. Behind the entrance gate, you can turn left and take the stairs downstairs, or turn right and cross the bridge to the living room. This bridge crosses the moat/ditch/ swimming pool. The pool, which was designed in such a way that railings are unnecessary, almost literally links the floor of the living room with the water in the bay. Lautner designed it as an infinity pool, where the water flows over the edge, so that the surface of the water visually turns into the water in Acapulco Bay. This makes it look as though the living room is right on the water. Once again, a radical-functional solution has created poetry here. Unfortunately, the second major disappointment awaits us here: shortly after the house was finished, the construction underwent differential settlement, as a result of which the edge is no longer exactly horizontal everywhere. The water level has since been lowered, so that the edge of the pool is visible after all, and the effect of the infinite space is lessened. In addition, the water basin with mosaic tiles has been given a light blue plastic lining.

But there is enough left to enjoy and discover. The living room is furnished with a combination of built-in and loose furniture. In the middle there is a large, round concrete sofa, which was

MARBRISA

originally conceived of by Arthur Elrod. We fan out through the house to explore. The walking route is much more complicated than we thought. The centrally located living room is accessed via three bridges: one from the front door, one from the wing containing the kitchen and the staff bedrooms, and on the south side there is a bridge that leads to a staircase which in turn leads to the master bedroom. Only the first bridge has a solid railing, which turns into the balustrade of the first space you enter when you come in through the front door. When the railing stops, it emphasises the openness of the living room.

Because we are allowed to stay all day, we can take our time to explore the house. First, we do a 'quick scan': from the outdoor stair-case back downstairs to the terrace next to the master bedroom. The full height of one of the concrete piers can be seen from here. At the spot where the pier hits the roof, there is a cutaway where the light comes in. Underneath this, alongside the rock face, there is a flight of stairs going down. The master bedroom is related to Lautner's other work, like the zigzag wall made entire-ly of glass, and the glass that has been built into the rock face. Under the living room, there are four more bedrooms in addition to the master bedroom, which are directly accessed from a patio. Each bedroom has its own bathroom. The character of the house is completely different on this storey than on the level above. The real surprise here is the presence of another large living room, the family room, where one can shelter from bad weather. The space is in open connection with the patio, which is directly accessible from the entrance by a flight of stairs. There are also a number of guest quarters. Pro-grammatically speaking, this makes the bedroom storey a complete house on its own. The rooms on this level all have large expanses of glass facing the bay and follow the fan shape of the roof above.

Lautner has accentuated the different functions: a large collective space that makes optimal use of its connection to its surroundings, in combination with private spaces that almost seem like separate units thanks to their bathrooms and built-in furniture. This is most noticeable in the master bedroom, which is spacious and has its own terr-ace, with another mini pool in the floor, from which there is a magnificent view. From the terrace, a

flight of stairs carved in the rock leads further down, into the garden. This is where the real swimming pool is; its sides follow the hill. There is a diving board at the highest point, which we all try. Behind the swimming pool, under the landing of the freestanding staircase leading upwards, there is a changing room with a toilet. All the stairs, which originally consisted only of cantilever steps, have by now been supplied with railings: pragmatism has prevailed over aesthetics. This staircase leads you back to the family room: there are several ways of walking through the house. From the family room, you can get to both the service patio and the patio next to the bedrooms. The service patio has a completely different atmosphere: because of how closed-off it is and the laundry hanging out to dry, it could just as well be a small square in the working-class district of a southern European town.

here. A central beam runs across the piers, with large cantilever fins jutting out from it. They carry the roof, which in fact hangs underneath them. The expressivity of the construction is purely in service of the spatiality of this floor; it is never pretentious. Perhaps this is one of the things that makes this house so extraordinary: total control in a free, organic expression. Lautner himself said he was only capable of attaining such precision after forty years of experience.

While the others stay in the living room, we walk around the neighbourhood to take some photos. Because there are people in the living room, the scale of the house is now clearly visible. Something we never read about anywhere is the acoustic (side) effect of the concrete shell roof. It works as a megaphone; we can almost follow the conversation in the living room from the street.

The hill is almost completely covered with large houses, where building high-quality architecture was clearly not a priority. A large cross in memory of two brothers who died in a plane crash towers over the house from high up. From a distance, it almost seems part of the composition of the house, a counterpoint to the stretched-out roof. When the house was built, it stood out as an alien object among all the green. Because of all the banal buildings surrounding the house, the contrast is even greater now. While the house's unusual form goes fantastically well with a natural landscape, its relationship with the cultural landscape is one of contrast.

You can also go back upstairs from the family room. This brings you back to the front door, so that you're back at the starting point of the route. So as to avoid feeling as though we missed anything later on, we step onto the roof through a trapdoor from the ramp. From here you can really see how enormous this house is. We walk to the hole in the roof where the fifth pier ends. The concrete construction of the roof can be seen well from up

It is time for lime and tequila. The staff provides us with glasses and salt. Their broad smiles and the practice with which they serve us make clear that our adaptation to the local culture is appreciated. With the changing light, the sculpturality of the house also changes: we can't put the cameras away just yet. We walk through the house again

The thunderstorms that had brought cool air the day before return, and the day ends with a terrific downpour. JRK: 'When we say goodbye to the staff, the caretaker tells us that in the twenty years he has worked here, he has never had this kind of visitors before. I suspect that it is once again thanks to Karol and Judy's presence that we have been received so

and again, only pausing to dive into one of the pools. We decide that the moat is very suitable for swimming. A lap of the living room is nearly a hundred yards. We do underwater swimming contests, which is actually pretty challenging, with all those bends. Only on the underside of the bridges can you still see the rough concrete.

When the sun has almost set, the reflection in the bay mixes with the reflection in the swirling water, and together with the reflection of the two tables in the glass, they form a continually changing abstract composition on the underside of the concrete roof. Christine remarks that the tables are placed in such a way that they seem to interact with the two islands outside the bay. The later it gets, the more beautiful the house becomes. The sky becomes an impossibly gorgeous colour and the living room seems to have been designed for maximum enjoyment of this. One of the most impressive things about Lautner is that he was able to keep the scale of the house pleasant and intimate despite its gigantic dimensions. The design never becomes intrusive or massive. Even the materials, concrete and stone, and the built-in furniture, which always come across as harsh in photos, have an atmospheric and tactile appearance. On Lautner's drawings, the design was even prettier: the bedroom patio was to have a water garden, and the roof was to be decorated with troughs full of plants hanging over the edge of the roof, which in the first place were meant to fulfill a structural function as counterweights for the cantilevered roof. It's unclear why this plan was never carried out.

hospitably. But I am surprised that they have never visited the house before.' We end the evening with dinner at the hotel, and from underneath the overhanging roof we see the rain pouring down.

previous: Hinerfeld
next: Harpel 3

MARINA FINE ARTS STORE

#140: Store remodel, 1989-1991, interior extant,
façade dismantled 2006
4716 Admiralty Way, Marina Del Rey, CA 90292

Tuesday, 15 July 2008

Not far from Helena Arahuete's office is the Marina
Fine Arts Store, a simple shop that forms part of
a mall, for which Lautner de-
signed the shop front and
interior. The characteristic front
needed to be replaced in 2006.
A study model of it was included in the exhibition at the
Hammer Museum. The two
interlocking half shells that
formed the façade of the gallery
clashed too much with the
beige plasterwork of the semi-
classical shopping centre, the
kind you can find anywhere in
the US. We've heard that the
shop front is in storage somewhere, waiting for better days.
Inside, the space is dominated
by a dropped ceiling, which
doesn't reach all the way to the
walls, leaving a gap. This allows
natural light to fall onto the
mounted art. The space also
contains a few elements used to
display artworks, a sitting area
and two counters. It appears
practically unchanged. We're
told it's not uncommon for
Lautner fans to visit the place.

previous: Schwimmer
next: Wolff 3 site

MARINA VIEW HEIGHTS HEADQUARTERS

#97: Office building, 1966-1967, extant
#116: Little, Dental clinic remodel,
1973, status unknown
34000 Via de Agua, San Juan Capistrano, CA 92675

Saturday, 5 May 2007

In May 2007 we drive south, to the Marina View Heights Headquarters, a building that was supposed to have marked the beginning of a whole residential neighbourhood designed by Lautner, including a shopping mall and recreational facilities. However, the project stranded shortly after the main building was completed, when the project developer ran into financial difficulties. Lautner felt embittered for the rest of his career, all the more so because he never again managed to build much apart from private homes after that. At a later stage, Lautner had the office converted into a dentist's practice for a Dr Little. These days it's a gym, which is closed on the day of our visit, compelling us to climb over the fence. A large hexagonal roof tops seven smaller hexagonal spaces, arranged in such a way under the roof that a covered open space has been created under each of the corners. The roof covering the central hexagon is lower than the upward sloping roofs of the six surrounding hexagons. The height difference allows natural light to penetrate deep into the building. One striking feature was a cantilevered tank with water cascading down into a pond at a lower level. When

we arrive, though, the pond appears to have been converted into a lawn, and the tank seems to have disappeared as well. The building looks neglected, which makes us fearful for its future.

previous: Jordan
next: Shearing

MAUER

Thursday, 3 May 2007

At the start of his career, Lautner carried out a couple of assignments which were passed on by Frank Lloyd Wright when the latter couldn't see his way to making a fitting design within budget. One of these, the Mauer house, now has the official status of 'Los Angeles Historic-Cultural Monument'. It sounds impressive, but all it really means in practice is that the interest it attracts is above average. Occupied by one of the two sons of the couple who had it built in 1946, the house's fame derives mainly from an article Alan Hess published in *Fine Homebuilding* in 1984. Because we'd failed to get hold of a copy through our usual channels, Hess sent us one, which was the beginning of an extensive correspondence via email. It's the first article we've read that actually focuses on the structural engineering aspects of a Lautner design, complete with coloured-in details. Lautner's work really deserves a publication that gives all his designs the same treatment.

For the Mauer house, Lautner managed to devise a very simple construction that actually consists of no more than a flat roof on a series of asymmetrical wooden trusses. These were made using cheap plywood boards. Below this, the floor plan develops independently from the roof. At strategic places, the walls and façade have been positioned at a 45-degree angle, creating a dynamic spatial interplay. It would have been so simple to place a straight façade under the rectangular roof, but Lautner decided to do things differently. This has resulted in lots of interesting places, like the spot where the living room juts out from under the roof, creating a skylight and softening the transition between the interior and exterior. For a large part the construction of the house was carried out by the clients themselves, with the help of friends. In his article Hess recounts that Mrs Mauer managed to drastically cut down the number of plywood boards

a contractor had calculated they would need, by piecing bits together here and there.

In all the years we try and fail to arrange an appointment with him, Michael Mauer picks up the phone just once. When we tell him what we want, he explains that 'it is all very complicated'. On Google Earth we have seen that the roof is covered with large blue tarpaulins. The house is in very urgent need of repair, he says. This could mean two things: the house is still in its original state and/ or the owner is ashamed of its state of repair. It is a feeling we sympathise with, but unfortunately one that keeps some occupants, including this one, from letting us in.

The house is nicely situated on top of a hill, at the end of a no-through road. These days, however, Mount Washington has lost all its original appeal. The surrounding area is quite a dump, and the site itself is surrounded by a construction fence. These effectively keep nosey types like us at bay, as very little of the house is visible from the road. Lautner's clients often had children roughly the same age as Lautner's own kids, the Mauers being a case in point. And it makes Judy and Karol, who accompany us in May 2007, rather uneasy seeing this impudent group of Dutch visitors assailing the property of people they used to know personally as children. On the one hand they are charmed by this show of European interest in their father's work, but they are also worried we may damage the

Tuesday, 7 April 2009

In 2009 we again do all we can to get into contact with the owner of the Mauer house, but to no avail. The once beautiful house looks just as deserted as it did two years earlier. We try to see more of the house by setting a camera mounted on a tripod on self-timer and holding it up as high as we can. This new technique works a treat. (A few years later we could have simply used a drone.) Instead of a buzzer, there's a note stuck to the fence inviting visitors to honk the horn on their car. About to drive off, we sound the horn just for the fun of it. We hear a female voice call out rather sharply, 'He's coming!' A somewhat dishevelled looking man in his sixties speaks to us in a friendly manner from the other side of the fence: Michael Mauer, the clients' son, apologizes for not answering our letters, but makes it clear he does not want to show us the house. Is this another case in which we must wait for the owner to pass away to take a look inside? And even then, the house may be beyond saving. It's a blessing of sorts that it is located on Mount Washington, an unattractive neighbourhood on the wrong side of Downtown. People are less likely to resort to demolition in order to put up new buildings here.

previous: Harvlan site
next: Henry's Alhambra site

precarious relationship they have with the owners of the houses, crucial as it is to preserving the work. The house itself seems to be in its original state, although pretty much falling apart. The fact that the fence doesn't have a buzzer but does have a large number of padlocks, suggests the house has not been inhabited for some time.

previous: Schaeffer
next: Dahlstrom

MIDGAARD

#3: Remodel and terrace addition, 1939, extant
Middle Island Point Rd, Marquette, MI 49855

Saturday, 17 September 2011

In order to complete our picture of Lautner we should also visit his birthplace, Marquette in Michigan. It lies in an area known as the UP, the Upper Peninsula on Lake Superior, just south of the Canadian border. The occasion suddenly comes up in 2010 when we are asked to lend visual material to an exhibition at the DeVos Art Museum in Marquette, part of the university where Lautner studied. Melissa Matuscak, the director of the museum, is planning an exhibition of eight of Lautner's houses that are representative of his work. She has arranged for the two of us to give a lecture at the school that Lautner himself attended.

The morning following upon our arrival we go to the History Museum of Marquette, where together with the big exhibition in the DeVos Art Museum there is an exhibition focussing on three generations of Lautners in Marquette. There is an interesting collection of old photos, furniture, paintings and other paraphernalia, like Lautner's original sailor suit. We are amazed also to find drawings and models of virtually unknown work of Lautner's, the Rumney house, that was to be built in Marquette. Lautner made two versions: a kind of cave and a teepee, both optimised for Michigan's harsh climate, compact and oriented towards to the sun as much as possible. There are beautiful models of each design, which perfectly display Lautner's ideas. Although this house is listed in the first Italian book about Lautner, by Pierluigi Bonvicini (1981), it does not figure on Lautner's own project list.

Five years after we began our research we are in Marquette, talking about our quest. It looks as if half the town is present, and among those present are several people who knew him personally. We describe our search for addresses and owners and talk about a few of our visits. We also make a start on describing Lautner's work in architectonic terms. TS: 'Afterwards Karol tells me

how wonderful it was to hear her father's work described from an architectonic point of view rather than in the kind of far-fetched cultural-historical speculations that have been surfacing here and there since the Hammer Museum exhibition.'

Midgaard, the log cabin where it all began, perched on a promontory with a view of a virgin bay of Lake Superior, is the key to understanding Lautner's life and work – a permanent search for ultimate beauty and connection with nature. Lautner helped

his father to build it when he was twelve years old, which left a lasting impression on the young boy. He would spend his holidays here and refer to the beauty of the unspoilt nature in this spot throughout his life. For us it is truly the last house we had not yet seen.

The road ends in a parking lot, from where you must continue on foot through the dense forest to climb the rock where the log cabin is located. We now understand why it was so difficult to determine the exact location on Google Earth. Shimmering at the foot of the terrace are the beautiful blue waters of Lake Superior. It's a perfect world. In order to bring Lautner's youth completely back to life we decide to take a dip in the lake. The water is crystal clear and ice-cold. But our desire to see the cabin from the water triumphs over the cold and we swim out quite far from the bank. It's becoming clear to us why he found Los Angeles so ugly he claimed

MIDGAARD

A central front door provides access to a low space with the kitchen on the right and the toilet and cloakroom on the left. Straight ahead is the main room, two storeys high, with a blue sky and clouds painted on the ceiling. A compact staircase in one of the corners leads to a wrap-around second-storey balcony, which is used as a sleeping area. From there, a hidden staircase provides

access to a crow's nest on the roof, with views of the landscape all around. Time has left its mark on the woodwork: two balconies were removed after rot had made them unsafe. In 1939 Lautner added a terrace with built-in seats.

Here in the log cabin, where time seems to have stood still, we have come close to Lautner's personal life. Everything breathes the presence of the master: the nameplates, the photo albums and the original furniture. His presence is almost a physical experience. Together with Judy and Karol we eat a local pasty, an old miners' speciality. We light the chandelier and Karol talks about the past, revealing during the conversation that the ashes of the entire Lautner family are kept here. Pondering the thought that we have been within six feet of the master, we go back down the unlit rock.

previous: Harpel 3
next: Taliesin

it made him physically sick. The cabin is perched on a '2.5 billion yr. old rock', as it says on a plaque dating from 1992, also declaring it to be a 'legacy to be enjoyed by all descendants of Lautner Ad Infinitum (Not to be sold)'. We speculate about how these surroundings may have influenced Lautner's work. Perhaps it was his love of nature that inspired his search for boulders under Elrod's level, bulldozed site or his use of tree trunks in the façade of Pearlman.

209

MIDTOWN SCHOOL

#81: School, 1960-1961, extant
4155 Russell Ave, Los Angeles, CA 90027

Thursday, 3 May 2007

In May 2007 we visit a building once thought lost: Midtown School, completed in 1960. The client was Kenneth Reiner, who also commissioned Silvertop and a large factory hall, Kaynar. As unstable ground made the site unfit for construction, Lautner designed a series of tent-like pavilions to serve as classrooms. Their construction consists of six laminated beams, similar to the roof of the Chemosphere. The floors, made of 'floating concrete slabs', were heated, making them warm enough to play on. Three overlapping pavilions make up a larger building, forming an interesting structure of interlocking rafters. Although the school was built on a budget, it contains a number of nice details, such as skylights and frameless glass corners.

When we invited Lautner's daughters to come with us, their reaction was, 'The Midtown School? Wasn't that torn down?' Google Earth had shown us that, although part of it had been demolished, most of it was still standing. The name had disappeared though: it's now the location of the Lycée International de Los Angeles. As in most cases, many phone calls have led up to our visit, only this time they were in French. The first thing we notice when we arrive at eight in the morning is the way the children are dropped off in front of the school by their parents. Everything is tightly organised: the cars file by the entrance and older kids take care of the younger ones.

Although the school shows clear traces of use, it still serves its purpose very well. It strikes us how Lautner has found a scale to fit the children. It's the kind of project that doesn't seem very exciting on the page, but makes a very different impression when you're walking through it. The whole school is shaped by the interplay between the pavilions and the space in between. The atmosphere is relaxed, open and inviting: it's the kind of place anyone would want to send their kids to.

previous: Reiner
next: Beachwood Market

#104: Kitchen remodel,
1969, disassembled 2006
731 Inverness Dr, La Cañada Flintridge, CA 91011

In 2009, we find drawings dating from 1969 for an
extension to the Mills house, which was, according
to the list included in the monograph, carried out.
It consists of an addition of a top storey including
a master bedroom. An interior sketch shows a
striking construction with large semi-circular
window openings in the façade. The extension
wasn't carried out after all, with the exception of
a Lautner-designed circular kitchen unit and an
accompanying lamp. These unique objects were
auctioned at Bonhams in 2007, after which we find
no further mention of them.

Guest House 'Eleanor's Retreat', 1940, extant,
designed in Frank Lloyd Wright's office
32436 Mulholland Hwy, Malibu, CA 90265

OBOLER

Wednesday, 8 April 2009

Some way behind Malibu, high in the Santa Monica Mountains, is the Arch Oboler Complex, far away from the outside world. This Frank Lloyd Wright project from 1940 consists, apart from an extravagant house called Eaglefeather, of a large number of outbuildings. Wright sent Lautner here to supervise the building works, but in the end only the outbuildings were built, and not Eaglefeather. When we reach the complex, we see that it is again a building site and that remodelling is in full swing: now we understand why our letters remained unanswered. The site is empty. We walk up to the top of the hill where Lautner and the contractor Paul Speer built a pavilion for Eleanor Oboler with their own hands. In the memorial book published after Lautner's death Speer reminisced about the time they worked on the building: 'John and I, without a drawing, took the materials available and built it. Out of this pile of lumber came a most unique design. That was the first time I was able to see John's ability to take the material at hand and make a beautiful structure from it.' In Wright's monumental three-part monograph (Taschen, 2011) there are a ground plan and a view of this building with notes recognisably in Lautner's scrawling handwriting. The heat and the perpetual wind blowing must be just the same now as when they were working here. As the pavilion is again under construction it feels as we might run into them any minute. Then a man approaches us and enquires, a little irritably, what we are doing here. It is the owner, who doesn't appreciate trespassers. But he relents when we tell him about our mission and we begin an animated conversation about Oboler, Wright, Lautner and the exotic blue stones set in the walls. He is living in a caravan on site and is working there too, just as many of Lautner's clients did when their houses were being built. He also believes that Lautner's contribution would not have been of much use here, as at the time he was not experienced enough to direct such a big project.

previous: Wood site
next: Bosustow Remodel

PACIFIC COAST HOUSE / MALIBU CLIFF HOUSE

#125: House, 1979-1990, extant
32402 Pacific Coast Highway, Malibu, CA 90265

Saturday, 28 April 2007

On the Pacific Coast Highway, behind high concrete walls, lies what is Lautner's most extravagant, but also his least accessible house. These walls contain a paradise that few people have been allowed to glimpse. Designed for a man who wanted an entirely unique 'garden of Eden' between the generic beach properties, it's a house Lautner worked on for ten years, forging a new and unequalled creation by combining successful elements from the rest of his oeuvre: the roof of the Turner house in Aspen, the swimming pool edge from Marbrisa in Acapulco, finished off with the flagstones and furniture from the Beyer house, which isn't far from here. The owner has done his utmost to keep the house out of the public eye. It's not included in the reprint of Barbara-Ann Campbell-Lange's Taschen book on Lautner (after Mr. Taschen was allowed a visit to the house), and neither does it appear in the 2008 documentary on Lautner's work, *Infinite Space*, because the owner refused all cooperation. All outsiders are regarded as intruders. At some point even Lautner himself was identified as part of the outside world that needed to be kept at bay. There are rumours that he even installed a system that envelops the house in a haze of mist by the push of a button, hiding it from sight if admirers gather on the beach. However, according to reliable sources this is a total fabrication.

None of our attempts to visit the house or even come into contact with its owner have ever been successful (then or in later years). We are clearly dealing with a person with unlimited financial means who wanted the best of the best and a place for his car collection. High, undulating walls shield off the house completely on three sides. The walls enclose a self-contained 'ideal world' with a tennis court, a guest house and a garden with water features and artworks, the only view being that of the infinity of the ocean and skies above. No wonder it is known as 'Contemporary Castle'. The roof of the house itself curves around the spaces, some of which are indoors and some outdoors, roof turning into wall in one flowing movement. Since the 1990s, when architectural firms made the shift from the drawing board to the computer, this has become a common stylistic device, but when Lautner came up with it, how to even draw such a design was something that needed to be invented from scratch. A large scale model was made and photographed, and slides of the images were then projected and traced. Andrew Nasser is the structural engineer who worked miracles here.

The house is known by a number of different names, one of them being that of the former business partner of the owner, Mr Harry Sagheb. When we contacted people with that name, they denied any involvement. The more research we do into the owner, the clearer it becomes that he wants no publicity whatsoever and does not want to share his private paradise with anyone outside his own circle of friends. We have pursued any hint we could find, such as the one that brought us into contact with an artist who made some sculptures for the garden. As soon as the reason for our interest became clear, he stopped replying to our emails.

The person who managed to get closest to the house was Bette Jane Cohen, who filmed it from a helicopter for her film *The Spirit in Architecture: John Lautner*. This documentary is unique, both because Lautner was still alive when it was made and because it includes a great deal of authentic interview material. We were in touch with her from the beginning of our quest but did not meet her for the first time until November 2011, in Enschede, where JRK had arranged for the two Lautner

sand asking to be let inside, along with our phone number. To our surprise we see the 'invisible' man, who hasn't responded to any of our requests, who stimulated the architect of his castle to create his best work, sitting on his terrace, calmly smoking a cigar with a sardonic smile on his face. His 'fort' has fulfilled its function splendidly, keeping out a group of potential intruders.

We have already met Duncan Nicholson several times and he does not refuse when we invite him to eat with us. We have a fantastic evening in a restaurant in Santa Monica where he tells us the most wonderful stories about Lautner and his practice. About his interview, for example: he was not only very intimidated by this great charismatic man, but also by the life-size portrait behind him, which made it look as if there were two Lautners sitting in front of him. The high point of the evening comes when we say how much we would like to see the Pacific Coast House, and Nicholson, who is also in high spirits, takes out his phone and calls the contractor, who was working on the swimming pool at the time, to ask him if we can come by tomorrow disguised as workmen. Of course we can, but it means staying in L.A. for a few more days, as the pane that has to be replaced in the swimming pool has not yet been delivered, so, regretfully, we have to leave L.A. the next day.

previous: Krause
next: Garwood

documentaries to be shown one after the other for the first time.

We leave a gift in the letterbox with our business card attached, in the hope that the owner might want to contact us. Then we try our luck on the beach side. We have found hints online pointing to a narrow public path leading to the beach a few houses down. We have looked up what time the tide is out, so we can walk around the rocks, giving us a view of the house with the concrete shell roof. In giant letters, we scrawl a message in the

Tuesday, 1 May 2007

The route to our appointment at the Boykoff house in May 2007 passes close by the Payne Addition, dating from 1953. We haven't managed to contact the owner before, and because the house didn't seem all that interesting, we haven't gone all out to arrange a visit. We drive past on the off chance, and luckily the owner happens to be in, even though he doesn't live there. He has bought the place as an investment, but hasn't decided what he wants to do with it yet. It's in a beautiful spot, in a not-so-great neighbourhood. This project concerns an extension, although it's not immediately clear to us where the original house (designed by Mrs Payne herself) ends and Lautner's addition begins. Inside the house there are also drawings Lautner made of a proposed extension to the living room, but this was never carried out. Lautner's design can be seen in a number of details: the coloured concrete floor, the timber cladding, the frameless glass, the fireplace made of large chunks of natural stone and the master bedroom, designed in such a way that it almost feels like you're sleeping in the open air. The house almost seems like a glass pavilion, so much glass has been used. The sloping windows are a direct reference to the windows in the kitchen of the Schaeffer house and the glass bay window in one of the other bedrooms is a striking precursor of the glass used in the bathroom of the Sheats-Goldstein house. In this way, the Payne Addition forms a missing link between designs that preceded it and those that followed. Although Lautner only mentions the house briefly in his book, without including any pictures, it can be considered a key work and a turning point in his career. This is where Lautner shrugs off the influence of Frank Lloyd Wright and starts unfolding his own personality.

previous: Tolstoy
next: Boykoff

Sunday, 29 April 2007

JRK: 'Two weeks before our departure in April 2007 I'm on the phone with Ms Pearlman, the clients' daughter. She tells me they visit Idyllwild regularly, but she isn't planning on going the weekend that we will be there. I tell her the thought of us missing out on seeing the house is unbearable. She's prepared to rearrange her schedule for us to make our visit possible.'

As it is generally regarded as one of Lautner's best works, the Pearlman Cabin is featured in all the books that have been published on him. The three books that document all of Lautner's houses – Lautner's own monograph, Barbara-Ann Campbell-Lange's book for Taschen and Alan Hess's book – give a good impression of the building. Taschen's *Big Series* edition includes a spread with a working drawing of the Pearlman Cabin. Studying it more closely, we see it features the whole house, supplemented with drawings of details.

However, being hidden among the trees, the house proved nearly impossible to track down using Google Earth. The road to Idyllwild passes through a spectacular landscape. This is before the benefits of GPS, so everything has to be found 'by hand'. JRK: 'Having learned our lesson from previous occasions and bad experiences with students driving (near-death experiences even), this time I myself am behind the wheel, with Tycho as my unerring navigator. We maintain contact with the second car via the walkie-talkies my wife has bought for us.' The highway turns into a trunk road, the trunk road into a side-road and the side-road into a dirt road. When we finally get to the village, the house turns out to be even further away than we thought.

We cover the final remaining yards at quick march. Exceptional architecture often goes with owners who have plenty of character, and this combined with a group of highly motivated young students always produces memorable moments.

A path leads to the front door on the higher side of the hill. The sand-coloured façades merge almost imperceptibly into the surrounding landscape. Originally, the path followed the façade, but this is a detail that seems to have been changed. Expectations run high as we approach. Is the owner there, is she really going to let us in, will we be allowed to take pictures?

All that is visible from the road is a modest, closed, round volume. The front door is situated in the single-storey side wing. Inside, two steps lead to the higher-level, circular living room. On one side the ceiling opens out to the surrounding view. When you enter the room, you suddenly find yourself surrounded by trees; glass panes fixed between tree trunks are the only thing separating you from the forest. The glass is virtually invisible because the panes follow the circle in a zig-zagging manner, and there is very little reflection as you usually look out through the glass at a straight angle. In addition, the way the glass is connected to the ceiling is hidden from view because the

JRK: 'While I was in the house I remembered the review Marc Schoonderbeek published in *Archis* of the reprint of Lautner's 1998 monograph and the book by Hess and Weintraub. With that review, Marc was one of the first people to write sensible things about Lautner in the Netherlands, one example being the way he traces Lautner's influence on Rem Koolhaas by referring to the columns made of tree trunks in the Pearlman Cabin and the Kunsthal in Rotterdam. Marc would have loved to have come along when he heard of my Lautner plans. I call him from the house to tell him about it, so he can sort of be there anyway, if only in spirit.'

From the central space there are two ways leading outside: via the back door, which leads directly to the forest, or via a balcony that extends out among the trees. Ms Pearlman takes us outside to get a view of the house from the slope. Seen from this side, the house rises up among the trees. It looks like all Lautner did was place a few glass panes among the trees. The owner tells us the fire brigade regularly orders her to cut down the trees around her house, but she says she'd rather burn in her own 'hut' than do that.

In April 2007 we also visited the cabin that was built for Charles and Altina Carey. We wonder whether this mysterious cabin could be the rumoured cabin for Marco Wolff. However, it turns out to be a copy of the Pearlman Cabin. The outside closely resembles

ceiling tilts upwards at the edge. It is incredible how well this concept of 'living in the forest' works; photographs don't do it justice. A better integration of living and nature is hard to imagine.

The grand piano in the room is a reminder of why this house was built in the middle of nature: to play music, which is the clients' passion. It truly is one of Lautner's best works, living up to its reputation as such. It may even be the high point of our journey.

the Pearlman Cabin, but it lacks refinement. The living room is exactly the same in terms of floor plan, but comes across very differently, on the one hand because the glass does not extend to the floor, and on the other because there is no ceiling, which means the complicated rafter construction is visible. The detailing also lacks the subtlety of Lautner's Pearlman Cabin. In fact, you really realise how brilliant the Pearlman Cabin is when you see this copy. The occupants rent the house from Carey, the owner who commissioned the building. They insist that this is a design by John Lautner, but honestly, we can't imagine that he would have made this copy.

For years, we hear nothing about the mysterious Pearlman Copy, but in the summer of 2011, the John Lautner Foundation receives a letter from Charles Carey. He asks why his cabin is not featured on the official list of Lautner projects and whether this can be remedied. Charles and Altina Carey had had a very pleasant stay in the Pearlman Cabin in 1971, so they decided to ask Lautner to design a copy for them, but with more bedrooms and a separate painting studio. Lautner didn't like repeating the same concept, but according to Carey he did agree to collaborate on this, although it is unclear to what extent. The studio was placed under the round living room, and the Pearlman bedroom wing could easily be enlarged without altering the concept. Lautner ensured that Wally Niewiadomski, the contractor who had previously built Silvertop, Elrod and Walstrom for him, did the building work. Lautner himself didn't keep a close eye on the construction process. According to Charles Carey, a young architect from the neighbourhood did become involved: Dennis McGuire, the architect who eventually built a cabin for Marco Wolff when Lautner's beautiful design wasn't carried out. During the construction, a number of changes were made. From the outside, the cabin bears great similarity to Pearlman, but it is clearly less successful, spatially. It looks as though the essence wasn't understood, so that the tree trunks simply

work as a gimmick here, rather than a continuation of the forest. After a discussion about the safety of floor-to-ceiling glass with the building inspectors, it was decided to make a one and a half foot ridge on the floor. The difference is enormous. The detailing is coarser, but the most prominent difference is the roof. Both in the original and in this Pearlman copy, a complicated construction was needed to create

the desired shape. In the copy, the temptation to keep the complicated construction visible was too great. The spatial effect of raising the ceiling towards the view is lost, this way. The construction also adds visual noise, which in fact draws the attention indoors. Here too, it is clear that the difference between good and excellent requires the direct involvement of the architect. Carey, who still owns the cabin, explains that he stayed friends with Niewiadomski and regularly went to look at the impressive sight of the construction of the Pacific Coast House in Malibu. According to him, that project more closely resembled a museum than a private residence.

When Carey gives the floor plan of his cabin to Lautner's biographer Frank Escher for appraisal, his

conclusion is that the house does not qualify as a real John Lautner design and so does not belong on the list of projects.

previous: Zimmerman
next: Wolff 2 'Wind Song'

#23: House, 1947, extant
3542 Multiview Dr, Los Angeles, CA 90068

Sunday, 6 May 2007

The semi-detached Polin house has been restored recently, but luckily the renovators have stayed close to Lautner's original. The owner is a famous radio DJ who didn't respond to any of our letters and isn't in the phone directory, for obvious reasons. When he sees us walking around he allows us to take a short look inside, after Bill Childers, the owner of the neighbouring Jacobsen house has vouched for us. This house shares a steel construction with the Jacobsen house, and like the latter it has an independent roof over a concrete base, but the division of space inside is completely different. Both houses explore the possibilities of a free floor plan under an independently supported roof, a recurring theme in Lautner's work that can also be seen in Mauer and Gantvoort. It looks like a fortune has been spent on restoring the house to its original state. The result shows us the potential of the Jacobsen house if restored properly. Childers comes with us and looks round with interest. It's the first time he's been inside too. It's a small house, but it doesn't feel that way because the rooms flow into each other via half walls. Between the house and the terrace is an ingenious sliding window, that can be folded away completely in three parts, making the living room a more sheltered continuation of the terrace. The whole group has fallen in love with this house; we couldn't have wished for a better ending to our 2007 trip.

Its subdued colours make the interior of the Polin house appear very similar to the black-and-white photographs that have been published. There's just one change that was made during the

renovation: the space originally created as an extra bedroom under the hexagonal roof, and which already looked a bit like a compromise on the floor plan, has been incorporated into the living room. On one side of the volume the kitchen sticks out, along with another spare bedroom. At the level of these wings there is also another small section of garden, bordered by a low wall. The view from this spot is fantastic. In the farthest point is an outside barbecue that looks a lot like a DJ booth, an appropriate touch given the owner's profession. There are photos on the walls featuring him and a couple of Hollywood stars in a small private plane. When we take our leave, we give him a small present, as we have done in the case of all the other home owners we have visited. In the Netherlands, one of the teachers supervising the trip, Machiel Spaan, had taken on the task of buying a small token for everyone and he'd found a series of foldable, inflatable vases – a Dutch design. The DJ, who is usually surrounded by people who want something from him, is visibly moved by this group of fanatical Europeans, who had never heard of him before now but have brought him a gift anyway.

previous: Jacobsen
next: Garcia

#73: Pool and house remodel, 1957-1962, extant
340 S Westgate Ave,
Los Angeles, CA 90049

Thursday, 10 July 2008

When we opened the roll of drawings for Preminger in the John Lautner Archive, several projects were revealed. The commission known as Preminger 1 turned out to consist of remodelling some interiors and designing a swimming pool. The house is a large villa in the early Hollywood retro-colonial style, with columns in front of the entrance. The client was Ingo Preminger, the producer of the *MASH* film, a close friend of Lautner's who gave him various small commissions, though he never went so far as to have him design an entire house for him. We ring the bell and a servant comes to the door. The house is no longer owned by the Preminger family, but it happens to belong to acquaintances of film director Murray Grigor's partner. However, the owner is in a meeting and can't receive us. After much urging, we are allowed to see the swimming pool Lautner designed, which is still in place. It's a rectangular basin with brick coping and a jacuzzi at one end. The visit is essential to our aim of getting an overview of Lautner's entire oeuvre, although we wouldn't have recognised his influence here ourselves, we think, as we stare at a green swimming pool. We aren't able to verify the rumours about interior remodelings as we are firmly requested to leave.

previous: Flowers That Bloom in the Spring Tra La
next: Sheats Apartments

Monday, 14 July 2008

JRK: 'During our search for the Preminger family I discover that there aren't many people with that name in the US, so I decide to call all of them. This brings me into contact with a Ms Preminger in New York City who is the daughter of the client we are looking for and who gives me the number of her brother in Los Angeles. The son of Ingo Preminger turns out to be a very friendly person. I ask him about the Preminger Pool that Lautner mentions in his monograph.' We arrange to meet up, but when we arrive at the address where his parents lived until recently, we find out we have been talking about two different projects. The first swimming pool Lautner designed for Preminger dates from 1957, but the swimming pool we see in front of us turns out to be the very final project he carried out. In April 1994 Lautner visited the place and sketched out a proposed design for a swimming pool on a piece of paper: a straight, elongated basin with a whirlpool at the front, surrounded by a brickwork edge that merges seamlessly into the bricks of the adjacent terrace. It wasn't included in Lautner's book because that had already been printed by then. The magnificent series of buildings, which started in 1939 with a house for himself and his young family, ended here, 55 years later, with a modest swimming pool for an old friend.

previous: Conrad
next: Schwimmer

RAWLINS

#122: House, 1977-1980, extant
804 S Bayfront, Newport Beach, CA 92662

Saturday, 5 May 2007

Like the Alexander house we visited earlier, in May 2007 the Rawlins house, dating from 1980, is also still inhabited by the wife of the couple who commissioned it. However, unlike Mrs Alexander, unfortunately Mrs Rawlins is not in any state to receive us. No longer able to communicate with visitors, she is cared for at home. We contact her daughter Pam, who tells us a visit is impossible at this time. This striking house, dating from a later period of Lautner's career, is situated directly on the boardwalk of Balboa Island, a water sports resort. Ironically, this is one of Lautner's few town houses, which makes it stand out among the traditional wooden houses around it. The façade features two curved copper clad forms, making it look a bit like the mouth of an enormous monster. The copper cladding conceals a sliding mechanism that allows the entire glass façade to slide open. When it's open, the terrace outside, which is slightly raised above the level of the promenade, forms an extension of the living room across the whole width of the space. The sides are made of cast-in-place concrete with formwork boards arranged horizontally on the north side and vertically, in a sawtooth pattern, on the south side. The level of detailing on the outer skin is unprecedented and makes us suspect the hand of a new collaborator. This proves to be the case.

Warren Lawson: 'I came up with the material palette and details. Now, regarding the exterior walls, I had them all board-formed horizontally. That worked well on the west wall, since it had the curve to accommodate the sliding door. But John, with his brilliant eye and sense of things, caught that the east wall with its ninety degree turn at the front door needed a different type of expression. Why not, he said, make the forming vertical? And even better yet, why not shiplap the boards and have those boards be 3 x's? Great idea, in my estimation. Was he exploring new territory? Always, at least when he saw

something that didn't feel right to him.' The living room and master bedroom on the first floor look out straight onto the water. The side walls of the master bedroom are three feet within the concrete side walls of the living room. Subtle strip lighting brings out the impression left by the rough boards used to form the concrete to maximum effect. This area also contains the stairs leading up. The house has a simple main design with highly characteristic detailing. Any further explorations of

the interior will have to wait until we can make an appointment, although all our attempts to do so on our subsequent trips have been unsuccessful.

When we meet Michael LaFetra in the Stevens house, we ask him about the Rawlins house on Balboa Island; he looks surprised and asks how we know that he has recently become its owner. We explain that we saw Mrs Rawlins in the house in 2007 and traced her daughter Pamela, who told us that a visit by a group of students to the house would be too much for her mother, who was suffering from dementia. TS: 'Although it did not seem likely that Mrs Rawlins had recovered since our first visit in 2007, I called her daughter from time to time during the next few years. But this year nobody answered the phone and I was shocked when I discovered that in the interval not only old Mrs Rawlins had died but her daughter Pamela too.' JRK: 'In the online obituary I found the name of a son who lives in Ohio. I called him and his wife told me that the house had been sold, shortly after Marjorie Rawlins's death, to a Michael LaFetra.'

The house is full of clever details on various scales, like the toilet-shower room that can be accessed directly from outside, and the ventilation holes in the concrete wall that can be closed with wooden pins. But the biggest eyecatcher in the house is the façade, of course, which gave the house its nickname of the 'Jaws House'. The story goes that the builders stuck large cardboard sharkteeth on the front of the house during construction, which of course only strengthened the association. When it gets dark and we are sitting on the balcony on the first floor with a glass of wine, taking in our surroundings, we realise that a visit to a Lautner house is not complete if you haven't seen it at night. The house seems to embrace you, and gives you the feeling there's nowhere else you'd rather be.

previous: Foster
next: Sheats-Goldstein

We ask LaFetra if we can visit the house but sadly he refuses: it is being restored and this week the whole house is being disinfected.

previous: Alexander
next: Johnson

Sunday, 12 November 2017

In 2017 the house has new owners, who receive us warmly. We arrive just before sunset, so we can experience the house in daytime and in the evening.

REINER (SILVERTOP)

#64: Reiner, House, 1956-1965, unfinished
#117: Burchill, Completion, 1974-1975, extant
2138 Micheltorena St, Los Angeles, CA 90039

Wednesday, 2 May 2007

Until the Sheats-Goldstein house was built, Silvertop (originally known as the Reiner house) was Lautner's most famous house after the Chemosphere. It's certainly one of the largest. The history of how it came into being shows how difficult it is to make something truly innovative. The commission was granted in 1956, and construction started in 1959. However, ten years into the project things went awry: the client, a successful business man called Kenneth Reiner, was swindled by his business partner and went bankrupt. In 1974 the house, which was nearly completed, was sold off at auction for a fraction of the money that had been invested in it. Philip and Jacklyn Burchill were the lucky ones to put in the winning bid. Construction had been halted back in 1967, leaving the house to the elements for a period of seven years. The couple hired Lautner and contractor Wally Niewiadomsky to finish the house. They lived in the house until 2014, cherishing it all that time and maintaining it in splendid, original condition. Reiner never got to live in the house himself. TS: 'During the preparations for our architecture excursion to L.A. in 1994, we came across Silvertop in various publications. We thought it would be worth a visit, even though we didn't know anything about Lautner at the time. After writing to them, the owners gave us a warm welcome. The timing of our visit was unfortunate though: it was only three weeks after the Northridge Earthquake, with a magnitude of 6.7. The house had been badly hit: there was a tear in the shell roof and a lot of large windows

were broken. Because the house was a temporary building site at the time, with plastic sheeting everywhere, the spatial qualities of the living room weren't very apparent. It was still a fascinating visit though, partly thanks to the house's many futuristic features, such as automatically operated skylights, revolving shutters, etc. The swimming pool also made an impression because it is one of the first examples of an infinity pool, appearing to merge seamlessly with the water of the lower lying Silver Lake. Thirteen years after my first visit, during our trip in May 2007, I see the house in its full glory.' We invited Frank Escher to join us on this visit, and without stopping, he vividly tells us how Silvertop [63] came into being, going into great detail. We spend an hour standing around him on the lower lying tennis court, listening to his stories. Because the lot was located on the top of a hill, Lautner had to deviate from Wright's rule of never siting a house on top of a hill. He solved this problem by creating an enormous shell roof that crowns the hill. The spatial quality of the living room under the roof is unprecedented: it almost

questions together with his client. You could ask yourself whether all this experimentation and technical gadgetry have benefited the house as a whole; in architectural terms, the added value is limited. In terms of spatial quality, this house's fame isn't in proportion to that of Lautner's better works.

In 2014 the house was sold and restored by the architect Barbara Bestor.

previous: Lautner
next: Midtown School

feels like you're standing outside, with a beautiful view on one side and an enclosed garden on the other. The house's design is pretty simple, really: two closed wings with an open space in the middle and a concrete shell roof spanning the gap. Years of work may have gone into constructing it; the basic idea looks like it was thought up in half an hour or so. Lautner spent the rest of the time coming up with experimental solutions to unconventional

#26: House, 1947-1948, extant
1430 Avon Terrace, Los Angeles, CA 90026

Saturday, 11 November 2017

During the years we spent making this book, some of the houses we describe changed owners or underwent serious alterations, one example being the Segel house. Now and then we receive unexpected news: in the summer of 2015, for example, we hear about the discovery that the Salkin house from 1947, only known to us through a photo of a scale model, turns out to have been built after all. Photos appear on Facebook via architectural historian Steven Price: it's unmistakably the house with the characteristic roof we've seen in the form of the model. The house has been altered slightly and is in a bad state. It is purchased by architecture lovers who have it immaculately restored.

Unfortunately, we don't manage to make an appointment with the owners, which means our visit in 2017 is limited to the outside of the house. It dates from the time when Lautner was experimenting with various constructions where the roof becomes a separate element, under which non-supporting walls can be placed independently, like in the Mauer, Polin, Jacobsen, Carlin and Gantvoort houses. The roof is shaped like an upside down flattened saddle roof, where the top part is flat and the peak points downwards. On the street side, the rectangular roof serves as a carport and rests on two large, U-shaped supports. Behind that, facing the view and the setting sun, a number of simple volumes have been inserted under the roof, which contain the living quarters. The space between the roof and the volumes has been filled with strips of glass, which are triangular on the street side, thanks to the inverted roof. Whether all this had the desired spatial effect is something we will have to investigate another time. Here too, the question remains why Lautner never recorded that this house had been built.

previous: Flower Shop for Mr. Samuel Morhaime
next: Darrow Office Building

SCHAEFFER

#29: House, 1948-1949, extant
527 Whiting Woods Rd, Glendale, CA 91208

Thursday, 3 May 2007

On 3 May 2007 we stop by the Schaeffer residence. Our appointment has fallen through at the last minute, but fortunately the house contains a lot of glass and we put our cameras up against the windows. Without doubt the house, which is owned by an architecture collector, is in showroom condition.

The 1948 Schaeffer house is arguably the high point of the first part of Lautner's career. Frank Escher calls it Lautner's first masterpiece and it's also one of Frank O.Gehry's favourites. It was built for the mother of Jim Langenheim. Langenheim worked as a draftsman for Lautner and brought in the commission for the Schaeffer house: Mrs Schaeffer was his mother. He now lives in the same street as the Schaeffer house, so we have asked him to go around the house with us. He is not very mobile anymore, so he cannot accompany us, but he invites us to his own house. He made the working drawings but in fact did not grasp much of Lautner's complexity. The first thing he asks is whether there is still that strange green corrugated material in the bathroom. 'Unbelievable!' His mother did not live to enjoy the house for long, dying a few years after it was finished.

The story of the Schaeffer house's genesis is similar to that of Wright's Fallingwater; Wright proposed constructing the house over the waterfall: 'I want you to live with your waterfall.' The clients who commissioned the Schaeffer residence had a favourite picnic spot in the shade of some oak trees and wanted the house to be built there. They had already consulted a series of other architects, who all wanted to cut down the trees to create a level building site. Lautner, on the other hand, left the trees where they were and constructed the house around them. He designed the dining room windows so

they looked out on the tops of the trees, using horizontal panes of glass to make the façade almost entirely transparent. This makes it feel like you are dining among the trees. The house has a complex, rotated plan, with dividing walls and roofs that look like independent elements. One section of the roof doesn't just follow the closed space, but extends to form a canopy overhanging the terrace; another section changes direction over the kitchen, folding upwards, making optimum use of the light

and surroundings. Things get really interesting when you get to the timber fence, which folds itself around the house. Parts of it form a fence surrounding the garden, but it also merges into the house's façade. It consists of horizontal wooden elements separated by 4 cm gaps, and constructed in T-shapes of standing and lying horizontal planks. The space between is sometimes left open, sometimes filled in using copper or wood, and sometimes fitted with a narrow strip of glass, depending on the desired relationship between the inside and outside. The true impact of this construction of the façade only becomes clear from inside, though. The lot is at a slightly lower level than the street, which makes the house seem far more modest than it actually is when you first approach it. This impression is reinforced by the fence, which partially hides the house from view. An opening in the fence forms the start of

the garden feel like a material extension of the natural surroundings. The glass openings vary from narrow strips in heavy frames to storey-high panes reinforced with glass ribs. The side door is fitted with enormous pivot doors, similar to the ones Lautner used in Mauer three years earlier.

previous: Gantvoort
next: Mauer

Friday, 11 July 2008

In 2008, we do manage to make an appointment where earlier attempts to visit this house have failed. The financial crisis seems to be affecting architecture collectors too: the fantastic Schaeffer househas been on the market for some time, just like the rest of owner David Zander's collection, including Wright's classic La Miniatura. We manage to arrange a visit via realtor Crosby Doe. Once again, the guiding theme in this house is that of dissolving the boundary between the interior and exterior. However, it does make a huge difference here whether you're standing with your nose pressed up to the glass or actually moving through the various spaces. The drawn-out floor plan means you are literally walking among the trees. Although the same materials have been used throughout, the house includes a number of spaces with a varying character. The diversity of façades and the gently sloping roof help to create different spaces around the central fireplace. The walls of the bathroom are made of green polyester corrugated sheets, showing how far Lautner was ahead of his time.

an inconspicuous path that winds around the side wall of the carport. The roof extends out over the carport, forming a porch. From the path to the front door you can see an enclosed outside space on the left, which is a visual extension of the master bedroom. The red colour of the wooden walls and ceilings fits in perfectly with the red bricks and the coloured concrete floor, wide strips of which extend deep into the garden. This makes

It's a strange feeling to walk around a house that isn't inhabited. Even though it's furnished, the place lacks soul. Some of that soul returns shortly after our visit, when Tom Ford uses it as a location for his film *A Single Man*, starring Colin Firth. The impression is created that the house is very near to the beach, as is the case with the Sheats-Goldstein residence in the Coen brothers' *The Big Lebowski*. In reality, the ocean is over twenty miles away. The

house was created in the same period as famous
ones built by Richard Neutra and the Case Study
Houses (late 1940s). A building such as this one
appears to come from a different dimension; above
all, it seems timeless.

previous: Speer
next: Gantvoort

SCHWIMMER

#129: House, 1981-1982, extant
1435 Bella Dr, Beverly Hills, CA 90210

Wednesday 2 May 2007

JRK: 'One of the strangest phone conversations I ever had was with the owner of the Schwimmer residence, a successful German fashion designer. It was a very short conversation: all my questions were answered with a simple "yes". Are you the owner? Can we come round? Would Wednesday morning be convenient? And "yes" is what we want to hear.' So there we are, early one morning, standing in front of a closed gate at the bottom of a steep drive. After punching in the code we've been given, the gate swings open.

Although the house was included in Lautner's book, it's an underrated work. It has a curved floor plan. Its arched roof also follows the outline of the floor plan, and is therefore doubly curved. The most striking feature, though, are its towers, which are like those on a medieval castle. The clients who commissioned the house filled it with heavy antique furniture that had nothing to do with the atmosphere of the interior of the house, which makes you wonder why they picked Lautner in the first place.

The current owner asked Frank Escher to renovate the house a few years earlier. After a difference of opinions, former Lautner staff member Duncan Nicholson took over and completed the renovation. The curved shape of the house enhances the relationship between the rugged stone floor and towers, and the wooden slats and white walls. The entrance is hidden, but a winding path leads visitors inside very naturally. Inside, the towers function as structural elements but also serve various purposes: they contain stairs (added by Nicholson), a shower, a DJ booth, etc. Outside, the towers block the view of the whole, creating the impression that the

house goes on indefinitely. The most intriguing feature, however, is the wall between the corridor and the living spaces, which serves as an outer wall. The recurring theme of the relationship between the inside and outside reaches its full potential here. The wall of the corridor is recessed here and there, reaching all the way up to the ceiling in some places but stopping short in others, and containing built-in cupboards and other elements. Its light,

playful character balances out the heavy quality of the towers. While the upper floor also has windows on the side facing the hill, the lower floor housing the bedrooms only looks out on one side, on the view. The corridor leads to a terrace alongside a swimming pool that sticks out from the slope of the hill, although this show of engineering strength is now hidden by the dense vegetation of the garden.

Visibly proud, but not boastful, Ms Harriet Selling Canepa gives us an informal tour of the house. It's a perfect start to the day. Nearby is the house that set this whole journey in motion, the Sheats-Goldstein residence.

previous: Sheats Apartments
next: Sheats-Goldstein

Center for Art and Architecture. It's a unique opportunity to experience the Schwimmer house under different circumstances. As the sun slowly sets, it again strikes us that Lautner's houses really come to life at night.

The owner regularly rents out the house for a few months while she is abroad herself. We doubt whether she realises that it is occasionally used to film pornography. In this country, pornographers apparently have a better eye for the sensual qualities of Lautner's architecture than the serious architecture press.

previous: Preminger 2
next: Marina Fine Arts Store

Monday, 14 July 2008

We end the evening with dinner at the Schwimmer residence. Harriet has cooked a wonderful meal. There are around a dozen guests from circles varying from fashion to modern art. They include Duncan Nicholson, who restored the house, his wife, and Kimberli Meyer, the director of the MAK

SEGEL

#121: House, 1977-1980, remodeled
#135: Studio addition, 1986, demolished 2016
22426 Pacific Coast Highway, Malibu, CA 90265

Saturday, 28 April 2007

The Segel residence, dating from 1980, has been owned by the actress Courteney Cox since 2001. In reply to our letter we received a vague fax message saying the house was private and not open to visitors. We decide to stop by anyway. It's located directly on the Pacific Coast Highway: a sculptural concrete wall separates the house from the traffic racing by. We walk up the hill on the other side of the highway to get an elevated view of the house. The wall features a wooden gate that has faded so uniformly that it's nearly the same grey as the concrete. From the highway, all we can see is a modest construction made of concrete and wood with copper roofs among leafy trees. We ring the buzzer and the PA who opens the door says we can't come in because she's clearing up before Courteney arrives.

previous: Lippett
next: Krause

Friday, 4 May 2007

Having noticed during this first visit how the Segel residence is hidden from view on the side facing the highway, today we make an attempt to get a look at the house from the beach on the other side. To access the beach we need to take account of the tide: when the tide is in, there is no public beach. When the tide is out, the public is allowed on the beach up to the high-tide line, to the great displeasure of the privacy-loving residents. The trick is how to get to it without having to pass through someone else's garden. We've made a careful study of the area via Google Street View, so we've already discovered a little path running in between two of the properties. The tide is favourable this morning and we make our way onto the beach lined by the houses of stars like Bruce Willis and Burt Reynolds.

The Segel residence has a beautiful, dramatic front facing the water. The façade is made almost entirely of glass, making it easy to look inside. This is probably why the owners have decided to apply a dark, reflective film, which disrupts the continuity between the inside and outside. The combination of reflective glass and concrete isn't very successful either. In addition, glass screens have been placed between the beach and the garden. We have heard that much of the built-in furniture was removed when Cox bought the house. She studied architecture for a while before her acting career, and she bought the house from Mrs Segel after seeing it while driving past one day. Mrs Segel weakened when Cox kept offering higher amounts. In the end, the price was set at 10.2 million dollars. Cox would later sell the house for 27.2 million. Lautner always had a loathing of 'bankers and lawyers' and 'for sale' and 'for rent' signs – he thought they should say 'for people'. It's ironic that Cox made so much money from a house by an architect who despised architecture being presented as marketable goods. Anyone familiar with the profession knows that masterpieces are often paid for by the blood, sweat and tears of the designers, and that many of them don't receive a penny of the profits that are made on the buildings.

Even if you compare all the photos that have been published of the house, its exact construction remains unclear. Even during the building process deviations were made from the floor plans as they appeared in Lautner's monograph. Two extensions

angle to the road, but Lautner placed this one at a thirty degree angle to the highway and the beach. As a result, you have a view of the sea from every room. The living room is on the side of the house, sticking out of the two-storey main volume like a tent, supported by a curved laminated beam, which also serves as the edge of the roof. This house marked a new turning point for Lautner. After creating his masterpiece in Acapulco, the Marbrisa house, in 1973, six whole years went by before he was able to build another work of significance. His form language changed: instead of the circles he frequently used in his earlier work, influenced by his mentor Wright, he now gave free reign to the free forms he first introduced in Mexico. JRK: 'I have to admit I'm disappointed we let ourselves be dissuaded too easily from the idea of seeing the house from the inside as well.' There's a glimmer of hope a year later when we're told the house has been sold to Dodgers owners Frank and Jamie McCourt, but it turns out to be in vain. Every year we try to contact the new owner, the former wife of the couple in question, who got to keep the house after an acrimonious divorce, but our messages go unanswered. In 2015 the house undergoes a drastic remodel: an indoor swimming pool is added and the studio wing that used to house the master bedroom is pulled down. We wonder what is left of Lautner's original design.

previous: Hatherell
next: Garwood

were later added to the main volume, which is positioned diagonally on the lot. As Lautner makes no mention of them, we don't know if they are his work. We later find out that Lautner did indeed design these additions in the mid-eighties.

The house is situated on a standard Malibu HWY1 lot: the front facing the four-lane highway, and the back opening out directly onto the beach, with fences dividing the lots from the neighbours' on either side. The other houses are all at a straight

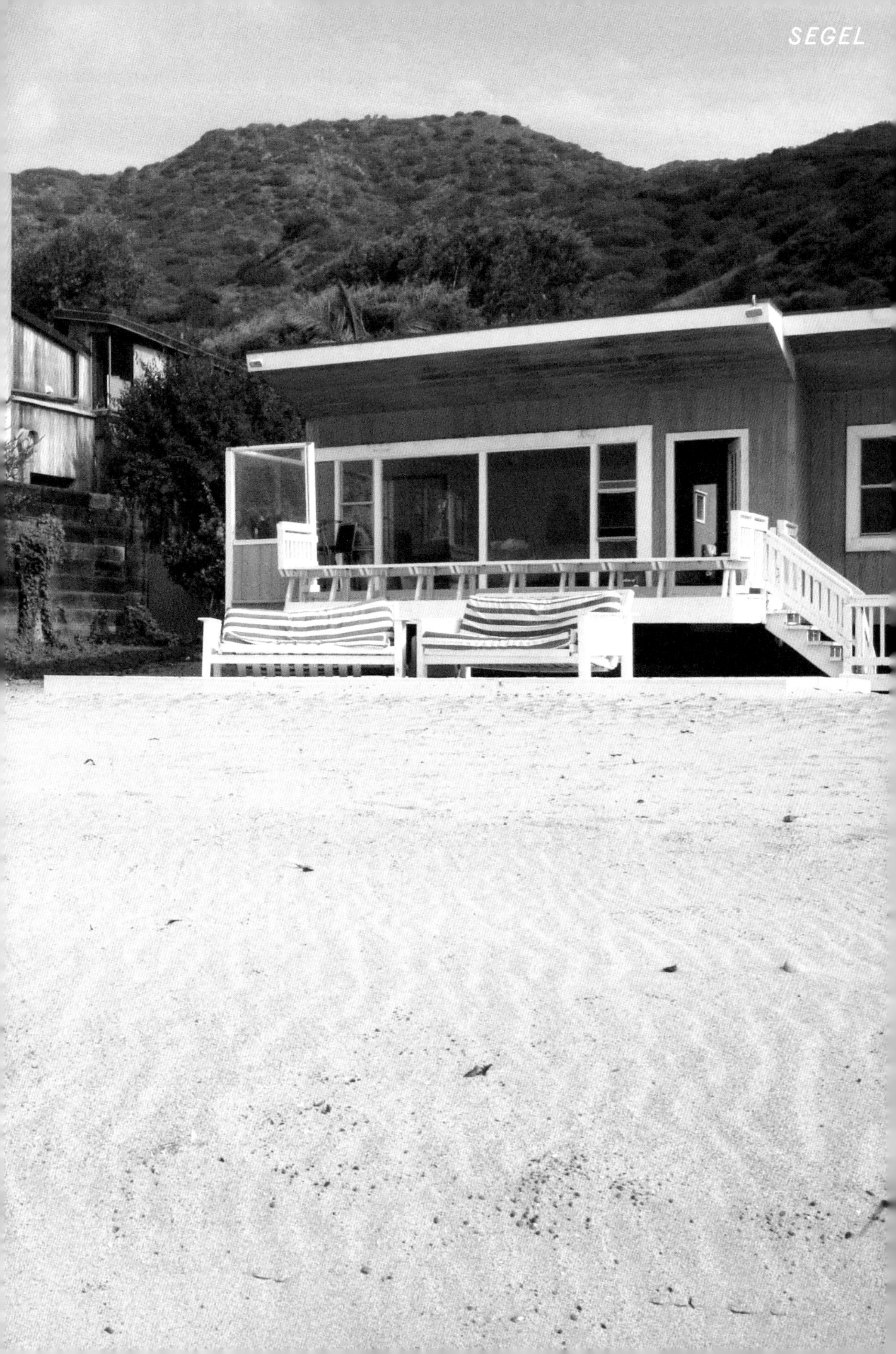

#41: Studio addition, 1950, extant
2515 N Commonwealth Ave, Los Angeles, CA 90027

Monday, 6 April 2009

We have submitted a wish list of drawings we would like to see during our visit to the archive in 2009, our top priority being the projects that were mentioned in Lautner's overview, but about which we don't know much else. One of these is the Seletz Studio. The roll in question contains various drawings for two different locations: an extension of an extant house on N Commonwealth Avenue designed for Dr Emil Seletz, and a completely new house for Jeanette Seletz on Dundee Drive. Both proposals are characterised by a semi-circular shape with pronounced rafters. Interestingly, neither of the addresses corresponds to the one known to us for the Seletz Studio. So this turns out to be another case where we sent letters to the wrong house.

When leaving the Getty Center at the end of the day we have fifteen minutes to spare, so we quickly make our way to the address we found on the drawing made for Dr Emil Seletz. It's one block further than the address we tried last time. When we get there we see a Spanish villa, and no trace of the semi-circular extension we are looking for. We ring the bell, but there's no answer. Walking around the house, we do see the contours of an extension, but we're doubtful whether it's one of Lautner's. JRK: 'I take a photo through the hedge, just to make sure we haven't missed anything.'

previous: Eisele
next: Harvlan site

The year after we come up with more inventive ways of getting hold of the remaining, more obscure projects. For example, we trace the children of the original clients to help us persuade the current owners to let us in. Our last visit to the archive produced the correct address of the Seletz Studio, after we'd been looking in the wrong spot for years. Although nothing we saw on the drawings had actually been realised, that one photo, taken through the hedge, did give us sufficient leads to continue our quest. The glass façade of the small building in the garden is reminiscent of that of the living room of the Bergren residence, as is the slope of the roof. The Seletz in question is

Dr Emil Seletz, a neurologist. The house has long since passed out of the family's possession, but we manage to trace a daughter of the original owner. She confirms that her father had a studio built, where he created oversized sculptures of celebrities. The woman is prepared to come to L.A. and brings along a picture of her father at work in the studio. We arrange to meet at the house and it turns out

hacienda-style house. The idea was that it would form one half of a whole, the other half being the house planned for Jeanette Seletz, Emil's sister (known for her 1943 novel *Hope Deferred*), which was supposed to have been built on the other side of the street. Years later another house was constructed there, spoiling the view for good. The fact that no plans have been found for the studio is presumably a result of the fire at Lautner's studio: some drawings were lost, while others still bear visible burn marks.

previous: Maloney
next: Hope

the extension we photographed a year earlier is indeed the studio designed by Lautner. The current owner is a musician and uses it as a recording studio. That required a few adjustments, but Lautner's design from 1950 is still basically intact. The studio can be accessed via an extra room.

We are standing on the spot where a semi-circular extension should have been added to the

Rabbi Jacob Kohn Sculpted by

Click image to zoom

SHEARING

#133: House, 1984-1992, extant
15 Green Turtle Rd, Coronado Cays, CA 92118

Saturday, 5 May 2007

At the end of the day, we have an appointment with the owners of the Shearing residence, the last house that Lautner carried to fruition. They were the first people to respond to our request. We're more than welcome; their only concern is that we should take enough time for the visit, because they have a boat and we should really see the view of the house from the water too. The house is located in a gated community in the bay of San Diego. It stands on a level, wedge-shaped lot among other houses at the end of a dead-end street. As all the lots border on the water, the residents all have boats. Looking at it from the street, the house divulges none of its secrets: it is almost entirely closed on this side. All we see is a garage door that spans the width of the façade. Although Lautner's work has a general tendency to dissolve the line between the inside and outside, here it seems a choice has been made to turn away from the outside world. Somewhat hidden on the right-hand side of the closed façade is the front door. Sticking to it is a note saying, 'WELCOME Lautner Admirers from the Netherlands!!'

Once inside, we see the house is surprisingly complex. It's like a small settlement with a pronounced outdoor space. The architecture looks remarkably current, and though the house has only rarely appeared in publications, it would form a high point in the oeuvre of any other architect. There's a parallel between the layout of the floor plan and that of the Segel residence: that also features a single story living room with an arched roof connected to a two-storey block. Where the Segel residence as a whole has been placed in an angle to the coast, to fully exploit its water-side orientation, in the Shearing house, an enormous mirrored wall has been used instead.

This covers the view towards the neighbours and extends the magnificent view of the bay to the other side, again maximising the house's water-side location. Again and again, Lautner's designs demonstrate his ability to draw out the best features of standard lots and make the most of them, making them even more attractive perhaps, in spatial terms, than the lots with the best views.

Going in through the front door, you walk past the patio, heading diagonally towards the mirrored wall, which draws your eye immediately to the view. The patio is the central hub around which the other rooms of the house have been arranged. The living room is formed by a suspended shell-shaped roof wing, separated from the rest of the house by a narrow strip of glass. The glued glass joins used here are little works of art. And there are more connections to other Lautner houses. The concrete outdoor area with jacuzzi, for example, shows a clear affinity with the outdoor space of the Beyer residence. The corner window of the study that slides open in its entirety is a feature that already appeared in the Stevens residence. And the skylight that can be opened automatically has its origin in the bathroom of Silvertop. Despite these echoes, there's a real difference in expression compared to the earlier works. We get the feeling that Lautner built into the wall on one side, right up to the panelling in the internal circulation space. After a comprehensive tour of the house, ending at a viewing platform on the roof, we are invited to take our drinks out to the boat. We cast off from the jetty and get a view of the house from the water. The slight curve of the roof sections gives the house a nautical look. We take a turn round the bay, but we don't see any other architectural masterpieces. The sun goes down on our last day of appointments. We're on a boat, a glass of white wine in our hand, accompanied by a group of students in fine spirits, as well as Lautner's daughter and the proud owners of the house: we can't imagine a finer end to our excursion. Back at the house, an elaborate meal is waiting for us. The Garcia family (no relation to the Garcias of the house of that name) owns a restaurant, and it shows. As we are in no hurry, we have time to let the architecture work in on us slowly. That night, we whiz back to our hotel in L.A., tired but satisfied. Three months later, after getting back to the Netherlands, we hear – to our great surprise – the owners have put the house on the market.

previous: Marina View Heights Headquarters
next: Wolff

set out the main lines, and then left it to the group of young architects he was working with to develop them into actual plans. When we asked the architects involved they categorically denied this was the case, but it seems obvious looking at the modern materials and details, which are in line with current-day designs: the plastered walls combined with raw concrete, natural wood frames alternated with frameless glass, a kitchen table

SHEATS (L'HORIZON)

#27: Apartments, 1948-1950, extant
10919 Strathmore Dr, Los Angeles, CA 90024

Tuesday, 1 May 2007

The last project we visit today are the Sheats apartments, built in 1949 for Helen Taylor Sheats and her husband Paul Henry Sheats, who later commissioned the famous 1963 Sheats residence on Angelo View Drive. The partnership between Helen Sheats and her architect resulted in Lautner's best work. Of the four projects Lautner designed for her, unfortunately only two were constructed.

The apartments are now used as student housing for the University of California in Los Angeles (UCLA). None of our attempts to contact UCLA by phone or in writing produced any results, so we resort to the old-fashioned method of ringing the doorbell. These apartments are one of a handful of Lautner buildings to have been given the status of Los Angeles Historic-Cultural Monument. Including the apartment of the Sheats themselves, the building originally contained six units (instead of nine, as stated elsewhere). It has a special place in Lautner's body of work, which mainly consists of freestanding houses. After visiting the complex we share his regret that he didn't get the chance to create many more of this kind of project.

All you can see at street level is a closed façade under an overhanging roof, with steps leading to a single entrance. But once you get to the top of the steps you enter a completely different world. The space between the building components follows the slope of the hill and its landscaping design includes planting, paths, water features and even trees. The whole has a structuralist character, with its endless variations on the circle. The dark yellow colour doesn't seem quite right combined with the dark blue windows, but we can't be sure because the famous original photographs were all in black and white. It's an unknown luxury for a student to be able to live here, just a stone's throw from the university. Voices from above and the muted

hum of a party ushering in the weekend lead us to the apartment that used to belong to the Sheats. Yes, the people living there did receive our letter and, yes, we're more than welcome to come and take a look around. The apartment would fit right in with the student houses we know in Delft, which are intentionally kept in as unattractive a state as possible. It's sorely neglected, filled with clothes, old couches and lots of mess lying around. Only in this case the place has unmistakeable character. Everyone feels at home immediately. Beers are passed round and the party kicks off. Visitors become residents. Lautner's magic reveals itself. The apartment is still overpowering in its forms and details. Its construction, using stacked mushroom columns, allows for a completely open façade. We visit the other apartments, one after the other, until we've seen them all. Although they all share a close affinity, no two apartments are the same. The communal courtyard is one of the best collective spaces ever built. It is a connective and truly shared place that doesn't encroach on the privacy of the surrounding units. The residents are vaguely familiar with the name Lautner, but to them this house is just a daily reality they take for granted.

The composition of circles and slopes intersected by straight walls isn't the result of a desire to create complexity for its own sake, but rather of a quest for 'real architecture' –

Thursday, 10 July 2008

A year later we pass the Sheats apartments again. The high quality of their design makes them worth a second visit. It's just as impressive the second time round, making us feel again what a shame it is Lautner never got another chance to make an apartment complex of this kind. It is a unique project that can't be compared to anything else.

previous: Preminger
next: Embassy Shop

architecture from within. Old photographs have been published of the building under construction, showing wooden constructions elegantly fanning out.

Night falls, giving us an alibi to pack up our cameras and get some sleep.

previous: Bergren
next: Schwimmer

SHEATS-GOLDSTEIN

#86: Sheats, House, 1962-1963, extant
#126: Goldstein, Remodel, 1979-1994, extant

Wednesday, 2 May 2007

Apart from the Chemosphere, the Sheats-Goldstein house is Lautner's best known house. It has been used in countless adverts, videos and films including *Time Bandits* and *Charlie's Angels* 2. Somehow, Lautner's architecture is always used as the residence of the bad guy, like adult-entertainment producer Jackie Treehorn in *The Big Lebowski*. Ironically, real adult films have been shot in the house, including *Unleashed* by Andrew Blake, a work of soft porn with aesthetic aspirations. This fact just serves as a distraction from the true meaning of Lautner's work, though. It was originally built as a fantastic family home.

The house has a fascinating history. It's now known as Goldstein's ultimate bachelor pad, but in 1962 it started out as a family home. Clients Paul and Helen Sheats had commissioned Lautner to design Sheats Apartments fourteen years earlier. The basic structure of the house is covered by a polygonal concrete roof that is composed of three triangles, with a coffered ceiling. One triangle ends in the slope of the hill and the other marks the narrow passageway to the floor below. This master bedroom suite, fitted with a lounge seat, bed, bathroom and closet, is completely concealed underneath the terrace behind the swimming pool. This makes it a secret spot, which can only be accessed via a covered outdoor area that starts under the large roof over the living room. The house brings together components with very distinct identities under one roof: the patio at the front with the low entrance, the kitchen/dining area, the bedroom wing, the living room with terrace, and the swimming pool and downstairs suite, with windows looking out

under the surface of the pool, establishing a connection with the level above. To avoid the necessity of a fence around the swimming pool, the floor slopes upward slightly around the edge of the terrace. The effect is that you instantly feel when you are at risk of falling off. This slope is also visible in the ceiling of the space below, where it serves as a way of bringing the outside indoors. The effect is comparable to that in the rooms in the Bubbling Wells Resort, the dining room of the Schaeffer residence and the retail space of Beachwood Market, only more subtle. The ceiling downstairs tapers into a sharp point, where the two glass façades meet. During Goldstein's alterations, the original wooden window frames were replaced by plate glass elements. As an added feature, these glass front slide apart soundlessly at the push of a button. It's like Gerrit Rietveld's open corner in the

Schröder house, only on steroids. This sharp quality has been applied throughout the whole house, which is remarkable when you think that the building was remodelled during the same period that the curvy Beyer house and Pacific Coast House came into being. The glass bathroom wing with its sink made entirely of glass has a shape that Lautner had already tried out in the Payne Addition over 35 years earlier. He's taken a good idea, reusing it and

perfecting it when the time was ripe.

When the house was built in 1963, instead of closing off the living room with a glass front, Lautner proposed installing no more than a curtain of forced air, as you find in shopping centres. This was another way of maximising the relationship with the exterior. Unfortunately this proved impractical. After a year, the curtain of forced air was replaced by plate glass after all. Jim Goldstein

bought the house in 1971 and, from 1979, commissioned Lautner to upgrade a whole series of elements, step by step. It's always fascinating to see people like Goldstein, who pursue their dreams without concessions and are able to realise them through the support of the right craftspeople. In our own country, this combination of personal cultural interest, sufficient financial means and a willingness to spend money on innovative architecture is virtually unknown.

Goldstein had the vision, money and patience to help Lautner expand his vocabulary. Lautner was fascinated by the process of taking a house he had lovingly designed for a specific client and adapting it to the lifestyle of a new owner, and didn't let feelings of nostalgia hold him back. When you compare the house as it is now to photos of the house when it was first completed, the first thing that strikes you is the 'tropical rainforest' Goldstein had laid out. The role Lautner's staff played in the development of the ideas shouldn't be underestimated. In this case it was Andrew Nolan, firstly, who worked out the detailed plans of parts of the house including the bedroom storey between 1979 and 1990. Subsequently, Helena Arahuete worked with Lautner on the entrance, the swimming pool and the pond with stepping stones. When Lautner died in 1994, he left behind lots of ideas that hadn't been carried out yet. Duncan Nicholson, who worked for Lautner from 1989, was contracted by Goldstein, together with Julia Strickland. Goldstein asked them to develop Lautner's sketches, which were roughly drafted but conceptually sharp. Work is still ongoing on various alterations and extensions for Jim Goldstein. After Nicholson died suddenly in 2015, the work is being carried on by his colleague James Perry. JRK: 'Initially, Nicholson was irritated when I asked him for a guided tour in 2007. He gets these requests so often he could fill his days with them. It's only when I told him Lautner's daughters would be there, as well as Bette Jane Cohen, that he arranged for his partner Michael Wirts to show us round.'

Our visit to the house in May 2007 is the first for TS. Wirts expects to be able to rush through our viewing in half an hour, but he hasn't reckoned with the students' interest. The group fans out to study all the building's nooks and crannies. In the garden we look at the building site where the Concannon residence once stood. All that's left is the garage, which is being used as a site hut. We study the plans for the new extension. To make the ongoing construction work bearable for the neighbours and hide it from sight, a jungle of greenery is being planted at the same time, including full-grown trees. As our guide tells us, this is happening at a rapid pace: one ditch that was dug for drainage pipes was accidentally filled with a stately row of trees the very next day.

JRK: 'For me this visit contrasted sharply with the one I paid to the house with my wife Christine a couple of years before. During the week, Goldstein is often absent and the paradise turns into one big building site, with dozens of construction workers and gardeners busy laying out a tennis court on the roof of a reception/party space. A second visit does help you understand the house better. It's a unique building you can visit endlessly and which deserves a prominent place in the history of architecture.'

previous: Schwimmer
next: Concannon

Saturday, 12 July 2008

The party celebrating the opening of the Lautner exhibition at the Hammer Museum slowly draws to a close; the bar has already closed. There's a rumour going round that James Goldstein has invited a select group of home owners to come back to his place for an after-party. It's 11 PM and Jan-Richard says, 'Come on, let's go to Goldstein's!' On second thoughts, we decide to call first. Goldstein picks up with a deep voice: 'Hello, you still got my number?', 'Yes I know who you are', finishing with: 'My door is open.' Tycho drives over to the Sheats-Goldstein residence right away. It's wonderful to see the house at night, very

different to the daytime view. Goldstein is just showing a group of people the garden when we arrive, and we're invited to join them. The visitors include Kelly Lynch, the owner of the Carling residence, the architect Bart Prince and Roban Poirier. We follow the group inside the *Skyspace*, designed by James Turrell, and sit around enjoying the light show. It turns out Lautner himself worked on the first sketches with Turrell. It wasn't until ten years after his death that the pavilion was finished though, supervised by Duncan Nicholson. By now it's past

midnight and we're the only guests left. Before we head back to our hotel in Silver Lake Goldstein's ladyfriend takes one last picture of us on the *Big Lebowski* sofa. It's been an amazing evening. It looks like Los Angeles has finally embraced Lautner as one of the most important architects of his time. Now for the rest of the world.

previous: Tower Motors / Parkway Motors
next: Wolf

TS: 'Six days later JRK is back home and my wife has arrived in Los Angeles. I have arranged for us to go along with a group visiting the Sheats-Goldstein residence. Every time you visit this house is an adventure, but the magic we experienced a week ago at night – well, it's not quite the same when you're there with a large group of people. But when you visit a house multiple times, you keep discovering new things: various details especially,

previous: Wolff 2 'Wind Song'
next: Taliesin West

Monday, 13 November 2017

One of the reasons to go to L.A. again in 2017 is Club James. The club, which is situated under the tennis courts of the Sheats-Goldstein house, is part of a complex including an office, a club, a museum and a library that the Concannon house was demolished for. The construction of the complex began when Lautner was still alive, but when he died, Duncan Nicholson took over the project. When he died too, James Perry took over, and he is the one who is showing us around now. We first met James Perry in 2007 – in ten years, he has progressed from intern to main architect of L.A.'s most challenging client. Since 2007, construction work on the complex has continued non-stop. The club can be reached by descending a staircase into a concrete space that allows access to the club. James puts on a deep house record and the beat guides our journey through these fantastic spaces. The club area was dug out of the hillside and has a spectacular view of downtown L.A. on one side. The steel dancefloor and the spacy furniture complete the effect. Outside one can reach Goldstein's office, as well as his bedroom in the house itself. A glass bay window protrudes from under the edge of the tennis court and seems to reach towards the view. Its design matches the sharp shapes of the house seamlessly.

Perry shows us scale models of the pool and the guest house that are still to be built. Reassured that the work is by no means finished and that we have plenty of reason to visit here once more, we walk through the main house again. It strikes again how

like the automated sliding roof over the toilet or the play of light you can see in the bedroom via the windows below the surface of the swimming pool.'

During our last visit to the archive, in 2010, we come across a folder containing photos of the Sheats house before Goldstein bought it. These show us the story about the living room initially being constructed without a glass façade are in fact true. The house looks curiously dated in the pictures; Jim Goldstein's influence has catapulted it into the twenty-first century.

homely it is. At night, you can see the lights of Los Angeles from under the enormous concrete roof in the living room, as though you're peering out from under a tent awning. A space has been created here that is both cave and tent: cave because of the solid construction, and tent because of the shape. The thick carpets and triangular cassettes in the roof construction contribute to the muted acoustics, which enhance the sense of intimacy. Because this is the Lautner house we have visited most often, it feels more and more familiar, even

SHEATS-GOLDSTEIN

though Goldstein's constant need to perfect the house does mean there is always something new to see. Now, for instance, there have been changes to the back entrance and the laundry room. The house is constantly kept in mint condition; not long ago, the floor in the bedroom was replaced.

It's still a magical place, which hasn't begun to feel dated in the least, throughout the years.

next: Bubbling Wells Resort

SHUSETT

#37: House, 1950-1951, demolished 2010
9340 Monte Leon Lane, Beverly Hills, CA 90210

Tuesday, 1 May 2007

The Shusett residence is located at the end of a cul-de-sac. It's hard to find, not appearing in many publications – the only known picture being a stamp-sized photograph in the list of works at the end of Lautner's book. Dating from 1951, the house's entire design is centred around a large cypress, which it surrounds in a semi-circular shape. It is striking to see how much Lautner and Frank Lloyd Wright influenced each other during this period. While Lautner was the one to lean on Wright's work initially, the roles gradually reversed, for instance in 1953, when Wright made a design for the Andrew B. Cooke House in Virginia Beach, whose floor plan showed great similarities to that of the Shusett residence Lautner designed two years earlier.

In 2007 the house is still there, but as a result of countless remodels it is far from its original state. A heavy portico has been added to the side of the house facing the street and the front door also looks like it's a few centuries off. We don't know enough about the house yet to realise how seriously it has been messed about. It consists of a curved part housing the kitchen, living and dining room, and, two steps up, a wing containing the sleeping area. The roof of the bedroom wing tilts up, letting in light from the north. The tree has grown to gigantic proportions, although you can still see the living room surrounding it.

during construction and just after completion. These show we got it completely wrong when we made an attempt to reconstruct the floor plan together with students in Tilburg, based on the material then available. The house's detailing is gracious and slender. The roof of the main volume, which is constructed around a tree, covers a subtle interplay of volumes, covered outside spaces and delicate frames under a band of circular ornaments, which seem reminiscent of Wright's work in the

The woman living there finds it hard to imagine why a group from Europe would come all the way to Beverly Hills to see her house. We get Lautner's book from the car, and she can't keep her eyes off the tiny picture. The dated and cluttered interior makes it difficult to see the original qualities of the house.

Then, in March 2010, we make a painful discovery in the Lautner archive. A folder turns up containing photos of the Shusett house, taken

final phase of his life. In other words, this was an exquisite house originally. When visiting it in 2007 we had no way of knowing the circle motif had been carried much further than could be seen then. Originally a large part of the space under the curved roof had been a covered outdoor area, creating a wonderful interplay between the inside and outside. The high point is the place where the bedroom wing connects with the living section, creating added height. All the misplaced elements, such as the coarse frames, the bulky portico and the awful front door, are later additions. It seems mystifying that only one photo, of the skeleton during construction, was included in Lautner's monograph, and that these photos of the final result were never published anywhere. Possibly if they had been it could have saved the house from its eventual fate. The folder also contains photos of perspectives of a complex with a 38-storey tower designed for Shusett in two variations. If you didn't

in his oeuvre. We answer that every Lautner house is significant and should be preserved. When it turns out a demolition permit has been requested, we immediately send the photos we have recently found of the house in the archive to various Lautner connections. We also contact Michael LaFetra to ask him if he could step in and buy the house. He seriously considers it, but the owner isn't interested and carries on with the demolition plans. An attempt is made to get a temporary stay via the courts, but to no avail: that same afternoon, on a date that is the same as the Beverly Hills postcode, 90210, the process of knocking down the house begins. We find out that the owner's mother died recently, freeing up a sum of money enabling them to replace the house with one better suited to their lifestyle. JRK: 'On the evening before the demolition work starts, I speak to the owner briefly on the phone. He asks me to leave him alone in a very irritated manner.' Mark H., the owner of Harpel 1, who also tried to persuade the owners to change their minds, sends us shocking pictures showing the demolition of a unique house that could have been saved. When we visited it, it was just a Lautner house in bad condition. It just goes to show the vulnerability of 1950s architecture in desirable locations. The newly built house is put up for sale shortly after completion.

previous: Familian
next: Baxter-Hodiak

know better, you wouldn't recognise it as Lautner's work at all.

When we're back in the Netherlands, we receive an email via Frank Escher from the Los Angeles Cultural Heritage Commission, informing us they have received an anonymous phone call about a house in Beverly Hills claimed to be a Lautner. They are investigating it and ask us if this house, known as the Shusett residence, is a significant work with-

#65: Office building, 1956, altered beyond recognition
#74: Addition, 1957, altered beyond recognition
3425 W Cahuenga Blvd, Los Angeles, CA 90068

Sunday, 6 May 2007

Contractor Paul Speer, a friend of Lautner who worked with him on Frank Lloyd Wright's Sturges House in 1938, built Lautner's earliest projects (Lautner, Bell, Springer). Later on, he built a few more of Lautner's designs, spread out over four decades. In 1956 he commissioned Lautner to design his office, and in 1973 they worked together one last time, on the building of the Crippled Children's Society.

We searched endlessly for this small office building while preparing for our trip in 2007, but nothing we came across even remotely resembled the clean space with laminated beams we'd seen in the photos in the back of Lautner's monograph. The contracting company does still exist, and the Lautner connection is referenced on the website, but it is no longer situated at the address Lautner indicated on his map of constructed works. When we arrive at that location, we find a dilapidated building housing a shop. Unfortunately it's a Sunday, so it's closed. Lautner's design is thought to have been lost, but through the window we catch a glimpse of what we think is a curved laminated beam. Could it still be there after all? Because the exterior blends in seamlessly with a series of cheerless commercial buildings alternating with garish bill boards, we never managed to find it on Google Earth. We're ecstatic that we've managed to find another Lautner, although the state it's in is a disappointment.

previous: Wolff
next: Jacobsen

Friday, 11 July 2008

In the centre there used to be a raised cylinder containing Paul Speer's own office. The place has undergone a whole series of transformations during the past decades. On the outside, there's nothing left that even points to Lautner's influence. Since the 1980s, the building has housed an arts supply store called World Supply. During our trip in 2008 we get to take a look inside. There, nearly everything is still as it was when it was built, only in a wretched state of repair and packed with

huge quantities of erasers, felt-tip pens, rulers and drawing paper. However, with a little imagination we can conjure up the black-and-white photos of the empty office space with its curved laminated beams. The shop has been extended a couple of times, but the central space on the floor upstairs is still recognisable. When we tell the elderly woman who owns the shop who we are, she offers us something to drink and proudly tells us Lautner himself used to come here to buy his pencils. It doesn't seem to have bothered him that the building was no longer being used for the purpose

he'd designed it for. It's a wonderful shop, of the kind you don't find very often these days, and we're afraid it won't survive for very much longer in this digital age. The huge advertising placards on the roof seem to be the most important source of income.

In the archive in 2009 we come across a roll that makes it clear what happened to the Speer Contractors Office Building. An additional bay had been conceived on the right-hand side and we find a number of proposed designs for the façade facing the street. On one of them the letters of the clients' name form the façade's support. The roll also contains a floor plan of an unknown Parking Structure on 730 S. Broadway Street in Los Angeles.

previous: Zimmerman
next: Schaeffer

Monday, 22 March 2010

A year later we find photos taken by Donald J. Higgins of the office, two of which are included in the back of Lautner's monograph. In the archive

after we made our discoveries in the archives, the old art supply shop has indeed disappeared. The building has been taken over by a company called Atlas Digital, which has painted the shop front black, making it impossible to see whether the last traces of Lautner's work have gone forever.

previous: Fischer
next: Deutsch

we find another ten pictures from the same session. This should be enough for a reconstruction. The glass construction placed on top of the contractor's personal office like a gun turret is a particularly wonderful feature, allowing him to survey the whole office but also providing a secluded space for meetings, with views over the surrounding area. The letters of the company name have been included, but not in the same way as in the drawing: not as part of the construction, but as free-standing letters made of rough cement.

When we happen to drive past there the next day

SPRINGER

#5a: Guest house, 1940, extant
#5b: Addition, 1940, extant
2215 Park Dr, Los Angeles, CA 90026

Sunday, 13 July 2008

On a beautiful Sunday morning, we visit a project that was Lautner's first commission as an independent architect, carried out in 1940. It actually consists of two separate commissions: an extension of the living room and a freestanding guest house at the back of the lot. The guest house is now the home of a successful musician/DJ and his family. He is crazy about the house: not so much because of the architecture as the acoustics! They're renting the place, but they're thinking of having a replica built somewhere else. The building's design can be traced back almost directly to the work of Frank Lloyd Wright. It's based on an interplay between axes of symmetry and 45-degree angular displacements, making it more dynamic than you would expect based on the floor plan. The shape of the plan is a large diamond. Because the roof has two peaks, placed at right angles to each other, each space is different, making the house look bigger than it actually is. The central living area reaches right up to one of the peaks. The high, narrow windows are reminiscent of those in Wright's Jorgine Boomer House. Some of the original clarity of the floor plan has been lost though, because at some point an extension has been added along one whole side of the building, as well as a balcony. The original plan is similar to one of the design options for the 'future house' on the Astor Farmin Indio.

We can't go inside the extension to the Springer house because the owner isn't in. Looking inside, we do see the cove above the window which is so characteristic for Lautner's work from this period. The view is emphatically framed by a protruding wall. With a little imagination, you could see this as a predecessor of Wolff. Although this project was featured in architectural magazines at the time, Lautner never mentioned it in his own book.

previous Wolf
next: Garwood

#100: House, 1966-1968, extant
#134: Remodel, 1984-1991, extant
23524 Malibu Colony Rd (78 Malibu Colony),
Malibu, CA 90265

Saturday, 28 April 2007

Our next goal is to visit the Stevens house, a Malibu 'beach house' dating from 1968. Practical considerations have led us to abandon our original idea of visiting the houses in the order of their completion. Dan Stevens commissioned a number of designs, two of which were carried out: a floristry shop called The Flowers That Bloom in the Spring Tra La after a song from Gilbert and Sullivan's comic opera *The Mikado,* and this building: a fantastic house with an extensive programme on a beach-side site that is relatively small for American standards. Two shell roofs extending the full height of the house mirror each other at the midpoint of the building. They cover a rich variety of spaces, from the swimming pool to the sleeping platforms under the roof. It is one of Lautner's masterpieces from the second half of the 1960s. The house is on the point of being sold, which makes it difficult to arrange a visit. Its concrete shell roofs stand out among the pimped 'beach huts' in the world's most expensive street, Malibu Colony Road. Although the houses have an average sales value of around twenty million dollars and are located in a gated community with residents including Sting and Tom Hanks, they're not particularly interesting in architectural terms. Security in the street is so tight there's really no point in stopping by without an appointment. The security guard does what he's paid to do, but he does let us phone the owner from his booth. The latter isn't home, but tells the guard to let us through, so we can at least see the exterior. The house is set back from the building line, with a black painted wooden fence facing the street, obscuring most of the view of the building. It doesn't take long before the first suspicious neighbours come outside to complain about our presence.

previous: Garwood
next: Harpel 1

In July 2008 we're back in Malibu, planning to take a look at the Stevens house from the beach, as we didn't get a chance to last time. When the tide is out, the beach is a public area, but the question is how to get there. They don't like people snooping around here. Naturally we've done our research, so as the sun goes down and the tide goes out we crawl through a gate and onto the beach of Malibu Colony. Although some photos of the house give

the impression that it borders directly on the beach, there's actually a height difference of sixteen steps between the garden and the beach below. We stick to the rules and stay on the beach. From here, however, we get a good view of the thin opposing concrete shells that give the house its unmistakeable shape. It's a remarkable sight among all the 'wooden huts' costing ten million dollars or more.

previous: Aldrich
next: Crahan

At the end of 2007 the Stevens house was bought by architecture lover Michael LaFetra and then carefully restored. We met LaFetra at the opening of the Hammer exhibition and have kept in contact. He is now living in the house himself. Over the past few years, he has set himself up as the saviour of high-quality West Coast architecture. He has bought, restored, and resold several houses by Schindler, Kappe and Lautner. He also had Pierre

van der Knijff of the Academy of Architecture in Amsterdam. The Austrian booklet that marked the occasion of Lautner's eightieth birthday places the house on the same level as Malin, Marbrisa and Sheats. We don't think this is an exaggeration. The house was preceded by Elrod and followed by Walstrom, both top-quality houses that were very different and were realised within one year of each other. Dan Stevens commissioned a number of projects, including the aforementioned florist shop for his third wife and an apartment in Paris. The characteristic feature of the Stevens house, on its narrow beach-side lot, is its two concrete shell roofs, in the shape of half arches. Lautner saw this concept as an alternative to row houses, the concrete shells serving to maximise the view while also creating privacy from the neighbours. At the halfway point of the house, there's a switch in orientation between the two opposing shells. As a result, the section facing the street also looks out over the ocean, and the ocean-side section also has a view of the mountains in the distance. The arch is always on your right, regardless of whether you're standing in the street or on the beach. Under these concrete shells, the house is organised on six different levels, creating a dazzling spatial spectacle. The number of materials has been kept to a minimum: the two soaring concrete half arches with large vertical openings, and, inside, a wooden framework of stairs, walls and ceilings, combined with a floor of beige tiles. The wood has been laid diagonally across all the horizontal planes, adding to the dynamic spatial quality. Even the wood components of the terrace have been laid diagonally. Beyond the entrance gate, a path leads us under the first concrete shell to a modest set of steps leading up to the front door.

Koenig's last design built on the site for which it was intended. His last acquisition is Lautner's Rawlins house on Balboa Island, which we haven't visited yet either.

The Stevens house now has a natural wood façade and gate, which immediately strikes us because they were a dark brown colour the last time we were there. The moment we step through the gate, in March 2010, is a magical one. We already got an impression of the house's spatial qualities from the 1:50 scale model made by Wendy

Under the large roof, we are now also under the protruding bedroom floor. This maximises the way you are led into the house. Despite all the constructive process that looks so dominant in the photographs, the house is very comfortable, with everything in its right place – from the protruding kitchen on the street-side to the beach-side living room, and the swimming pool to the built-in lofts in the bedrooms intended as guest accommodation.

Although its programme is compact, the house feels spacious thanks to the many views and open spaces. This effect is enhanced by the fact that the space under the shells isn't completely filled in with construction. On one side the garden extends into the space under the roof, and on the other the swimming pool connects the house to the beach. Once again, Lautner shows himself a master of scale: the house feels like a suit that has been made to measure, not a single part feeling too large or small. Its dynamics result from the soaring heights and the connection between the different floor levels – the stairs with their sculptural quality, which provide a different perspective on the same space. However, the stairs also have a secluded character when you go down to the lowest level, which used to house a painter's studio, later converted into a sauna by Lautner. In the corridor, wooden slats shape the space, but don't close it off. The fish-scale-shaped slats in the concrete over the swimming pool block the view from the neighbouring lot, while still letting in light. Michael LaFetra tells us that during the restoration he carried out a number of details that Lautner had designed but that hadn't come off during construction, such as two sliding doors that meet in one corner of the living room, so that the corner disappears when both are slid back. Dan Stevens trusted Lautner implicitly, and the two men remained friends for the rest of the architect's life. Lautner came back many times to carry out adjustments. On the photos taken by Shulman shortly after completion, the sand of the beach reaches right up to the back of the house. Now, the beach is at least six feet lower than the garden and a terrace has been created, the curved concrete shapes of which look like they were a finger exercise for the nearby Pacific Coast house. Stevens's daughter Gwen Neidlinger tells us her father considered the house his heart and soul, and that he regularly invited famous rockstars to their home, including Robert Plant, Jimmy Page, Steven Tyler and Mick Jagger. 'He always said the one thing he wanted to be

remembered for was this home.' When he was in the hospital, knowing he was going to die, there was only one thing he wanted: 'He just wanted to be home, in that fabulous bedroom overlooking the ocean, when he died.'

previous: Weinstein
next: Fischer

SUNSET PLAZA GATE

#132: Entrance gate, 1983-1987, extant
2300 Sunset Plaza Dr, Los Angeles, CA 90069

Tuesday, 1 May 2007

On 1 May 2007, we drive to a project we have never found any trace of apart from a rumour on the internet: it's the entrance gate of a house owned by the same person who co-mmissioned the Pacific Coast house in Malibu. The gate is the entrance to a hill with a neoclassical villa at the top. While Lautner was working on the design for the new villa in Malibu, the client asked him to make a few alterations to his house in Hollywood. The plans went so far that a completely new villa was supposed to have been built here too, but in the end only a wall and gate were actually constructed. Lautner may also have been involved in various other conversions the villa underwent. The gate is so heavily dimensioned it could stop a tank. The surface cover-ing of flagstones is strongly reminiscent of the pyramid in front of the Familian house. A large, black, sliding steel door closes off the gate. The first letter of the owner's last name, which happens to be that of Lautner's too, has been cut out in monumental proportions. Angular but not perpendicular, the shapes are characteristic of Lautner's designs in the late seventies and early eighties. A tiny camera next to the door buz-zer watches us. We press the buzzer repeatedly, but the gate remains shut.

previous: Baxter-Hodiak
next: Garcia

TALIESIN EAST

designed by Frank Lloyd Wright
5481 County Road C, Spring Green, WI 53588

21 September 2011

Spring Green lies in beautiful surroundings, reminding of an English landscape. Spread across the hills are the various buildings that make up Frank Lloyd Wright's Taliesin.

It was Wright's autobiography (1933) that made Lautner want to go to Taliesin. Working with Wright meant 'learning by doing': cooking, to teach the students how a kitchen works, bricklaying, carpentry and drafting Wright's projects. Lautner later said that no contractor ever needed to tell him whether something was feasible or not. There is a famous photo of Wright surrounded by students, with a self-confessed shy Lautner in the background. Wright was later to say that Lautner was his best student, the second-best architect in the world. Taliesin East is an idyllic decor for the classic master-apprentice relationship. We have already visited Taliesin West, the place where Wright spent his summers, and the location of Lautner's first design of his own: a shelter among the cactusses. However, since we're in the neighbourhood anyway, we also want to see Taliesin East, where Lautner spent his formative years, with our own eyes. Wright's 'kingdom' is big business: in the visitor centre/gift shop tickets are sold for various tours of the buildings, which are still partly in use as a school of architecture, and we have booked a so-called highlights tour at two o'clock. We see Wright's private quarters, work room, theatre and the drafting room with its black triangular rafters, and we finish in the guest wing, made specially in the fifties for Solomon Guggenheim, who came here to talk about a new museum. Although we get an excellent tour through the most important parts of the complex it is frustrating to be herded around and have to stay back behind wire barriers. In one of the rooms is the above-mentioned photo of Wright in the drafting room with John Lautner directly behind him. Lautner lived and worked here for six years. Wright used to send his apprentices to the sites where his projects were being built to supervise the work, and this is how Lautner found himself in Los Angeles, supervising projects like the George Sturges House and the annexes to the Eaglefeather project for Arch Oboler. In a 1986 interview with Marlene Laskey Lautner said that he had a very happy childhood, with affectionate parents who loved art and culture, surrounded by beautiful nature. Judging by the films and

photos that can be seen all around here his stay in Taliesin must have continued in the same vein.

previous: Midgaard
next: Wolf

288

#01: Temporary drafting / sleeping shelter,
1937, demolished
12621 N Frank Lloyd Wright Blvd,
Scottsdale, AZ 85259

TALIESIN WEST SHELTER

Saturday, 19 July 2008

TS: 'At the end of the day my wife and I arrive in Scottsdale, Arizona, just in time for the last tour of Frank Lloyd Wright's Taliesin West, a complex built in 1938 and a fine example of architecture which

bricks of the walls of the drafting room himself.'

It was here that Lautner designed and built his first own project, the Taliesin West Shelter. Every student there was given the task of making their own sleeping and studio space. He chose a spot under a large Saguaro cactus to build his tent-like construction, which provided shelter from the sun during the day, with an opening above the bed providing a view of the stars in the desert sky at night.

Lautner's temporary construction was a precursor of his later masterpieces.

previous: Sheats-Goldstein
next: Turner

has become one with the landscape. In a 1986 interview with Marlene L. Laskey Lautner waxed lyrical about the time he spent here. Unfortunately, the tour does not include the drafting room, as this is still being used by students. Lautner's contribution to this building was important: he preferred tasks like steam fitting and bricklaying, in which physical and mental work were combined, to drafting, and said that he had laid most of the

TOLSTOY

#82: House, 1961-1974, extant
9540 Hillside Rd (Tolstoy Ranch Rd at Norbrook Dr),
Rancho Cucamonga, CA 91737

Tuesday, 1 May 2007

As we drive back to L.A. from Palm Springs in May 2007, we stop in Rancho Cucamonga, at a house we have searched for endlessly. During the course of the year in which we prepared for our excursion, we both became a father for the second time. We spent many sleepless nights trying to soothe a crying baby, while scanning Southern California on Google Earth at the same time. We each had our personal favourites we were determined to track down. JRK: 'One of mine was Tolstoy.' The house is the opposite of the Chemosphere. Where the latter rises into the air on a single stalk, the Tolstoy house is anchored to the ground with cables. The actual design consists of just three concrete piers, covered by steel cables that form a star shape and are anchored to the ground in three points. Once this skeleton of steel cables was in place, the owners built most of the rest of the house themselves. It took thirteen years to complete it. The steel cables have a dual function, supporting the light-weight polyurethane roof and defining a beautiful outdoor area between the three volumes, accommodating hanging plants that provide shade in this warm location. When we looked on Google Earth in 2006, the image resolution for this part of California wasn't very high, which meant the creeper-covered cables made the house nearly invisible. Looking at it now on Google Earth, it's hard to imagine we had such trouble spotting the house. It used to be surrounded by nothing but orange groves, but it has recently been completely encircled by a multitude of houses much too large for their small lots. The Tolstoy house is hidden in the centre of a lot dotted with trees. As we haven't

managed to contact the owners, all we can do for now is take a tour round the periphery. This is enough to show us the house is built up of circular elements. An arch cut out of the curved outer wall of the living room is mirrored in a circular pond. A circular shower is situated in the point of this section of the house. The only element that breaks with this geometrical pattern is a new swimming pool, which has replaced the previous, heart-shaped one. The second circular wall houses a recording studio, and the third a covered outdoor area. The cables that support the construction have a wonderful added effect, serving as a support for climbing plants in the centre of the house. It's clear that nobody lives here permanently.

Our surprise at the versatility of Lautner's work

grows with every house we visit. But this house really is one of a kind: it's unique, even within Lautner's oeuvre. The encroaching surroundings make us fear the worst. The size of the house is such that you could easily divide the site into four separate lots.

This striking house within Lautner's oeuvre is also one that the client helped build, like the Mauer

Monday, 14 July 2008

The current owner, a project developer who is now covering the surrounding orange grove with tightly packed houses, kept the Tolstoy house for himself after buying the house and land from the original owners. In 2007 we were already impressed by this paradisiacal oasis in the midst of a growing suburb. When we meet them in July 2008, the owners are clearly proud of their house and very pleased to receive a visit from Lautner's family: they have asked a large number of people over for the occasion.

We are especially keen to experience for ourselves the transition from the living room to this central area. The façade is set back under an arch-shaped window, creating an inverse bay. At this point, the raised seating area meets the circular fountain, which extends indoors from outside. The cables that support the roof are visible from inside. Wooden boards have been laid on top, covered in insulation. The floor plan of the living area ends in a point, where a shower is located. Lautner never used this construction method again; it is truly unique, and a brilliant idea. The house is currently being used as a weekend retreat, but we ask ourselves how long this will last. It is relatively unknown and can't be seen from the public road: it could easily just disappear suddenly. The only way to protect these projects is to make sure Lautner's work becomes better known. At least the house has become easier to locate now, as the dirt track

and Malin houses. Lautner's book only contains construction photographs of this project.

previous: Hope
next: Payne

that used to be there has now become a proper street called the Tolstoy Ranch Road.

previous: Johnson
next: Henry's Pomona site

Saturday, 12 July 2008

In July 2008 we are standing at the crossroads where Lautner's first design for the Henry's chain used to stand and, across the road, the showroom of Tower Motors. Both buildings were demolished in the 1980s. The client who commissioned the Tower Motors Lincoln Mercury Showroom was Arthur Eisele, who had had the Eisele Guest House built shortly before. A number of drawings of the showroom are on record, but not many photographs. Nobody really knows what this design looked like precisely. Unfortunately visiting the site doesn't produce much useful information either. In 2010 we find a series of photographs in the archive that finally shed some light on the design in its built state, which turns out to be slightly different to the abovementioned drawings. We also find colour slides taken just after completion. They look like snapshots, and their age can be deduced mainly from the appearance of the cars on display. In his own list of works Lautner marked this project down as 'Good one', but only included a single, miniscule, nondescript photo in the book. The Tower Motor Co. itself, meanwhile, advertised as 'The finest, most strikingly modern automobile establishment in America...'

previous: Henry's Glendale site
next: Sheats-Goldstein

Thursday, 24 July 2008 (TS)

The Turner house, built on the edge of ski resort Aspen in the Rocky Mountains in 1982, is a milestone in Lautner's later career. For the first time, he created a floor plan that consisted entirely of free curves, under a large concrete shell roof that touches the ground at three points. From the side facing the road, the roof follows the slope of the hill, hardly standing out at all – all you can see is the grass-covered roof and edging. On the other side, the roof opens out to the ski slopes with large curving glass façades. Designed around 1980, the house was commissioned by an unusual client, who worked with Lautner to create a kind of hippy's retreat. The most striking feature was the curved wall along the stairs, which is carpeted. There's a gap between this wall and the ceiling, letting a strip of light into the bedroom. Another interesting detail is a plateau on hydraulic hinges, which makes it possible to convert the dining corner into an outdoor terrace when the weather's fine. This simultaneously creates a sunken sitting area covered in deep-pile carpeting.

After the client died twenty years after the house was completed, it stood empty for a long time, seemingly impossible to sell. There were even plans to tear it down, but according to Lautner the concrete construction would make this far too expensive. In his own words: 'I am very happy that I was able to make so many buildings out of concrete. Because I get a kick out of that, I tell people they are going to be there a long time. Not because there is any

understanding of architecture but because they are too expensive to tear down.' The house was eventually sold, but the current owner has made a number of alterations, toning down its original character. All the finishings have been replaced with hard materials and the soft colours that were used originally have gone, detracting from the natural

feel of the curves and language of forms. TS: 'My wife and I are given a friendly welcome by the housekeeper. Initially I am not allowed to take pictures, but once the ice is broken I am told to go ahead.'

vorige: Taliesin West
volgende: Baldwin

JRK: 'In July 2009 my wife and I visit Aspen, where the slopes are seamlessly integrated into the street pattern of the resort town. The Turner house was built in 1982 as a home for the winter months. In the classic qualification of dwellings as either tents

or caves, the Turner house unmistakeably belongs to the second category. Invisible from outside, the house is oriented towards the surrounding landscape with surgical precision. The shape of the roof has been created by cutting a section out of a sphere with two small arches and one large one. You enter under one of the low arches, while the other one provides a view from the kitchen over the valley, where thunderclouds are gathering in the distance. The tall arch frames a view of the mountains surrounding Aspen. The house, which looks very closed off from the outside, consist almost entirely of glass on the inside. It deviates from the photos in Lautner's book in a number of places. For example, there's a door that leads from the kitchen, via a small platform and up four steps, to the garden. In the drawings that access way leads outside via an underground tunnel leading from the bathroom. An additional room has been added over the garage and the carpet that used to cover the curved wall has been removed. The kitchen has been changed too: the built-in cupboard that used to be at the top of the stairs and kept the view hidden for just a little longer has gone. Alterations are rarely improvements, unfortunately. In the furthest corner of the living room we spot an echo of the Carling house, built over thirty years earlier. With one press of a button an entire sitting area swings out into the open air. The idea was that you could sit outside on a sunny winter day, without the need to clear the snow off a whole terrace or haul a load of furniture out. In fact, apart from a few smaller spaces in the basement, all the important living func-tions are connected to each other under one enormous concrete dome. The wall dividing the master bedroom and the rest of the house is convex and is not connected to the roof. The route from the front door to the living room leads past this wall. A platform is built into the stairs at the point where a door leads to the bedroom; high above it is a magnificent skylight. If you turn around at the top of the stairs you get a spectacular view of the enormous, cave-like space. From the master bedroom five steps lead down to the bathroom, which receives natural light via the window under the small arch. A utility room leads to an extra bedroom, which in turn leads to the entrance hall. The housekeeper offers for us to spend the night in the house, which we happily accept. When the sun goes down the house feels even more like a cave. I wander through the house at night, which gives off sounds as the concrete shell, which has warmed up during the day, cools down again, shrinking in the process. It's the second time I've been given the chance to sleep in a Lautner. As always, a longer stay always makes more of an impression than a fleeting visit.'

vorige: Bosustow
volgende: Maloney

#52: House, 1953, extant
3612 Woodhill Canyon Rd, Studio City, CA 91604

Thursday, 3 May 2007

Although our contact with the owner of the Tyler house is friendly, we aren't able to arrange a date before our trip in 2007, meaning we don't get to see it from the inside. When we arrive with the group it looks so new it seems freshly built, despite the fact that it dates from the 1950s. At the same time, there's something that doesn't seem quite right: the balance between the house's open and closed qualities seems to have been lost. The characteristic triangular terrace outside the living room has been enclosed.

previous: Williams
next: Brooks

Friday, 11 July 2008

The year after, we do manage to make an appointment with the owner. It's a spectacular looking house from the street and it still looks like it's just been built. This is in fact partly the case. The current owner, who spent a year living in the Chemosphere first, bought the place in a bad state of repair, just before the earthquake in 1994. The house was heavily damaged, but the insurance money allowed him to renovate it completely. He hired Tracy Stone to do the job. She carried out a few alterations, changing some of the finishes of the materials and adding a skylight in the living room, which make the house look very modern. It now has natural wood cladding and frames inside and out, combined with white plaster. Because the cladding extends from the inside out, and the glass panels disappear into the walls and roof without any visible frames, the interior space merges seamlessly into the outdoor area. You approach the house via a driveway that passes underneath the house to the front door, which is at the back. The floor plan is entirely made up of triangles. The living room originally ended in a triangular terrace, but Lautner indicates in his book that this was enclosed a few years after the house was built, although we don't know when

exactly or whether he was involved himself. It has now become part of the living room. It still forms an important element within the house, with a sofa in the point of the former terrace. The windows slide back automatically to let the breeze in, like the corner in the bedroom storey of Sheats-Goldstein. Slightly detracting from the effect, though, is a column in this same corner. The house has a wonderfully light and spacious quality. Even more striking is the sequence of different levels, with two steps leading from the street level to the living room, and the kitchen a few steps higher again. This has the effect of defining different zones under the same roof. We visit the house in the company of Lautner's daughters Karol and Judy, their children and grandchildren and a handful of friends who also help out with the Lautner Foundation. Mentioning that Lautner's family would be present made it much easier to arrange visits to some of the more famous works.

previous: Coneco Corp
next: Zimmerman

UPA STUDIOS

#30: Office building, 1948-1949,
demolished 1980s
#79: Addition, 1958-1959,
demolished 1980s
4440 W Lakeside Dr, Burbank, CA 91505

In 1948 Lautner received a commission to build the animation studios of UPA (United Productions of America). Lautner also carried out several extensions in the subsequent decades, until the building was demolished in the eighties to make way for a Disney studio. The owner, Stephen Bosustow, built up a long-lasting friendship with Lautner and in 1972 he asked him to design the Lake Almanor cabin we visited in 2009. The design of the UPA Studios alternates between large, closed façade components and all-glass parts and a characteristic corrugated roof with a curved edge detail. The roof is level with the façade at some points, overhanging at others. This is a detail we came already across in the Harvey house from the same period. On photographs we found in the archive you can see the animators at work behind the huge expanses of glass.

VALLEY ESCROW OFFICES

#25: Office building, 1947-1948, demolished
15446 Ventura Blvd, Sherman Oaks, CA 91403

To complete our overview of all Lautner's built
works, we resume our search for lost works in the
photo archive. The only reference to the building
he designed for the Valley Escrow Company in
1948 included in Lautner's 1994 monograph is
a small black-and-white photo. In the archive
we find another photo of the exterior and two
interior shots, showing a one-storey building with
heavy brick side walls and a floating roof with a
substantial overhang, which appears to rest only
on the jambs of the window frames, allowing
an uninterrupted flow of space from the interior
to outside. Like most non-residential projects
designed by Lautner, the building was demolished
in the 1980s.

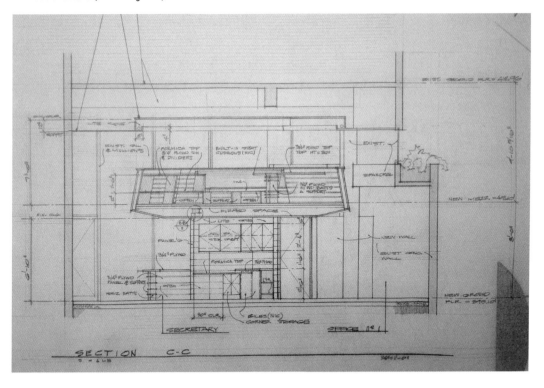

Wednesday, 2 May 2007

On our way to the Harvey house, we pass a commercial complex on Vine Street for which Lautner designed a number of different interiors in the 1960s. Our focus during this trip is on the main works, so we don't have time for obscure remodels at this point. Later we find a set of interesting drawings in the archives.

One of the roles that we open in 2010 contains various interior designs for the complex at 1777 Vine Street. Frank Escher tells us he has taken a look inside there in the past, but hasn't found any remaining traces of Lautner. The designed units are mainly square spaces of approximately 10 x 10 m, which Lautner managed to make more interesting by positioning the dividing walls at an angle. Drawings include one dated 8 and 21 November 1961, for a unit on the third floor for the Robbins Music Corporation, publishers of sheet music including the soundtrack of *Dr. Zhivago*; one dated 19 September 1961, for Zulch & Zulch Advertising in suite 400; and one for hairdressing salon Percolor in 'Room No. 101'. The sketch plan for the latter is dated 16 May 1962 and the work plan 4 June of the same year, indicating the projects' quick turnaround time. The salon was situated on the ground floor, which was two storeys high. Lautner designed a two-storey-high, freestanding element for the space, with stairs providing access to an extra office space inside. Initially designed as office space for Capitol Management and Realty Co, just a few alterations were needed to make it suitable for this company specialised in hair colouring treatments. There's another office design for Bear Advertising in suite 209, consisting of '4565 square feet', which has been divided up into five separate workspaces by placing a system of orthogonal dividing walls at a fifteen-degree angle to the façade. Studying these plans closely, you might conclude that these small assignments served as finger exercises for later works such as the office designed for Goldstein in 1989. At the start of the sixties, Lautner placed the walls at an angle to the façade; in the eighties, he went even further, placing the walls at an angle to the floor as well. This created an entirely dynamic world between the floor and ceiling, thirty years before this became a mainstay of architectural design.

previous: Concannon
next: Harvey

WALSTROM

#101: House, 1967-1969, extant
10500 Selkirk Lane, Los Angeles, CA 90077

Tuesday 1 May 2007

When we visit the Walstrom house it is still occupied by its original owners. By the time we started our research project, the address wasn't generally known. We spent weeks searching for it. But because so few addresses were public knowledge, it was relatively easy to persuade the owners of the houses we did find to let us come and visit: 'Students? Well, they'd better see some good examples!' The Walstrom house, built in 1969, belongs to the incredible series of masterpieces Lautner built in the second half of the 1960s. Never before (and never again) did an architect build quite such an extraordinary sequence of varied works of such high quality in such a short amount of time.

The house is constructed on a steep slope, just under the flat crown of a hill, following Wright's commandment 'Never build on top of the hill but on the slope.' The house is suspended slightly above the ground, built between two gigantic trusses that form the main construction. The house just touches the upper ground at the higher end of the slope. A switchback path leads upwards, past the carport and under the house, bringing you to the front door in three turns. Inside, the path continues, leading between the façade and the kitchen on a higher level, up to the back door. There you can choose to go outside again or turn left into the living area. This takes up the entire floor and contains a kitchen block and a toilet block surrounded by bookshelves, on top of which is a lounge area that can be accessed via a narrow set of stairs. The landing of the stairs extends into the canopy covering the entrance. The whole house is made of wood. The frame consists of large, diagonally placed beams filled in in a variety of different ways. Because the façades aren't parallel to each other, the roof is lightly slanted. The bedrooms are under the living room, five steps down from the front door. At this point, the outdoor area cuts into the

volume of the house, creating a patio along the bedroom corridor and under the living space, ingeniously lit along the side of the slope.

When the house was being designed, Lautner was working on a number of different projects at the same time. Instead of each individual house being overloaded with ideas, this resulted in a series of balanced works. The owners, who are well into their nineties, are a great example of the

group of creative clients Lautner managed to collect around him. 'The house has kept me young', Octavia Walstrom tells us, effortlessly climbing the stairs without bannisters.

previous: Boykoff
next: Familian

WEINSTEIN

Thursday, 10 July 2008

The remodel of the Weinstein house is a Lautner project that nobody has visited yet, as far as we know. Like a number of other works on our list, we know it has been carried out, but we don't know what it looks like. It's an extension of a house in Hollywood at an unknown address. Having searched the archives, not only have we found the address, but we have also learned that the project involved not one but two extensions, on either side of the house. When we ring the doorbell in July 2008, nobody answers and all we can see from the road is in the point of the east-facing extension. It has a bay window with an interesting twist to it, which we immediately recognise as early Lautner.

previous: Carr
next: Aldrich

Sunday, 21 March 2010

This time we have an appointment. The gate is open to us. The remodel, dating from 1945, is above all an extension. A study has been added on one side, and a bedroom on the other, making the house surprisingly spacious. The floors of the added rooms are not level with the rest of the house. Built-in furniture has been installed in the transition zones between the levels, as Lautner did in his own house and in Harpel 1 and Alexander. It's fascinating to see how Lautner makes an orthogonal house more dynamic by introducing a 30-degree angular rotation. He applies this to the desk, which is positioned at an angle within the study, and the bedroom, where a bay window twists away from the volume, embracing the garden. The form language resembles that of the Springer house and the home he built for himself five years earlier.

In terms of the materials used, this house stays close to the work of Frank Lloyd Wright, with its stone accents of horizontal strips of natural stone. The gently sloping roof, which includes modest skylights in various places, combined with large mirrors in the bathroom, adds spaciousness. The

horizontal section of glass above the parapet wall folds out to form a bay window. The bevel siding used on the façade is another reference to Lautner's own home. The house is a collection of ideas Lautner would later develop, like the entrance hall with frameless glass walls, one side consisting of corrugated glass in this case. The owner would like to build a new living room in the part of the house left untouched by Lautner. We strongly advise him to consult one of Lautner's former members of staff. Looking at the house again on Google Maps in 2016, though, we question whether he took our advice.

previous: Bubbling Wells Resort
next: Stevens

#48: House, 1952, extant
3329 Ledgewood Dr, Los Angeles, CA 90068

Thursday, 3 May 2007

The Williams house is less than a mile away from the Beachwood Market. Again, the only documentation of the project included in Lautner's book is a tiny black-and-white photograph. It isn't always clear to us why Lautner chooses to discuss certain projects at length instead of others, but in this case the omission is truly mystifying. It's a small house with a simple programme, and yet it looks completely different to all the other small houses with simple programmes. Lautner has managed to integrate a complex spatial puzzle, forging it into a dynamic whole. There are differences in height, skylights in unexpected places, wooden beams running across the ceiling in a variety of directions, and so forth. The kitchen, the heart of the home and the place where people eat, is light and opens out onto the terrace. The sitting room is sheltered, in a lower lying section of the house, though in open connection with the kitchen. The house is closed off to the street, but opens out to the garden, and feels spacious despite its limited surface area. The main volume is Z-shaped and is built on a slope. The complex interplay of different volumes and the resulting spatial quality make it a direct precursor to the work of a subsequent generation of Californian architects such as Frank O. Gehry. Starting at the front, where it forms a carport, the sloping gable roof extends over the entire house in one expanse. From the street you can see how the slightly set-back main volume rests on a short beam supported by stilts, emphasising the airy quality. At the highest point of the roof, a lower volume containing the kitchen extends outward, allowing light to penetrate deeply into the house. Because the entrance hall is also at this level, you enter into a door-high space, which then proceeds to explode, in a manner of speaking. A number of

steps divide the space into different zones, but the roof follows the Z shape with a pronounced ceiling whose beams extend outside, forming a pergola. A skylight in the middle of the roof, surrounded by mirrors, lets light into the kitchen and bathroom. The inward angles of the Z contain a formal garden at the front and a sheltered terrace at the back. The sloping terrain leaves room for an additional lower storey at the back. The client has been living in the house very contentedly for nearly sixty years without making any essential changes. We are shown a set of original drawings they have kept. Studying these, we see the floor plan is more regular than you would think. We remain surprised Lautner didn't pay more attention to this house in his book.

previous: Beachwood Market
next: Tyler

#54: Guest house, 1953, extant
2869 Durand Dr, Los Angeles, CA 90068

Sunday, 13 July 2008

At the top of one of Hollywood's hills stands a kitsch castle with the curious name of Wolf's Lair, after project developer L. Milton Wolf who had it built in 1927. Lautner designed a guest house for this place in 1953, about which virtually nothing is known. We have arranged a visit in May 2007, but another appointment gets in the way and we decide to skip this house for now, thinking we'll be able to visit it another time. It's not until ten years later that we finally manage.

In July 2008 we are unable to arrange an appointment. That doesn't stop us from driving past to get an impression of the place. Very little of it can be seen from the road. By coincidence we run into the owner, a TV celebrity who quickly locks her car when JRK walks up to her. Naturally she doesn't let us in just like that. We do manage to get her husband's phone number from her. Because the couple are getting divorced, the castle is up for sale: the real estate website also includes a couple of pictures of the guest house, which has the unmistakeable look of a real Lautner. It was built as late as 1982, which makes it even more interesting to us. Later, we hear the castle was sold in 2010 to the musician Richard Melville Hall, known by his stage name Moby, who lets us know we're welcome to visit. But before we're in the neighbourhood again, he's already sold it, after building a recording studio in Lautner's section.

previous: Sheats-Goldstein
next: Springer

Saturday, 11 November 2017

In 2017, we get in touch with the current owner, who invites us to come and visit. The 'castle' turns out to be situated on a fantastic piece of land, which stretches far back and has a view on two sides. Lautner's contribution is a remodel of the gatehouse, to which he also added a section.

Because of the frequent use of veneered walls, the house has the same atmosphere as the Harvey house. The building houses the bedrooms and the kitchen, which has a wonderful detail: a revolving cupboard in the corner turret. Because the ceiling has been kept very low in the bedroom wing, and the hallway is very narrow, you feel like you're on a ship. You get the same feeling when you're standing by the railing that runs past the living room; that living room is situated in the newly added volume. Large expanses of glass between the stone columns

reveal a view of the valley down below. A spiral staircase attached to the outside wall gives access to a roof terrace, part of which can be partitioned off with large sheets of canvas. It's still hard to imagine that Lautner doesn't mention the project at all in his own monograph. The spatiality and the details do make it a real Lautner. Another interesting detail is the combination of luxury and cheap industrial materials, like the veneer and the natural stone, the coated Styrofoam for the ceiling and the corrugated sheets of plastic around the stairs. You could see Lautner's use of materials as a forerunner of that of Rem Koolhaas.

previous: Midgaard
next: Harpel 2

#90: Pool and addition,
1963-1964, extant
9228 Hazen Dr, Beverly Hills, CA 90210

Sunday, 13 July 2008

One project that brought Lautner to the attention of the wider public for negative reasons was a swimming pool he built for Bernard Wolfe in 1964. Three years later Wolfe, who was an editor at *Playboy Magazine*, wrote an article titled 'How not to build a pool. Swimming in red ink'. This is a witty description of all the things that went wrong during the construction of the pool in his back yard, focusing on the kinds of things contractors are still known for today: not turning up at arranged times, dumping construction waste in the garden (in this case, a rubber hose filled with waterproof concrete), and charging everything up as additional work on top of the agreed price, such as digging the hole, supplying the pipes, etc. One problem affecting Wolfe's pool was that its intended site was at the bottom of a steep slope, a spot that wasn't accessible for a truck mixer. Apart from this physical obstacle there was another unusual circumstance. The swimming pool wasn't being built behind just any old house, but one designed by Richard Neutra, on which Lautner had carried out a few improvements as well. In the article Lautner isn't the target of criticism himself; his design is described as follows: 'Pool? It was a miniaturized Lake Como they proposed to install in my back yard, a 40-foot-by-26-foot bit of wavy waste laid out for me alone.' Despite the lavish praise for Lautner and staff member Guy Zebert, the negative note stuck around, damaging Lautner's reputation. Lautner wanted to forget this project as quickly as possible and never talked about it again. This turned it into a 'mystery project': nobody knew where it was, what it looked like or even whether it still existed.

Having found the address in the archives, we drive over there one evening in 2008. The house is in a terrible state; it is clear no one has been living there for some time, which explains why

our letters were never answered. It doesn't take us long to decide to go into the garden. Looking through the windows, we see the house is being renovated again. Built on a slope, the house has four storeys on the street-side, and three on the side facing the garden. The swimming pool behind the house is beautifully nestled between the hillside and the terrace. It's located at the level of the second storey. A bridge leads up to the wooden terrace, which in turn leads up to the swimming pool, a trapezium-shaped container with a natural stone coping that is slightly curved on the outside. It's not quite the same as in Lautner's drawing, which doesn't surprise us given the difficulties of the building process. But the wave of negative criticism unleashed at the time doesn't seem in any proportion to this modest design. It is fantastic to be here, more than forty years after the notorious article. But the swimming pool awaits an uncertain fate, because an unknown Neutra in a bad state of repair is bound to be torn down soon, and it seems unlikely the pool will be spared.

previous: Googie's site
next: Johnson

#84: House, 1961, extant
#91: Guest house, 1963-1964, extant
8530 Hedges Place, Los Angeles, CA 90069

Sunday, 6 May 2007

On the last day of our trip in 2007, we start at the Wolff house. TS: 'This is the house I fell in love with thirteen years earlier. I had no idea what to expect when I visited the Wolff house for the first time in 1994. We had seen a photo of the façade in a guide book and it looked kind of interesting. In the end, the house made an indelible impression on me, marking the beginning of my interest in Lautner's work, which has fascinated me for over twenty years now. The house shows a clear debt to the work of Frank Lloyd Wright, but there's more going on here than just that. The integration of nature and the landscape in the house is much more direct than in Wright's work. The scale of the house feels as pleasant and comfortable as a bespoke suit. The refined manipulation of the landscape is easily visible here; it is to be a recurrent theme in Lautner's work. At the time of my visit, the second owners of the house have been living there for twenty years, and they have kept it in perfect condition. When you look at it from below, it is a striking sight. There's a kind of tower built up against the hill, with various stacked volumes at an angle. The concrete wall that hides the swimming pool from view is now completely overgrown, so that the house blends into the landscape beautifully.'

Although the house was built in 1961 and Lautner had distanced himself from the form language of his mentor by then, the client wanted a house that looked as though Wright had designed it. He had died two years earlier, so it wasn't possible to ask him. Still, Lautner and Wolff managed to build up an excellent relationship,

although it eventually hit the rocks in 1975 over the design of the Wolff Cabin in Idyllwild, which was never built.

The entrance of the house is at the north side of the lot, on Hedges Place; but the base of the house and the walls of the swimming pool are situated on Miller Drive, four storeys below. From below, the house towers upwards, and the expressive pool and the protruding roof command one's attention. We drive up the hill, from where the house looks totally different. Here it is the long, low roof that dominates. The roof connects the original house to an extension, a guest house, which was added only two years later. A high wall, covered with flagstones, rises between the two volumes. The folded wall, which zigzags back and forth three times, completely hides the house from its neighbours. A concrete zigzag wall, reminiscent of the side walls of the Rawlins house, borders the stairs down to the entrance, which is illuminated by triangular skylights. There is a flagstone-covered triangle, which looks like a precursor to the pyramid in front of the Familian house and forms a visual link to the sturdy flagstone walls. The

heaviness of the stone dramatises the contrast with the frameless, floor-to-ceiling windows.

Undisturbed, we sneak around the outside of the house and follow a path that leads to the pool, which looks very inviting. Because we'd like to be able to visit one day, it's not a good idea to be found in the pool, should the owner come home unexpectedly. At first glance, the house seems in perfect condition, but upon closer inspection, all kinds of things turn out to have been changed. And here too, changes are seldom an improvement. Although you can look in here and there, the real qualities of the house largely remain hidden. We don't know a lot about the extension at that point. It seems to lack the refinement of the house.

It's clear that we're not done with Lautner, by the end of this trip. The Wolff house is generally considered one of the high points in Lautner's career, but if you only see the outside of a Lautner house, you often miss its essence. The history of the ownership of the house has been rather turbulent since the mid-nineties. There was a quick succession of owners, who sold the house at a great profit. For instance, the Hollywood star Vincent Gallo (famous from the film *Buffalo '66*) made $ 850,000 on the house in eight months' time.

previous: Shearing
next: Jacobsen

Sunday, 5 April 2009

Three owners later, we have finally managed to make an appointment with the owner of this house, the Lautner that has changed hands most often. It is in perfect ondition, but unfortunately, a number of features have been considerably changed. It was briefly owned by an interior architect, who was of the opinion that she knew how the house could be improved. It belongs to the ten best houses Lautner ever built. The entrance is phenomenal. From the street, all you see is a low carport. To reach the front door, you go down six steps from the street, and then you are standing under the large horizontal roof that connects the house and the guest quarters. From this lush, verdant area you already get a limited view of the city. A slanting volume rises up at an angle, so that no railings are needed.

Our tour begins in the guest house, which

319

Lautner added two years after the house was completed. Although the full spectrum is on display here, it is entirely lacking in character compared to the original house. We suspect that the guest house was altered later, but because we have never seen photos of the original situation, we can't verify this. Inside the house, a disproportionately large glass front door leads to a hallway, which leads to a staircase, at an angle. The stairs, which are jammed between a wall and a glass façade, descend one floor down to the two-storey living room. Because the view of the neighbouring houses is blocked by a 20-foot folded wall, it seems as though the house looks out over the city from an isolated spot. Since this wall is situated outside, at living room level, and does not form the boundary between inside and outside, the outdoors is involved in the indoors. In the small patio this creates, there is a large eucalyptus that the house is built around. The living room extends outwards on two sides, towards the patio with the tree, and to a covered outdoor area, a triangular terrace that is wedged between the high wall and the slope on the other side. From this terrace, which has a built-in bench in the balustrade, there is a fantastic and unobstructed view of the city. The terrace is accessed through two doors, both two full storeys high, and made of a single sheet of glass. Again, Lautner shows here that this is structurally possible, and that it will last fifty years. The façade is made of glass, two storeys high, with bronze frames, in a wall with frameless glass corners. The outdoor space turns out to consist of different levels, so that there is a second, outdoor way of going downstairs.

Inside, it turns out that quite a few changes have been made to the house: the original staircase from the living area to the bedrooms has been moved, so that the balance between the internal spaces has been disturbed. Because of the new position of the staircase, at the back of the house, the master bedroom has become a kind of main street intersection. We wonder how it's possible that someone who has spared no trouble or expense manages to miss the mark completely. When we descend another flight of stairs, we find the swimming pool, where the closed concrete railing has been replaced by a tempered glass one. While this looks very slick, it means everything

can be seen from the street below, while this closed wall was meant to ensure privacy. In terms of size, this is a modest house, although it feels very large because of how spatial it is.

We make the interesting discovery that Lautner made an extension plan for the second owner of the house, Dr Kaufmann, which was unknown until now. The drawings are present in the house, and

the owner dreams of having it built someday. However, a year later, the house has changed hands again.

We have always been curious what the Wolff
house looked like before the guest quarters were
built, because the design is very unified. In the well-
known publications, the house has never been de-
picted on its own. In the Lautner archive, we first
see photos of a free-standing Wolff house in 2010.
The entrance is formed by a glass box stuck up agai-

nst the house. This doesn't look like it was intended
to be temporary, which reminds us of the story of Mrs
Boykoff, who told us that when making an extreme
proposal, Lautner sometimes said that it was possible to change it back if the clients weren't pleased.

previous: Jacobsen
next: Eisele

WOLFF 2 'WIND SONG'

*#98: Cabin remodel, 1966-1968, extant
48700 Twin Pines Rd, Banning, CA 92220*

Sunday, 29 April 2007

When we are on our way to Desert Hot Springs from Idyllwild, we drive through a desolate area where a forest fire has raged just earlier. Here and there, a chimney is still standing. There should have been a cabin here, remodelled and extended by Lautner for Marco Wolff, who commissioned the Wolff house from 1961 and later also a cabin in Idyllwild. We fear the worst for the Wolff cabin, which is nicknamed Wind Song, and we have no pictures of it so we also don't know what to look for. When we arrive, we see the house in the distance, behind a sturdy fence. A large roof is visible, resting on the house like a cap. The house lies on a hilltop with a fantastic view all around it. For now, this is where our research ends. We haven't managed to make an appointment, because the owners are in their house in Arizona. However, we are warmly invited to come by next time we are nearby.

previous: Pearlman
next: Bubbling Wells Resort

Wednesday, 16 July 2008

A year later, we get to go inside. We are accompanied by Alan Hess. We invited him to join us to share in our discovery of a virtually unknown work of Lautner's. In the archive, we found several drawings labelled 'Alterations for Marco Wolff's cabin'. But it's not clear to us whether it's a remodel or a completely new building, and if it's a remodel, then what exactly has changed.

The owner takes us through the house and tells us what she has changed herself. What we see is dramatic. The coving above the windows, where the roof soffit seemed to continue indoors, was too low for her husband; he kept bumping his head. It was sawed out and thrown in the fire. JRK: 'Hess,

who walks through the house examining everything carefully, his face a mask, asking apparently neutral questions, holds up the last piece of wood in his hand as I take a photo of him.' Because of a number of extensions and additions, the outside has also changed unrecognisably, perhaps with the exception of a zigzag wall, behind which there used to be the garage, now the master bedroom. The owner shows us a photo album with lots of detailed pictures of

the original condition. She systematically changed or removed everything she didn't like about the house. Unfortunately, those are exactly the things Lautner had added. Because of her changes, Lautner has almost completely disappeared from the house. Glass bricks have been added, and funny details, like a normal window that has been placed in the façade crookedly. Triumphantly, she tells us that she did what Lautner would have done. Maybe she's right: Lautner had no trouble 'perfecting' his designs to fit better with someone else's lifestyle. You can hardly call the house a Lautner anymore, but a few years later, when it is for sale, it is emphatically praised as such.

The sun has almost set when we decide to get something to eat with Alan Hess at Desert Hills, the huge outlet mall on Interstate 10 in Banning.

collected over the years. Hess is impressed, and becomes the second person after Murray Grigor to encourage us to write a book. In turn, we have always been very impressed by Hess's own book, so the evening ends in mutual expressions of admiration before the security guards politely throw us out of the mall.

previous: Wolff
next: Sheats-Goldstein

The mall is empty but we can still sit outside on the terrace. The atmosphere is surreal: in the middle of the desert a lot of beige plasterwork provides an illusion of walking through a small town, an enclosed walking area surrounded by enormous car parks, with a warm desert wind enveloping us. With Hess we go through the files that Tycho made as a prelude to the database in which he compiled all the information about the projects that we had

YOKENO

House, 1990-1992, unbuilt
1156 Lachman Lane, Pacific Palisades, CA 90272

Wednesday, 8 April 2009

The building of the Yokeno house had apparently started but stopped when the clients became involved in a difficult separation. As we arrive at the address in a not very smart area we find the site hidden behind a row of houses; it is still undeveloped and affords a fantastic view of the bay of Santa Monica. The ten large concrete pillars for the foundations that were sunk into the grass some fifteen years ago are still there. Vaughan Trammell had shown us photos of the model, so we have an idea of how it would have looked. For some time, there was still hope that one day it would be built, but the site was recently sold to an unknown buyer. We resolve to approach this new owner and get him interested in Lautner's design. The design consists of a one-storey construction in the shape of a semi-circle. Closer inspection shows that it's the round side that faces the slope. The bedrooms are located on this side, while the living room is in the heart of the circle. The straight side of the semi-circle crags out over the slope and is oriented towards the view in a gentle curve. The living room gets daylight from the back side too, through a strip of skylights that follow the radius.

previous: Howe
next: Wood site

#62: House, 1955-1957, extant
#143: Rodman / Friedberg, Remodel, 1992, extant
2880 Hollyridge Dr, Los Angeles, CA 90068

Friday, 4 May 2007

In 1992, Lautner remodeled the Zahn house, which he originally built in 1957, according to the wishes of the current owners, Howard Rodman and Anne Friedberg. In Lautner's monograph, it is listed as his last completed work. While we immediately receive a positive response to our request to visit the house, the appointment is moved several times. In 2007, we arrive with Karol and Judy Lautner and the rest of our group just as a party for teenagers is ending, and parents are here to pick up their children, so the house is bursting with people. Anne and Howard remain unruffled.

The Zahn house is in a remarkable location: when Lautner was called in to design the house, the client had already been piling up boulders to level the ground for construction for years. Usually, Lautner did his best to use the natural properties of the land as much as possible. The house that Lautner designed for this location shows parallels to a modernist villa, with a glass entrance on the ground floor and a floating living area above it. Even the materialisation of a white box with white aluminium blinds is atypical for Lautner. Rodman gives us an enthusiastic tour, as if he was used to giving them every day. In this house, Lautner tried out all kinds of modern technologies. Rodman mentions the electricity in the house, which switches on a low voltage: 'terrific when it works, but impossible if a diode needs to be replaced.' He calls it 'the history of yesterday's future, today'. He tells wonderful anecdotes about working with Lautner, about the remodel of the glass entrance wall, for instance. Lautner suggested making it out of one piece of glass. The clients found this too

expensive and suggested making it from two parts. Lautner responded: 'When you split it in two, you look cheap, when you split it in three parts it looks like intended', but that's not what they wanted, so one large sheet of glass was used. This entrance and the flower beds in the floor ensure that there is very little in way of a boundary between outside and indoors. This level of the house has a trapezium shape and is reached from the fully glass entrance hall, where a monumental staircase under a central skylight leads to the next floor. Here you arrive in the heart of the living area above, and your gaze is immediately directed towards the view. The entrance hall ceiling, made of strips of wood, blends into the sides of the open space around the stairs. Various rooms are clustered around this open stairwell. Off the living room there is a large balcony, which sticks out over the entrance. While the layout of the house is simple in terms of design, the central open space makes it very spatial.

Full-window blinds, like the ones we have seen before in the master bedroom at Silvertop, give the house its characteristic appearance. Since they are all linked, they can be operated with one hand. Rodman demonstrates: with a simple movement

an office. By the time the remodel was complete, Lautner was no longer able to climb the stairs. He passed away two years later.

Slowly, everyone leaves, so that we get to see the house both full of people and almost empty. The space seems made for both situations. While we are drinking wine on the terrace, we watch the sun set over L.A. In the distance, we see the Wolf's Lair guest house. We leave the house, driving backwards down the impossibly narrow and steep driveway, which was made, strangely, when cars had monstrous proportions.

previous: Deutsch
next: Kaynar Factory

of the hand, the atmosphere in the house changes completely. Entirely shut off from the outside world, you can enjoy the spectacular view. The house, which is completely white, is lit up at night, so that the flaps stand out nicely against the dark sky and the Hollywood sign in the background.

Lautner's remodel was relatively limited: a few changes were made to the entrance hall, and the storage room next to it was transformed into

ZIMMERMAN

previous: Malin
next: Howe

#95: House, 1965-1968, extant
3848 Berry Dr, Studio City, CA 91604

Friday, 11 July 2008

Saturday, 28 April 2007

The Zimmerman house is a round house on a steep slope. Just like at the Chemosphere, this house was built on one column, but now with walls that go straight down, enclosing the lower floor. The current owner is the son of the original client, by now elderly himself. It is interesting that the clients who commissioned Lautner's best works were often single men; that is the case for this house, but also the Elrod house, the Sheats-Goldstein house and the Pacific Coast house.

The owner of the Zimmerman house responded to our first letter quickly: 'no visitors'. Aside from all kinds of obvious motives not to be disturbed, we try to think of reasons why the owners can be so uncooperative. In a few cases, it is because they are embarrassed about the poor structural condition of the house, which seems likely when we arrive at this house. The fact that to us, a run-down but original condition is highly preferable over a sloppy renovation doesn't seem to sway people. Because this time many owners do welcome us into their homes, a negative response from time to time is not the end of the world – at least not until a few years later, when we have seen almost all of Lautner's work, inside and out, apart from a handful of houses.

When we look in through the windows in 2007, we see that the interior is covered with the dust of at least ten years. At first sight, you'd say the house was unoccupied. That would explain why our phone calls go unanswered.

The client wanted a party house, and Lautner didn't pass up this opportunity. The round living room at the top has a similar view to the Chemosphere, while the lower floor consists of one large two-storey space with an indoor pool in it. But it doesn't look like anyone has swum here recently.

Our attempts to visit houses with reluctant owners, like this one, are sometimes conducted outside of the 'official' channels. In 2007, we were fobbed off with a fax from the original client's son, which said 'The house is not in viewing condition.' The house is situated on Berry Drive, on a plot of land that was originally the back garden of a house on Richmond Drive, much lower down, where Wayne Zimmerman lived with his wife and son. When the couple divorced, they split the garden in half and Lautner was asked to build a house for Wayne in the upper part. His ex-wife stayed living in the lower part. By now, Wayne has passed away, and his son R. owns the house. Unlike his father, he has absolutely no desire to let strangers into his house. JRK: 'When he finally answered the phone in 2008, after dozens of attempts on our end, he literally said we would be welcome after his death.' We didn't want to wait for that. On the internet, we found a phone number for the neighbours, whose garden extends right up to R.'s house. The neighbour told us that there's a treehouse from where you can look over the fence, into the house. She could see the funny side of it and couldn't

our longing to see the inside of the house. It is a house with a unique design, and what's more, it's Lautner's only house with an indoor pool.

To see this house from another angle, we go to the neighbours of the neighbours, who live in the house Mrs Zimmerman stayed in after her divorce. When we tell the neighbour about the empty pool, she finally realises that's where the tsunami came from that flooded her garden a few years earlier.

previous: Tyler
next: Speer

Tuesday, 7 April 2009

Another year later, we drive past the Zimmerman house again. We wonder whether anything has changed, whether the son is still living there like a hermit, but it looks just as desolate as the last times.

Later, in the archive, we find plans an extension to the Zimmerman house. Lautner was faced here with an interesting challenge: how to add an extension to a round house? The answer is to be found in a miniature version of the house, also with a round plan.

previous: Henry's Arcadia site
next: Deutsch

have said a truer word. Her garden runs almost to the façade of the ground floor of the Zimmerman house. From the treehouse, you look right into the swimming pool on the spectacularly high-ceilinged ground floor. There is no water in it; there are only some unused things lying under a thick layer of dust. But the two-storey space with the indoor pool is beautiful. Thus, this visit, too, provides us with more information, which only serves to increase

ZIMMERMAN

Tuesday, 16 October 2007
In the autumn JRK receives this email:

'Dear Jan-Richard: Hello! We are making a feature documentary about John Lautner as well as six short films for the Hammer Museum exhibition that opens summer 2008. Everywhere we go, you guys have been there first! We love hearing about the 10 or 12 or many Dutch architecture students who found the Lautner buildings through Google Maps. Amazing and always a fun moment in our travels. We'd love to know more about you and are wondering if you documented your travels in video and/or stills. If you're interested in furthering this conversation, please contact me.

Best, Sara

Sara Sackner
Producer
John Lautner Project
The Googie Company'

Thursday, 13 March 2008

On 13 March 2008 the Scottish director Murray Grigor and cameraman Hamid Shams come to the Netherlands to interview us. We pick them up at Schiphol and go straight to the American Hotel on Leidseplein in Amsterdam, where a meeting has been arranged with Jessica Raspe of AVRO TV, which will eventually be broadcasting the documentary. The next morning, we take the train to Arnhem with Murray and Hamid. JRK: 'I was asked to prepare a field trip during a train journey to Munich on an end of the year excursion of the ArtEZ Architecture Academy where I had been teaching that year, in the end I chose Lautner because his work is very diverse and his buildings are close to each other. This was all inspired by Lautner's book, which was the beginning of it all, and so the first scene is now filmed in the train: me looking through the book.' At Arnhem station, we re-enact the meeting with Tycho. Almost everything is filmed in one take, even how we talk to each other as we enter the building, designed by Gerrit Rietveld, in which the school is housed. Almost all the students who were on the trip are present and are interviewed at the school, each one in a different place. We finish with a scene in which we walk in single file through the woods, as if we were at the Pearlman Cabin.

Saturday, 26 April 2008

Following our 2007 trip TS started setting up a Lautner project database to document all our discoveries. After we had shared the first results of this with Judith Lautner the board of the John Lautner Foundation decided to appoint us advisers. On 26 April 2008, this decision was officially notified to us by post and on the website our names were added to an impressive list of advisers. Holding this official status will, we hope, make the integrity of our mission clear, and perhaps also open the doors of Lautner houses to us more easily in the future.

Monday, 7 July 2008

On 7 July, we again board the plane for Los Angeles. The immediate reason for this trip is the opening in the Hammer Museum of the big Lautner exhibition curated by Frank Escher and Nicholas Olsberg. We want to do some archive research this time but that will not be simple as the Lautner archive was recently handed over to the Getty Museum. Of course we would also like to see as many as possible of the Lautner projects that we did not reach or visit on our last journey. We have managed to make appointments at five houses at the front doors of which we stood in vain in 2007. We also plan to go to locations where formerly Lautner buildings stood, to see their context and to be sure that there is nothing left of them.

After visiting the Familian house we drive on to Ojai, some two hours north of L.A., one of those wonderful hippie towns that you only find in the US. This is where the film producer Sara Sackner lives, and where she and director Murray Grigor are editing the documentary *Infinite Space. The Architecture of John Lautner*. We have been invited to a preview of the 90-minute documentary, which will be premiered in September the same year. We are welcomed with the sort of hospitality you only meet in America. Sara lives in a wonderful Mid-Century Modern house, built in 1963 by Fred E. Hummel Jr. Only one room has air-conditioning and there, people are working hard on putting the film together. Also present are Murray Grigor with his partner Carol (not to be confused with Lautner's oldest daughter), and Anna Thomas, the co-producer. After lunch, we watch the raw version of the documentary together. As it is actually impossible to experience the richness and complexity of Lautner's architecture without physically moving through it, we are extremely curious about the film. Lautner's work is shown chronologically, starting with the Lautner family's weekend house in Marquette, which Lautner worked on as a twelve-year-old, through archive pictures of Frank Lloyd Wright, and visits to some thirteen houses, three of which we had not yet seen ourselves.

*Director Murray Grigor & cinematographer Hamid Shams
in the train from Amsterdam to Arnhem*

We see Frank O. Gehry talking about the Schaeffer house and fantastic archive pictures of Leonard Malin who commissioned the Chemosphere, 'proud owner of a $10,000 concrete column'. Lautner's work has been beautifully filmed by cameraman Hamid Shams. The pictures of the houses that we have already seen are a fine addition to our own experience but it is the houses that we have not yet visited that fascinate us the most. The documentary ends with the 1982 Turner house, as the owner of Lautner's last great work, the Pacific Coast House refused permission to film inside. 'Dr No' has successfully excluded his house from history. Therefore, the film ends perforce just before the great final chord which in reality brought Lautner's oeuvre to a close. Of course we are also curious to see how we ourselves appear in the film. Before he came to the Netherlands Murray Grigor told us why he wanted us in the film: 'You laid a happy trail.' He visited the houses after we had been there and got the feeling that every visit had been a delight for us, and it appears that the inhabitants felt the same.

It is clear that our role in the film is primarily intended to show that Lautner is also relevant to a younger generation of architects outside the United States.

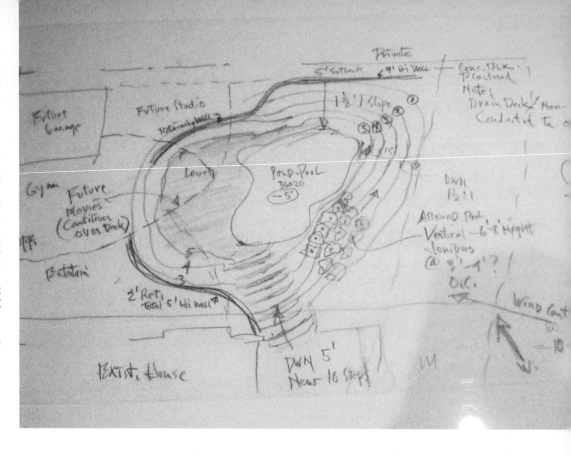

Sketch of pool for Miles Davis in Malibu, 1990, unbuilt

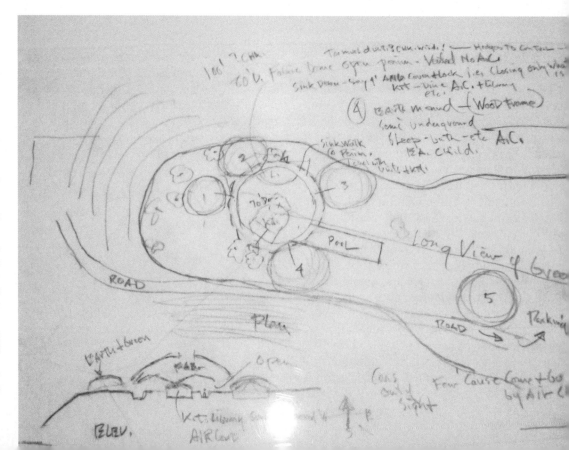

Sketches for Arango Ranch House in Paso Robles, 1992, unbuilt

Saturday, 12 July 2008

This is the day we came here for: the grand opening of the exhibition *Between Earth and Heaven* in the Hammer Museum. It is announced all over the city: posters hang along Sunset Boulevard, newspapers and magazines are full of articles. One thing is for sure: Lautner is *hot*! Frank Escher had already told us a bit about the organisation of the exhibition. At its heart are original drawings, very many drawings, each one exhibited at a slight angle on its own stand, so that visitors can study the drawing carefully from the same perspective as its maker. In this way, there is no distinction at all between built and unbuilt work, and the focus is on the design and to a lesser degree on the execution of the designs. We are quite surprised: we had expected the exhibition to be aimed at the general public, but through the large number of original drawings, which are only interesting when you study them closely, it seems rather to be intended for professionals. Of course, exhibitions about architecture are always a tricky business, as the representation very seldom approaches the physical experience of an actual visit. To overcome this difficulty the curators have had a few very-large-scale models of Lautner's best work made, with random sections cut so that you can literally stand inside the buildings. There are models of Walstrom, Malin, Marbrisa, Elrod, Pearlman and Turner, made in a warm grey tint without too many details so that the emphasis is on their use of space. In addition to these the film essays of Murray Grigor and Hamid Shams are projected beside the models and drawings. This is certainly much more effective than only a photo or a drawing, but because of the diversity and complexity of Lautner's work it comes nowhere near an actual visit; in this way, the exhibition is reassuring for us. But it is also an incredible treasure house of information. In this museum setup photography is forbidden and the drawings have been transformed almost into art, which seems extraordinary to us, as less than two days ago we were pulling similar drawings out of their cardboard tubes with our own hands. It is wonderful material, the original plans for masterpieces like Sheats, Pearlman and Marbrisa, and also sketches for lesser known works like Shusett. What makes the exhibition especially interesting, is that many addresses are clearly marked on the drawings.

Saturday, 20 March 2010

Two years after the exhibition is on show at the Palm Springs Art Museum, where to our surprise it is more effective, as the exhibition spaces are very different. The accompanying book, *Between Earth and Heaven. The Architecture of John Lautner,* contains almost everything that is to be seen in the exhibition: an inexhaustible source of information. The study models with pencilled remarks and notes are particularly fascinating as they show how Lautner's mind worked. This is also the case for the rough ground plans with notes, like the swimming pool design for the trumpeter Miles Davis from 26 September 1989, with dotted lines showing later developments like 'future garage', 'future studio', 'future gym' and 'future movies'. Gwen Neidlinger, the daughter of Dan Stevens of the Stevens house tells us that Miles Davis often visited their house in Malibu. The 1993 sketch of the A. Ranch in Paso Robles for the client of the Marbrisa house is also interesting; it consists of six concrete domes, with a written note: 'closing only what is necessary'.

Now that we have seen almost all the built work our interest turns to the unbuilt work, like the sketches for the Roven residence from 1986 at 805 Cord Circle in Beverly Hills. This residential house annex painting gallery was intended for a flat area in surroundings with free standing houses situated in the centre of the lots. As a reaction to this Lautner designed a house that was entirely turned in on itself, with in its heart a large sunken living room, completely surrounded by an outdoor space. The living room ceiling is round and reflective, so that the garden is mirrored in it. Around the ring-shaped patio is the gallery space, into which the other rooms open. Here Lautner invented a new typology.

The exhibition gives us still more answers to open questions, like the extensions to the Segel house. This house already diverged from the drawings during building and later on more extensions were added on two sides. The original model of one of these extensions is exhibited.

John Lautner Archives, J. Paul Getty Museum,
Los Angeles

&

Lautner Archive of Andrew Nasser,
Pasadena

LOWER LEVEL PLAN 1/8"=1'-0"

MASTER BATH

Condense

No Basement

Master

Make

View

Void

Silk Trellis

Terrace

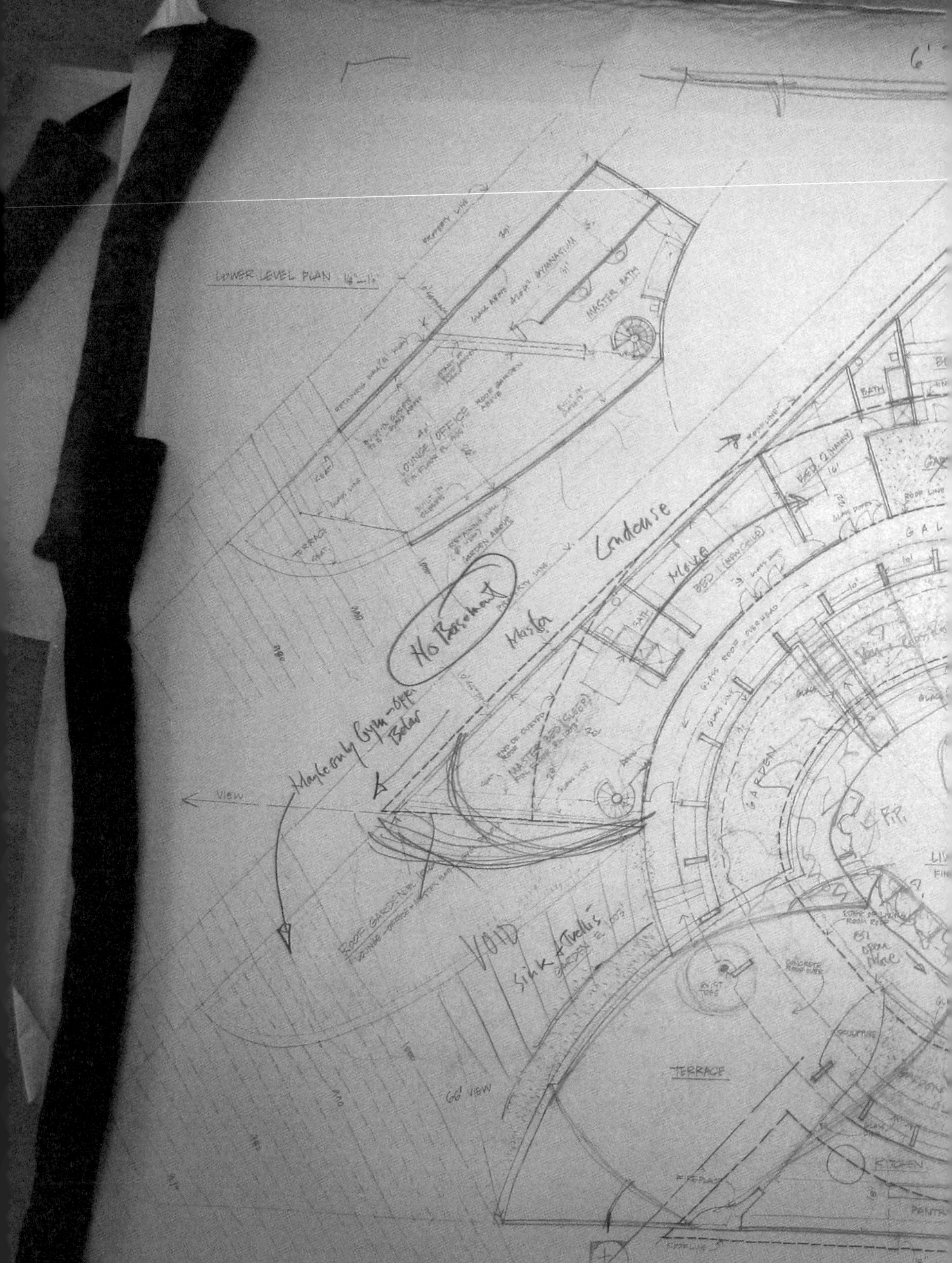

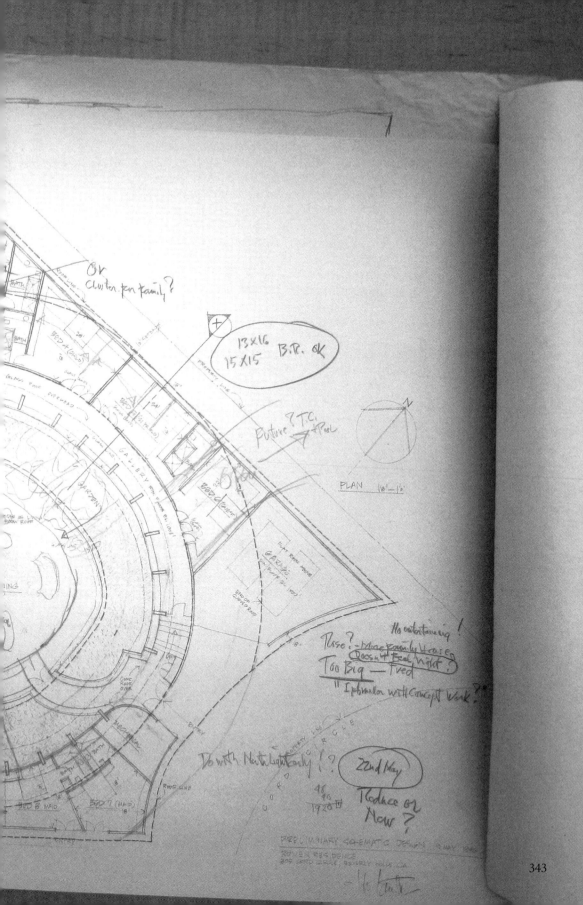

343

Wednesday, 9 July 2008

After lying many years in the back of Frank Escher's office the John Lautner Archive was handed over to the Getty Center in Los Angeles in 2006. At the moment, the drawings are waiting to be inventoried and catalogued, a process that may take years, and the archive cannot be consulted until this is finished. Through Murray Grigor we got in touch with the Head of the Department of Architecture and Contemporary Art at the Getty Center, Wim de Wit, who is, as his name suggests, a Dutchman. He is very happy to have visitors from the Netherlands with an interest in one of his collections, which is why we are given access to the archive. We have an appointment at the storage depot, a bleak hangar in the Van Nuys area in 'the valley', where the archive is temporarily housed. We had already sent a list of the projects we want to examine: our 'mystery list'.

There are several projects that appear in Lautner's monograph about which nothing further is known. The extension to the house of Alex Weinstein is one of these. There is an address on most of the drawings, so that afternoon we go through the many rolls of drawings and in the evening we look up the addresses on Google Earth. The question each time is whether what we see on the drawing was really carried out and whether anything remains of it. At last we get a clear picture of the remodel for Mr and Mrs Ernie Adams, and the remodel for Fern Carr at 233 S. Palm Drive in Beverly Hills, for which we now have an exact address. All of these are very precise and detailed pencil drawings on transparent paper. And, at last, drawings of the Bosustow Cabin in Lake Almanor. It feels like the discovery of the treasures in Tutankhamun's tomb. In the next roll of drawings there are plans for a cabin in Idyllwild for Marco Wolff, the same Wolff who commissioned the house on Hedges Way in Los Angeles; on the drawings, one can see how this house was planned around the extant boulders. Now that we know the exact location we will have to go back to Idyllwild to check if anything was built and if so what. In the same roll, we also find drawings for a country home for Marco Wolff, this time in Banning, which looks like a conversion. On other sheets the design is titled 'Alterations to Mr Marco Wolff's cabin'.

We find a remarkable number of designs for swimming pools; sometimes just a simple tank, others are roofed over in a completely new building. An example are the alterations for Mr and Mrs David M. Conrad', a new wing for an extant house. We see several variations, each one more spectacular than the one before – and with addresses. We race through the rolls, hungry for new finds.

It is already evening and we have only studied a small number of the rolls that we wanted to look at. We are able to make another appointment to continue our fascinating work in the archive on Saturday.

Next to the visit to the archives we have appointments with two former collaborators of Lautner's: Vaughan Trammell and Duncan Nicholson. Trammell worked with Lautner from 1977, on Hope, Schwimmer, Krause and Boykoff, among others. He left in 1988 to start his own practice. Nicholson started with Lautner in 1989. We reach a building housing several businesses, belonging to Santa Monica airport, where Nicholson's office is situated. At first conversation is stilted: Nicholson and Trammell sit rather withdrawn on a sofa and ask, 'Do you have specific questions for us?' When we show them the database that we set up last year and they realise that our interest and knowledge are greater than those of the average Lautner fan, they unbend slightly and provide us with some information.

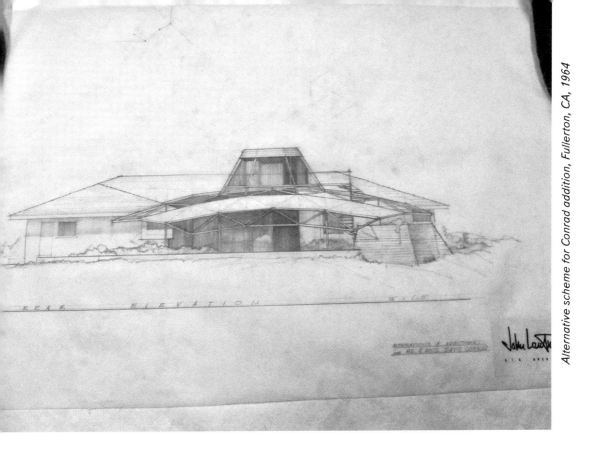

Alternative scheme for Conrad addition, Fullerton, CA, 1964

Model of Yokeno house, Pacific Palisades, CA, 1990

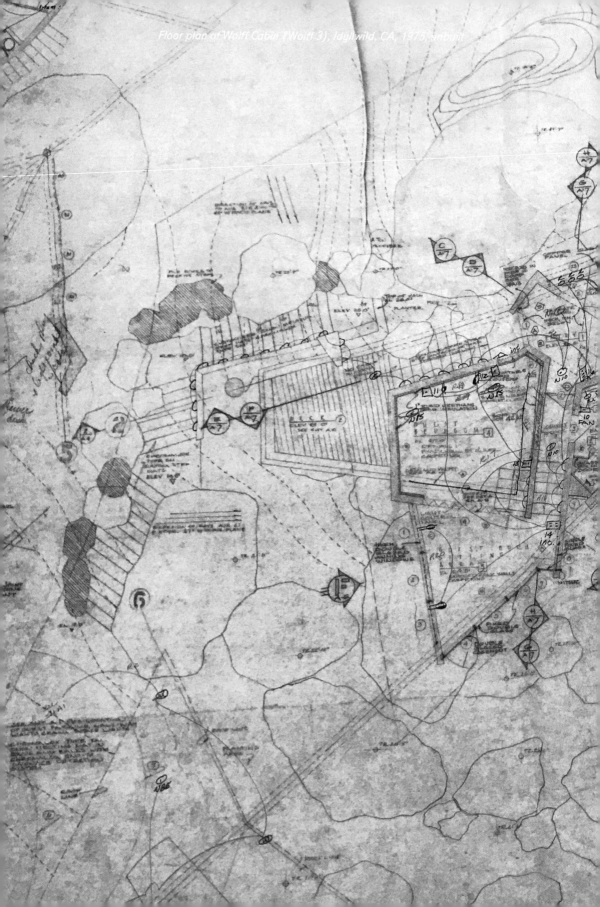

Floor plan of Wolff Cabin (Wolff 3), Idyllwild, CA, 1973, unbuilt

FIRST FLOOR PLAN

Cabin, 1975, unbuilt
53590 Rockey Way, Idyllwild, CA 92549

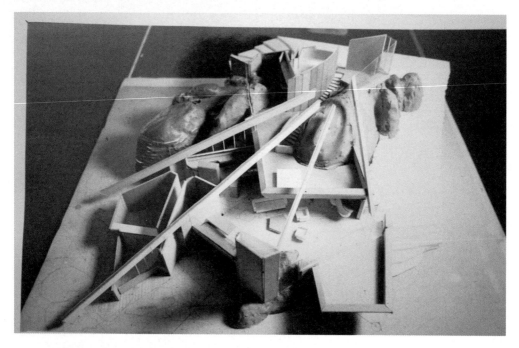

Wednesday, 16 July 2008

In Idyllwild, we go in search of the location of
the Wolff Cabin designed in 1975, of which we
now, as a result of our archive research, know the
exact address. There are rumours that the cabin
was actually built. From the photos of the models
and the drawings we know that it was a beautiful
design, embedded between huge boulders and
under a large roof following the slope of the hill.
After some searching we find the large boulders
that figure on the drawing. A little lower down the
hill than Lautner intended there is indeed a cabin,
not Lautner's design but that of Dennis McGuire,
a local architect. He was given the commission
because Wolff was afraid that Lautner's design
would be too expensive; this brought the long
collaboration between Wolff and Lautner to an end.
Fascinated, we clamber over the boulders and try
to imagine how it would have looked if Lautner's
design had been executed: this would certainly
have been one of Lautner's most daring buildings.
Making the confusion still greater we later find, in
the archive of Julius Shulman at the Getty Center,
photos of this house with an attribution to Lautner.

previous: Marina Fine Arts
next: Wolff 2 'Wind Song'

Wednesday, 8 April 2009

We know the location for the Kirk Wood residence from Bette Jane Cohen's documentary. Lautner stands on a hill high above Malibu, looking over the ocean. This is where Lautner's last big project would be. The first drawing shows a widely spread-out house, three levels which follow the slope, with vaulted roofs. This concept worked very well with the natural incline in the landscape but permission was refused as the building would limit the neighbouring houses' view. A new concept was developed lower down on the site: a house in which the living room was conceived as a large glass greenhouse with a swimming pool flowing from inside to outside, thereby providing a thermal buffer. Whenever Lautner was asked what his favorite design was, he would invariably reply: the most recent one. This is the last complete house designed by Lautner himself; we are therefore standing on the spot of what would have been the house Lautner loved the most. In the documentary Lautner walks around the site, talking about his design as if it was actually there. Now we do the same as we try to determine its exact position. Lautner died not long after the design was finished. At first the client wanted to go on with the project but after a few setbacks, among them a large forest fire, he decided to sell the lot.

previous: Yokeno site
next: Oboler

Second visit to the John Lautner Archive

Saturday, 12 July 2008

Today for the first time we are at the Getty Center; Wim de Wit has bought the rolls we wanted to see from the storage depot in Van Nuys. As it is Saturday, the complex is packed with visitors. We find drawings with the exact addresses of the Lippett Remodel and the Wolfe Pool, working drawings of the definitive design for Goldsmith and a curious social housing project in the form of some cooling towers, called HUD.

Later that day we visit Helena Arahuete (née Dobrovolsky). After Lautner's death in 1994 she continued the practice under the name of Lautner Associates, first with Duncan Nicholson and Julia Strickland, but as their ideas about the future of the practice diverged the extant commissions were divided up and Duncan Nicholson was put in charge of the Sheats-Goldstein house, which his office is still working on now, eighteen years later. We had spoken to her briefly in 2007 when we visited the Harvey house, where she supervised the renovations. She started with Lautner in 1971, working on the Marbrisa house, and worked on all of Lautner's best projects, like the Pacific Coast house, until his death. In her office, there are beautiful models made of corrugated cardboard, like the ones she made for Lautner himself. The model of one of Lautner's last projects, the never built Whiting house in Idaho, is among them. Helena Arahuete tells us that she showed this model to Lautner when he was in hospital shortly before he died and he was enthusiastic about it. The design shows a wonderful series of spaces with many surprises: a double-curved wall that leads the visitor from a cave-like space to a fantastic panoramic view from the living room. The son Henry of the clients who commissioned this house wrote a detailed article about Lautner in the issue of *Global Architecture* that was dedicated to Lautner's last work. JRK: 'He told me that his parents finally decided not to build the house because they thought, once the contours of the house had been sketched, that the site it was to be built on was too small.'

On the walls of her office hang many photos of the work she did with Lautner and that she continued to work on after his death. On one building site photo of the Pacific Coast house we see for the first time what the mysterious client Dr L. looks like: with a wide arm gesture the young Helena is demonstrating something to Lautner, Dr L. and the contractor Wally Niewiadomski. This is a golden team that executed Lautner's magnificent swansong. Helena tells us about a house in Alaska that she is working on, at the heart of which is a large waterfall, and about the Roscoe house near San Francisco, which is on top of a hill dominating its surroundings. In 2017, the Roscoe house was destroyed by a wildfire. At the moment, she is working on a commission for a house on Mulholland Drive, directly opposite the Garcia house. Talking to her, we are closer to Lautner than we ever thought possible.

She was and remains a patient source of endless information. We show her the database we made in the past year, review all the projects in it, and Helena provides us with interesting extra information. Finally, she remarks that if she ever needs to know anything more about Lautner, she will apply to us. When she hears about our plan to write a book her greatest concern is that, after so many publications in which Lautner and his work are wrongly represented, we set the record straight. We are grateful to Helena for her critical reading of our manuscript, and for the improvements and additions she made to it.

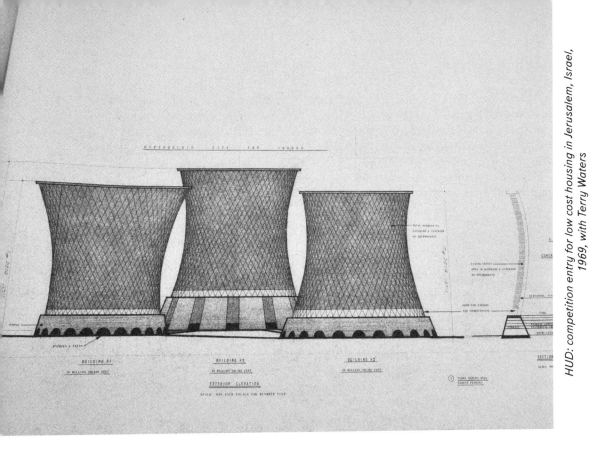

HUD: competition entry for low cost housing in Jerusalem, Israel, 1969, with Terry Waters

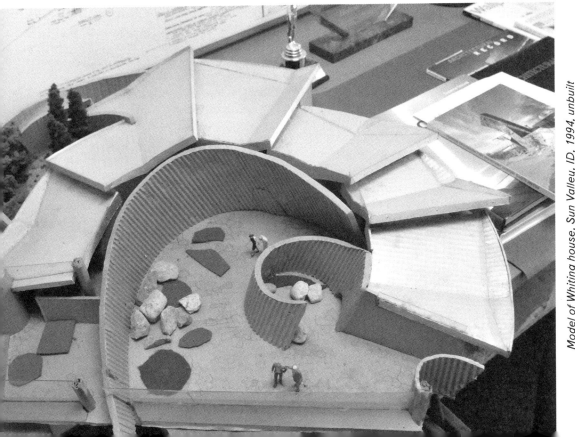

Model of Whiting house, Sun Valley, ID, 1994, unbuilt

Monday, 6 April 2009

We spend the whole day in the Getty Center doing further research in the archive. We have the building almost to ourselves, as the museum is closed to the public on Monday. Lautner's archive is fascinating, with its thousands of drawings and sketches, most of them rolled up in cardboard tubes. Every tube we open contains new surprises. Once again we have made a wish list. It would be beyond the scope of this book, which is intended as an account of our visits to houses that were constructed, to describe every drawing that we found in the archive, but there are a few projects that are significant to our quest.

We look at a large number of drawings of work that was not built and which, as Lautner's oeuvre develops, becomes ever more exaggerated, with a high point in the seventies. Each house that comes out of the rolls is more fantastic than the one before. It was at this time that the Acapulco house (Marbrisa) was built, and in the decade following Lautner hardly built anything else, but made many designs. One of these is a design made in 1971 for the Lueck house on Elaine Way in San Diego, a two-storey house with a circular roof, half buried in a hill, which is entered from the top floor. The space in the house is defined by arcs and a cylinder which contains the kitchen. The drawings are extremely detailed; the decision not to continue must have been taken just before building was to be started. The burden of disappointment formed by an accumulating number of unbuilt designs is something that non-architects can barely imagine. This is the last house in which Lautner used a purely circular plan. The set of drawings from 29 April 1972 with Lautner's last handwritten corrections is the most fascinating: the shape of the swimming pool has been adjusted, and the contour of the terrace. On this drawing, the exact position of switches and power points is marked, and an extra window has been added.

Another project from this period is the Lucy house on Horseshoe Bay in Texas. The Lucy house has a quarter-circle ground plan, its structure formed by fifteen curved concrete ribs, above which is a sheet of glass, like the first design for the Goldsmith house. JRK: 'When I got in touch with Cheron Hurd Lucy by email in April 2012 she told me that they found the design wonderful but it was not executed because they thought it would cost much more to build than they could afford at the time.'

In the next roll is the second project on Horseshoe Bay, for 'Mr and Mrs Norman Hurd', in Marble Falls, Texas. There are several dates on the drawings, all in 1974. This was an extravagant house, planned on the tip of a peninsula in an artificial lake. With the drawings, there is also a large black-and-white aerial photograph, with pencilled notations like 'lighthouse' and 'not so good view', illustrating how Lautner started work on a new project, making notes on the spot on a detailed contour map or aerial photograph. In *Infinite Space* his daughter Judy, who worked in his practice for six years, describes how he used to stare at them for days before putting the first lines on paper. The Hurd house was supposed to be so close to the tip of the peninsula that water could flow right into the centre of the house. The dish-shaped roof hangs on an enormous concrete ring, in its turn held up by a circle of pillars, three of which stand in the water, with very expressive shapes strongly reminiscent of the work of Oscar Niemeyer. With its curved concrete disks like breakwaters in the water, the house conjures up the image of a cactus flower, with its own world inside. The Hurd house is one of the most extreme examples of Lautner's unbuilt work. It is unclear why it was not executed, although there are rumors that Hurd did have the house built, but without Lautner. On Google Earth, you can see that there is a house on that spot, but it does not look in the least like Lautner's design. JRK: 'When we got home I wrote to Hurd to ask him about the design and what happened, he replied that he could not remember anything about either Lautner or the design, which considering the details in the drawings seemed unlikely, but possible in the light of his age. So the doubt remained: how could someone forget about

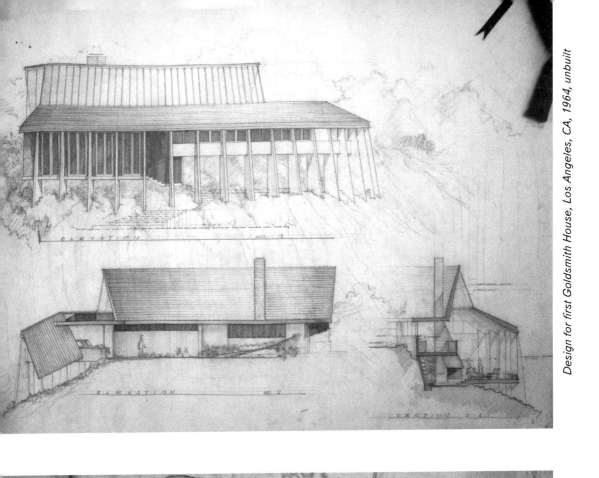

Design for first Goldsmith House, Los Angeles, CA, 1964, unbuilt

Lueck residence, Dwane Avenue & Elaine Drive, San Diego, CA, 1971, unbuilt

BERNARD LUECK'S RES.

PLAN   JOHN LAUTNER ARCHITECT

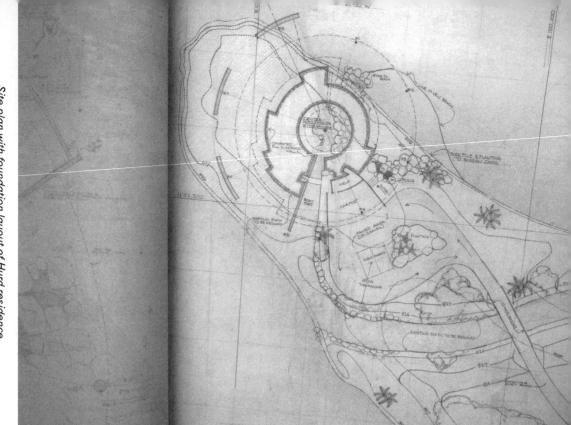

*Site plan with foundation layout of Hurd residence,
Horseshoe Bay, TX, 1973, unbuilt*

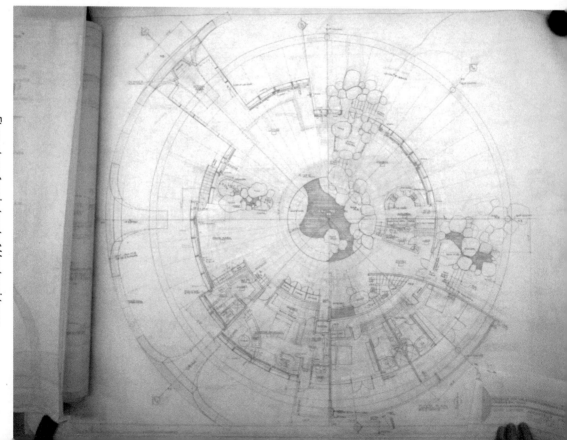

*Floor plan of main level of Hurd residence,
Horseshoe Bay, TX, 1973, unbuilt*

this house, about which there must have been intensive discussions, as it was worked out to the smallest detail. Through my contact with Cheron Hurd Lucy it became clear that it had been her father, Norman, who had commissioned the house, but the letter I got was not from Norman but from his brother Wayne. Norman was dead by then.'

Frank Escher, who has seen most of the drawings in the archive, is helping us today. Last of all comes the roll with drawings from 1990 of the Beverly Hills Bridge over La Cienega Boulevard. This bridge was cited as one of his last works in the Austrian book published in honour of Lautner's eightieth birthday in 1991. Lautner occasionally entered competitions, like the one for this bridge, mostly in order to get commissions other than houses for private clients. We are very curious how Lautner would go about designing something like a bridge, so this is an interesting side-track. There are some five different concepts in the roll, each more spectacular than the one before, all completely different from each other, but very expressive for such a simple assignment as a footbridge over a boulevard. So we are not surprised that Lautner didn't win; here too he was far ahead of his time. A few days later we drive past the spot where the bridge was to be, and indeed there is now a simple, unobtrusive, small bridge.

As the Getty Center is close to Brentwood, we drive past Frank Lloyd Wright's Sturges house, built in 1939, one of the projects for which Lautner came to Los Angeles, where he was sent by Wright to direct and supervise the building of this spectacular house that seems to be cantilevered straight out of the hill. We had long thought that Lautner carried out another conversion for the present owner, Jack Larson, but archival research showed that this was quite a different project. The story goes that Leland Burns, a professor at UCLA who wanted to buy the house in the early seventies, approached Lautner and asked if it would be possible to convert the house in such a way that there would be room for his beloved church organ. Most architects would have answered in the negative, as the Sturges house is a low one-storey building with a large cantilever, into which a vertical element of this kind would simply not fit. But Lautner answered, 'Sure.' But Burns apparently wasn't convinced, as in 1974 he commissioned Charles Moore to build a house around the organ, with marvellous results.

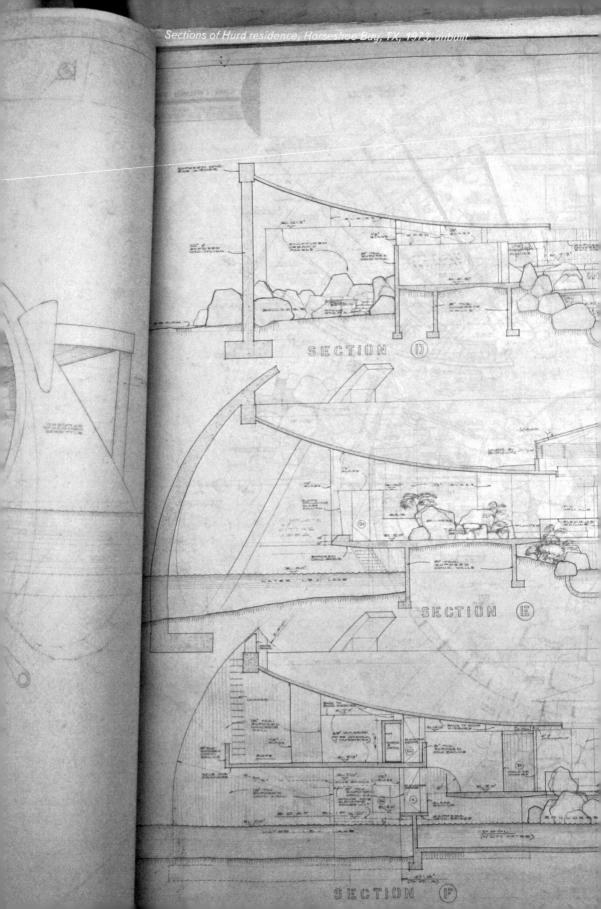

SECTION D

SECTION E

SECTION F

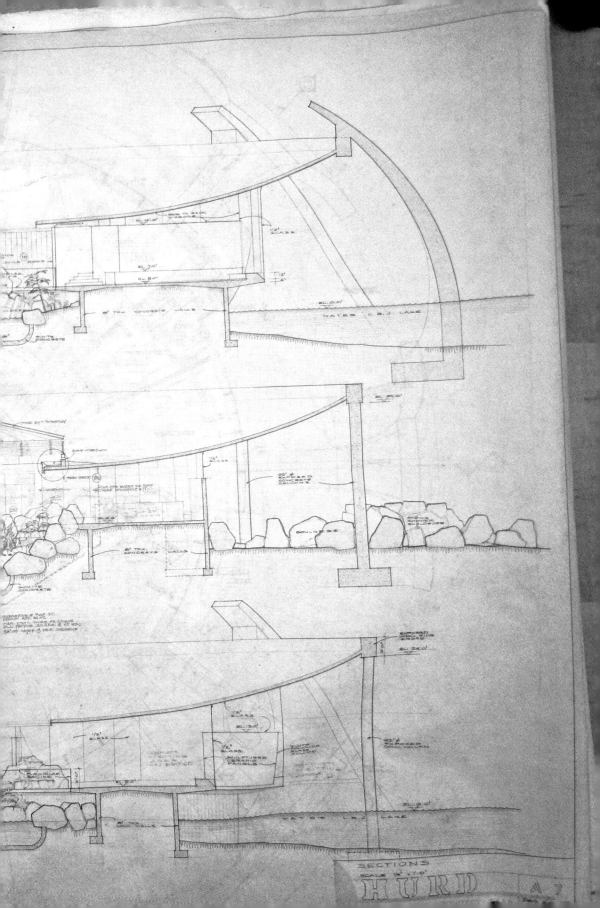

SECTIONS
SCALE

HURD

A 7

Wednesday, 8 April 2009

Andrew Nasser, Lautner's main structural engineer from 1972 onwards, has invited us to visit his Lautner archive at his office in Pasadena. Nasser is a friendly man who likes talking about his time with Lautner and we have asked him to unroll the drawings of all the projects he worked on with Lautner. Archives again, but this time with a full explanation from the maker. The style of the drawings is unmistakable, with crisp pencil lines and the constructive parts filled in in light blue. We page through the drawings of an incredibly complicated house that will later be nicknamed the Contemporary Castle, and see for the first time the wonderful construction drawings of its concrete shell roof. TS: 'Also the drawings for the Allan Turner house in Aspen, which at that time I had seen already, but Jan-Richard had not.' Apart from insight into the work, Nasser also gives us a lecture on construction principles. Executing Lautner's ideas was only made possible by builders and advisers like Nasser whom Lautner had assembled around him. Here is the never built Familian beach house, and a set of drawings for the Townsend house, consisting only of a concrete shell structure. The shell is raised up above the ground, completely open at the front, and runs on continuously to protect the street side. Nasser shows us working drawings of the reinforcement but does not know why the house was never built. The modest conversion to the Stevens house comes up, and Nasser asks us why we are interested in such details. We see the 1987 drawing for a never built extension to the Wolff house at 8530 Hedges Place for Dr Kaufmann, who lived in the house for twenty years with Dr Pleasant Waverly Davidson III. On the drawing, it looks as if the living room is to be enlarged to the side and a pavilion has been added. To our surprise Nasser says that he has never shown these rolls of drawings to anyone before, nor indeed has anyone shown any interest in them.

The biggest surprise comes last: a set of drawings made in 1958 for an unknown guest house for Willis Harpel.

Nasser, a fanatic tennis player, tells us that he often played tennis with the owner of the Pacific Coast house on the court at the house, and offers to ask the owner if he would allow us to visit the house. Unfortunately, we hear a few days later that the owner prefers not to receive us in order not to create a precedent for other enthusiasts.

Master engineer Andrew Nasser explaining the structure
of the Turner residence

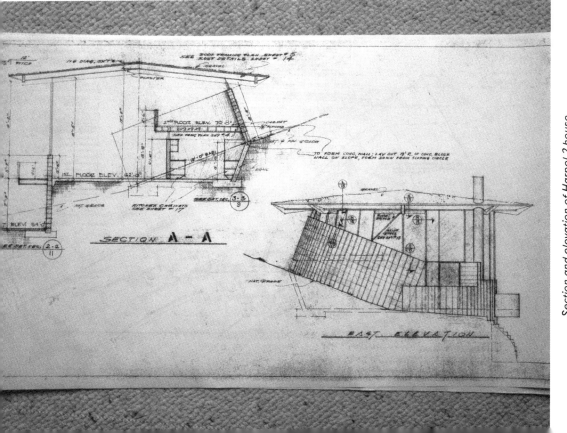

Section and elevation of Harpel 2 house,
Los Angeles, CA, 1958, under construction (in 2018)

Monday, 22 March 2010

We spend today and tomorrow in the archive at the Getty Center and have asked Frank Escher to go through the drawings with us on the first day. The archive has not yet been classified and as the drawings are all in – sometimes very full – cardboard tubes, unrolling them is very time-consuming. Tycho had the brilliant idea of also asking to see the photographic archive, which we are very curious about, especially photos of the lesser known projects. During these two days, we unlock a treasure trove of information, which answer many of our questions and bring up some new ones. The true list of works turns out to be much longer than we thought. This time our focus is in particular on the lost work, like Henry's restaurants.

A great deal of unknown and unbuilt work passes by, photos of models taken from the roof of his studio on Hollywood Boulevard, where his practice was established after the office at 1820 El Cerrito Place burned down in 1960.

There are photos of models that show the Franklin house in Argentina, the house that was intended for a race course, in four different variations. There was a studio model of it at the Hammer Museum exhibition. Helena Arahuete: 'In 1973 Lautner got a phone call from Dr Robert A. Franklyn, a hip plastic surgeon from L.A., who had decided to breed polo ponies in Buenos Aires. He asked Lautner to design a house for him beside a training ring. Lautner had the fantastic idea of making concrete, umbrella-like ribs to hold the house up. In this way, the façades were not attached to the construction, so there was a wide view of the racetrack. Several studies were done, and a big model made, that was shipped to Argentina. But we never heard anything from the client again, nor was the bill ever paid.'

Curious about something we believe to be a proposal for a conversion for the Frank Lloyd Wright Sturges House which was built under Lautner's supervision, we have requested a roll with drawings for a certain Larsen, ex-pecting this to be Jack Larson, who has owned the Sturges House for some forty years. In fact, it contains something quite different: drawings and photos of models of a house in Maricopa County, Arizona, for a Mr and Mrs T. Larsen. It is a very exciting design, with a roof construction built up from a series of arches standing beside and behind each other. The drawings date from February to April 1979. Interestingly we also find a letter from the clients describing what they wanted: a house with three bedrooms and two bathrooms. These simple desires proved no barrier to Lautner's imagination, and the house deserves a place in the series of high-quality unbuilt houses, like Hurd, Roven, Franklyn, Lueck, Yokeno, Wood and Whiting. That these projects were never executed must have been a great disappointment. When we look at this design for the Larsens we are again amazed: how can someone be so creative that he neither repeated himself in the hundred buildings that were built, nor in the countless projects that were not built?

JRK: 'When I happen to be in the neighbourhood in the summer of 2017, I drive past the spectacular location on the E Red Rock Drive in Phoenix, AZ where the Larsen house should have been built. Instead, there is an ordinary house that Lautner clearly had nothing to do with. When I take a few photos, the current owner comes to inquire suspiciously what I'm up to. The names Larsen and Lautner mean nothing to him.

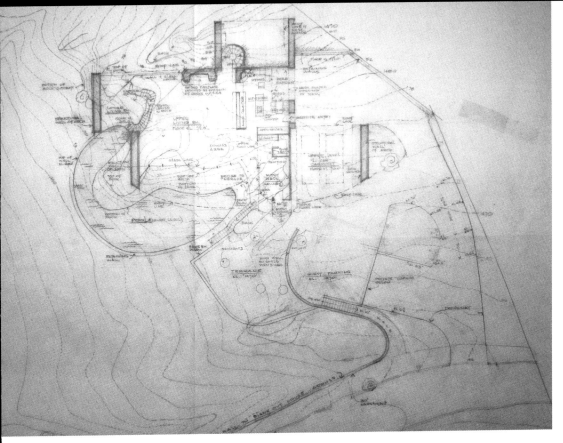

Preliminary plan and model of Larsen house in Maricopa County, AZ, 1979, unbuilt

Tuesday, 23 March 2010

Today is the last day of our visit to L.A. As
work in the archives has surpassed our
wildest dreams we again return to the 'holy
mountain', this time to concentrate on the
photographic archive. It's the two of us again
today, and a trolley is brought to us with the
boxes of photo files which we want. As this
will be our last visit for a long time, we go
through the material like mad men. The staff
on duty, who have never seen this kind of
'scientific research' before, are aghast. Wim
de Wit, the head of the department, comes
by and smooths ruffled feathers. We work
our way through an enormous amount of
photographic material, focussing today on
the blank spots in our knowledge. All sorts of
things come up, but we limit ourselves to a
few high points.

In a box of photos of the Pacific Coast house
we also come across photos of models of an
unknown design for Sunset Plaza: the client
who commissioned Lautner's most extreme
design must also have commissioned one for
another location. This house is more like a
composition of shapes piled on top of each
other, contrasting with the free forms of the
Pacific Coast house. Finally, the decision was
made only to carry out some renovation work;
we do not know to what extent Lautner was
involved in this.

Obviously, the archive is a gold mine,
where one could easily spend several months.
As with all architects the unbuilt projects are
often at least as interesting as the work that
was carried out.

Entirely covered backyard of Carr house in the 1950s

Original Wolff house before it was extended by Lautner with a guest wing in 1963

Contact sheet with model pictures of two different houses for the same client, 1987; Pacific Coast house, Malibu: built, Sunset Plaza Drive house, West Hollywood: unbuilt

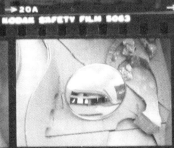

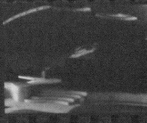

Monday, 13 November 2017

Because of the discovery of Samuel's Florist we have become even more curious about projects that appear to have been built without there being any information about them. In the six years since our last visit to the archives, we have found a few more projects we are very interested in. We have given the custodian of the 'special collections' a list of the projects we would like to see. What did the Bergren Studio look like, for example? In addition to the drawings we have seen, are there any other drawings of the Flower Shop for Samuel Morhaime and how do they compare to the actual building? Where exactly was the house for Franklyn the pony breeder located, if it was really built? Aside from floor plans and cross sections, we find a drawing of the area and the location, the latter with notes in unfamiliar handwriting, but with the usual information Lautner always used to get started, like the view ('lousy'), the path of the sun and the dominant direction of the wind. The house was designed for an area that now houses the Club de Campo Armenia, in a suburb of Buenos Aires called Manuel Alberti. Besides the familiar oval-shaped version, we also come across a tamer round version. We see many variations for the Burrell Ranch in Texas, which gradually become more moderate.

We also find drawings for a house for the notorious gangster Frank (Lefty) Rosenthal in Las Vegas, and for the Lindenberg house from 1959, which was to be built opposite the Foster house. Judging by the drawing style, the working plans were made by the same person who did the drawings for the Harpel Guest House. We also find perspective drawings for this last house in the Lindenberg folder, which is rather confusing. The confusion mounts when we find a beautiful, coloured-in perspective drawing of what we recognise to be the Jacobsen house; on the back it says, 'Robinson house, Lautner'.

Then we throw ourselves into a folder with a design for a house for 'Mr. & Mrs. John Lynn', situated at 1332 Las Palmas Drive, Hope Ranch, Santa Barbara – from Lautner's own 'rough schematic, showing basic concept' dated 3 December 1979 to working plans from 1988. When we check Google Earth later, to see whether something was built after all, it seems not to be the case, although we do discover a roof shape that shows some similarities, a bit further on. That also applies to the Raintree Inn, in Grand Junction, Colorado. There is indeed a hotel on the corner of Interstate 70 and Horizon Drive, but it doesn't remotely resemble Lautner's design. We make one wonderful discovery after another. A 1958 design for the Islander Motel on N. Sepulveda Boulevard, for instance, looks an awful lot like what Google Earth shows at that location.

We won't be done with 'the Chief' anytime soon.

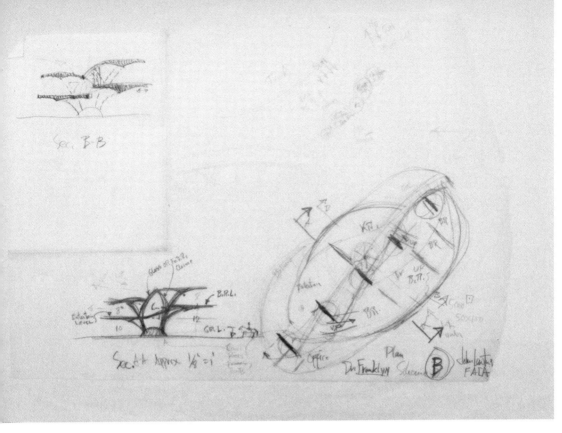

First sketches and floor plan for Franklyn residence, Buenos Aires, Argentina, 1973-1975, unbuilt

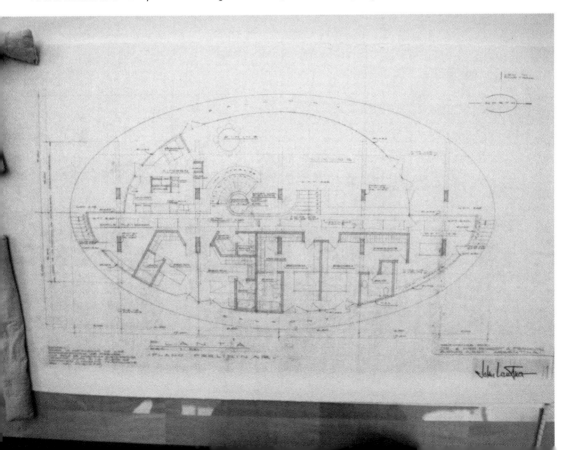

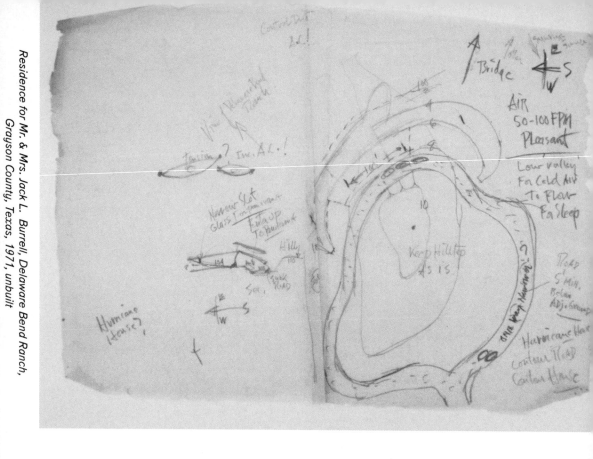

Residence for Mr. & Mrs. Jack L. Burrell, Delaware Bend Ranch, Grayson County, Texas, 1971, unbuilt

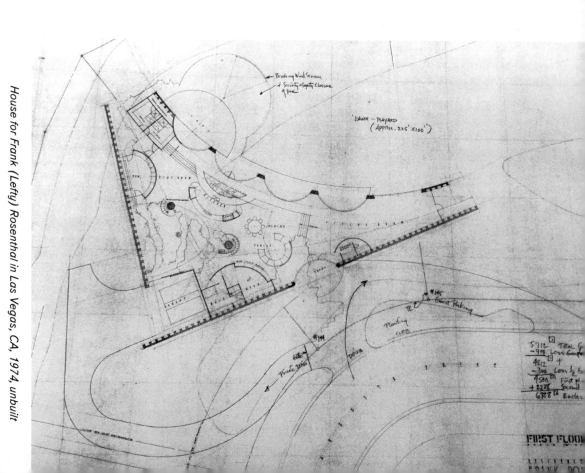

House for Frank (Lefty) Rosenthal in Las Vegas, CA, 1974, unbuilt

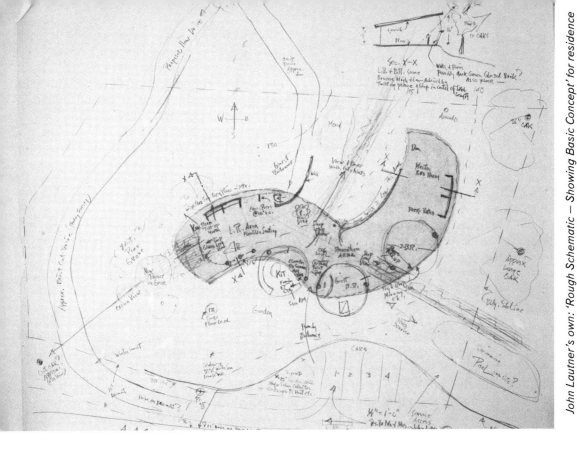

John Lautner's own: 'Rough Schematic – Showing Basic Concept' for residence for Mr. and Mrs. John Lynn, Hope Ranch, Santa Barbara, CA, 03 Dec 1979, unbuilt

Islander Motel, N Sepulveda Blvd, Los Angeles, CA, 1958, not built under Lautner's supervision

Conclusion
Tycho Saariste

Having spent almost every day of the last ten years engaging with Lautner's work in some way, it's time to take stock. Visiting the houses gave us an invaluable amount of insight into Lautner's work. Earlier visits of the work of Adolf Loos and Le Corbusier, for example, taught us that the real spatiality of a building can only be experienced when you walk through it. Photos are incapable of capturing this effect. While Neutra's houses can be disappointing when you've seen Shulman's photoshopped wide-angle shots, Lautner's work, and Wright's work to a lesser extent, always turns out to be much more dynamically and logically constructed than you'd think, when you visit it. Lautner used the language of his mentor, Wright, to develop himself, but permitted himself many more liberties by letting go of geometry, for instance, while this always played such an important role in Wright's work. Initially, Lautner still used grids and circular elements in his floor plans, but later he became freer and freer in his spatial compositions. At first sight, Lautner's houses seem completely different to one another. In terms of outward appearance, that's certainly the case, but upon closer inspection, the themes are the same every time. Something that's central to Lautner's whole oeuvre, starting with his own house in 1939 and carried through to his last design in 1994, is the link between the house and its surroundings and nature. He screens off the house from the street as much as possible, to create privacy for the occupants. At the same time, the link to nature and the view are maximised. Lautner manages to manipulate the site in such a way that even an average lot seems like a fantastic one from the house. Any view of the neighbours is screened off as much as possible, and the view is carefully framed. This mastery of dealing with the site is unparalleled in modern architecture. In order to link the house itself with the landscape, he designs the floor plan as an open structure with a flowing space, with as few closed-off rooms as possible. Many houses have an independent, dominant roof construction, with the walls placed freely below it. This is a kind of extension of Le Corbusier's *plan libre*. Where Le Corbusier limited himself to detaching the interior walls of the construction, Lautner extends this principle to the exterior. The boundary between outdoors and indoors is usually formed by a covered space, half inside, half outside, where he literally brings the landscape into the house with plants or rocks. This makes the relationship to nature tangible.

There is another aspect of Lautner's work that stands out in comparison to that of his contemporaries: he makes an integral design. Lautner's houses are always tailor-made for a certain client, where each specific question received a specific answer. In his designs, Lautner managed to bring together all the different factors, like the client's wishes, programme, surroundings, view, spatiality, construction, interior, daylight, installations and budget, creating a complex whole again and again, where it was totally impossible to predict what it would look like beforehand. The remarkable thing is that decisions about the design, which initially seem random, turn out to be very pragmatic when you see the house in reality. Lautner's choices were often unconventional. The radical designs were not always received positively. For instance, in the archives we found an A4 with the requirements for the design of a simple house. Lautner used these to make a fantastic design that can't be compared to any other house ever built. I suspect that the clients were so shocked that they quickly went to a 'normal' architect to have him build the house they had in mind.

I studied at the Faculty of Architecture at Delft University of Technology. When the building designed by Van den Broek and Bakema burned down on 13 May 2008, this marked the end of an era of architects who were schooled according to the 'form follows function' method, where there was little room for frivolity. At that time, I was fascinated by Le Corbusier, who broke with contemporary dogmas in his villas and introduced spatiality within a simple enclosure. Now, when I look at a design, I am much more focussed on optimising the qualities of the location and how buildings can be embedded in the landscape: organic architecture, but not the anthroposophic direction taken by Rudolf Steiner and Alberts and Van Huut, with which the concept is often wrongfully associated. No, organic architecture in the sense that Frank Lloyd Wright described first: architecture that grows, from within, and where everything is connected to everything else. I was able to use this form of organic architecture in the extension of my own house, which would have looked very different without Lautner's influence. Lautner's work has made me conscious of what's really important in architecture and life in general: the desire for added value and connection to the landscape.

Lautner's work gives a unique snapshot of a different kind of architecture of the post-war twentieth century, as a counterpart to functionalist concrete architecture. He was misunderstood and ignored by architecture critics at the time, but he is slowly being rediscovered now. This book aims to contribute to ensuring that Lautner is duly valued for his impressive oeuvre. At press time, 95 of Lautner's designs are still standing. How many will there be in twenty years? Three factors threaten the houses. Some of them are in a fairly bad state, often because the owners do not possess the means to restore them. On the other hand, they cannot part with them, because their whole lives are interwoven with their houses. When they eventually die and the house is sold, it has become so run-down that it is too expensive and complicated to save it. In addition, some home owners have no idea what they own. As a result, they renovate the house poorly and adapt it to their taste, without any comprehension of Lautner's intentions. For that matter, Lautner didn't have any problem with remodels of his work; he preferred to look forward to new challenges. The third threat is formed by the fact that personal property is highly valued in the United States, as is the freedom to do whatever you want with it. When a house gets a new owner, there is no guarantee that it will be kept. Sometimes a Lautner is bought not because of the house, but

because of the location, and it is replaced by a flashy McMansion. House prices in the US still seem to be determined by the location and the number of bathrooms. This way of thinking will have to change if we want to keep extraordinary architecture for the next generation. The houses need to become world famous, in the hopes that owners and neighbours become aware of the fact that they own something special, and that this comes with responsibility. During our search, that mission has become clearer and clearer: as far as I'm concerned, John Lautner belongs in the list of most important architects since 1900: Le Corbusier, Frank Lloyd Wright, Ludwig Mies van der Rohe, Alvar Aalto, Frank Gehry, Rem Koolhaas, Herzog & de Meuron and Kazuo Sejima and Ryue Nishizawa from SANAA.

For me, the quality of Lautner's work can be summarised in these two examples:

Harpel 3
Anchorage, Alaska, 1966

Sitting on the sofa in the middle of the house, with the enormous clerestory behind you, ficuses several yards high growing underneath it, you feel as though you are simultaneously in a tropical country and in a snowy winter landscape, because you have an almost unobstructed view of the snow-covered lake. The impact of this room can only be experienced in real life and can't be captured in photos.

Marbrisa
Acapulco, Mexico, 1971

When you come in, something extraordinary happens: you step into a surrealist décor, and you feel as though you're floating on a disc with a 180° view of the Acapulco bay. It is a unique experience: there don't seem to be any neighbours – they have been carefully hidden from view, and the hill on which the house is located doesn't seem to exist either. The edge of the living room is marked by a circular swimming pool, which reflects the light and seamlessly blends into the ocean in the distance. But even though a number of changes have been made, like the painted concrete, the bannisters and the PVC swimming pool liner, it is still the most remarkable house of the twentieth century!

It is incomprehensible that these houses barely figure in the architecture history books; it is time for them to be rewritten. Lautner was an unparalleled genius of a calibre that we wouldn't have thought possible when we first encountered his work.

Conclusion
Jan-Richard Kikkert

In the past years, we have visited nearly all of Lautner's oeuvre, spoken to his family and colleagues and consulted the archives. The aim of all this was to get a complete overview. Now that our amazement at Lautner's relative obscurity has faded away, only our outrage has remained. The mechanism of development through recognition barely occurred in his case. The period when he built one fantastic house after the other, in the second half of the sixties, with highlights like Harpel 3, Elrod, Stevens and Walstrom, came to an end when he completed Marbrisa, which is generally seen as his masterpiece. Although he completed three houses after this that are also seen as high points in his career – Segel, Turner and especially the Pacific Coast house – many of his works after that time were never built: Hurd, Roven, Franklyn and Larssen. We looked at these houses in the archives incredulously: some designs were so far developed that they could be built right away.

Exactly because each work is completely different to the last, it is interesting to see how much the works have in common. However different they are, the fixed ingredients are always the location, the client and the technology. The aim to create a perfect world in relation to the surrounding landscape is a central theme in almost every design. The Southern California climate contributed greatly to breaking down the barrier between indoors and outdoors. A complete fusion of the house and the location seemed to be the ultimate goal in many cases.

Architecture as applied art derives its distinguishing force from the very fact that it is applied. It has given a place to the autonomous position of the masterpieces of twentieth-century architecture, and an almost divine status. In Villa Savoye, Le Corbusier's most famous private home, which was situated in a pastoral place between fields and meadows, the main volume is one level higher up in order to emphasise its autonomous position. The same situation exists in Mies van der Rohe's Farnsworth House, although in this case it was done for a different reason:

the Fox river frequently burst its banks. Here, the perfection of the design and its execution is just as famous as the fact that the client eventually broke with Mies and sold the house a few years after it was completed. It is precisely their autonomous character that gives these two examples their place in architectural history. Without putting this last point up for discussion, I am forced to conclude that the architects who designed these houses in no way took into account the people they designed them for. The fact that these houses are fawned over so much while Lautner's are ignored raises questions about architecture criticism.

Most people who are interested in Lautner first get to know his oeuvre through the books that have been published about his work. This immediately highlights the diversity of his production, while it mostly consists of private residences. This picture is slightly inaccurate, as most publications appeared after the demolition of his public buildings. The car showroom, shops and especially restaurants have all vanished over the years because of the economic dynamics paired with this kind of enterprise. Preserving this kind of building is only possible when the building adapts to meet changing demands, which is of course at odds with keeping the design in its original state. An example is the hotel Lautner designed. Because of a number of drastic changes, it was possible to breathe new life into it.

What remains of Lautner's work, then, are the private residences, most of which are still used as such. The private residence has turned out to be a crucial aspect of the development of architecture, because of the fact that it is so relatively simple and has such clear parameters, from a programmatic point of view, but also because living needs have barely changed in the last hundred years. Staff quarters disappeared and appliances came in, where the advent of air conditioning likely had the biggest architectural impact. This is precisely why private residences are so rewarding to design and study. And since the relationship between the client and the designer of a private residence is so direct, the possibility of making something unique –

unadulterated and without compromise – is great. A private residence most clearly does justice to the designer's personal outlook. Almost all of Lautner's houses turn out to function perfectly still. The changes that have been made to the houses were mostly for other people than the original clients. What stands out is the unbelievable variety in the work.

In the aforementioned interview with Marlene Laskey, Lauter talks about his relationship with the 'businessmen, who don't give a damn, the lawyers and the bankers', and his heroic battle with institutions. And his deep abhorrence of Los Angeles, which he found so ugly that he wanted to destroy it with huge boulders. He established his position by turning away from colleagues and critics, and shaping his architecture as an autonomous object, where the occupants are consistently given the sense that they are alone, surrounded by wilderness, from which they need protection. This idea reaches its apex in the Pacific Coast house, where Lautner was forced to face up to the fact that in the perfect world he had created, he himself would eventually be considered part of the big, bad world outside and was no longer welcome. Paradoxically enough, Lautner is at his best when the protective shell stretches across a larger number of residences: the collective outdoor space for the Sheats Apartments. This is one of the best outdoor spaces ever designed worldwide, and in L.A. there is nothing that even comes close to it in terms of quality. Of course, the emphasis on the individual has to do with the individualistic mentality of American society. The pioneers' heroic battle against the elements, the impossible climate and the hostile local population is also a key theme in Lautner's work. Indoors is the perfect world, where one feels safe and secure. For Lautner, this indoors was always the starting point for each design: 'I have never designed a façade.' Lautner's pursuit of a perfect world is supported by an uncompromising focus on details. When rocks shape a space, like in Elrod, the glass simply blends into the rock. When the construction runs from inside to outside, the glass follows seamlessly. When the furniture forms the boundary between indoors and outdoors, like in the Dahlstrom house, the glass follows its impossible contour. In a few cases, there is no physical boundary between indoors and outdoors at all, like in Marbrisa, and the original situation in the Sheats house. The virtuosic detailing isn't there for the sake of the detail itself – no self-referential virtuosity in Lautner – but always to support a spatial idea. Frank Lloyd Wright's conviction that you should never do the same thing twice is something Lautner took very seriously right up to his death, much more seriously than Frank Lloyd Wright himself ever did. Lautner's virtuosity at coming up with new solutions for the same problem again and again is unbelievable. A fellow architect is best placed to appreciate the value of this.

The more research we did, the clearer it became that Frank Lloyd Wright was a lifelong inspiration for Lautner. The form language and use of materials of Bell and Carling still lean heavily on what Lautner did under Wright. In 1951, Wright designed a house with pool (which was never built) for Edgar Kaufmann's wife, who wanted more than a rectangular basin to do laps in – instead, she could swim circles around the living room. One could see it as a precursor to Marbrisa's moat. Lautner's genius was characterised by the fact that the swimming pool in his design also served as a railing to prevent you from rolling down the mountain, simultaneously offering an unobstructed look at the view.

Lautner really began exploring new paths after Wright's death in 1959. The light, tent-like character of his first works – excluding the Bubbling Wells Resort and the first sketches of the Eisele Guest house – reaches its high point in Jacobsen and Polin. One could see them as a continuation of the hut Lautner designed for himself in Taliesin West. With Silvertop, he introduces a concrete roof, which covers an enormous living room here. All the extra elements, like the kitchen, study and bedrooms, are located in two side wings. This also happens in Elrod, although the kitchen is also located under the concrete shell of the living room here. In Stevens, all the rooms are grouped under two shell roofs. And in Marbrisa [107], from 1974, the roof evolves into an enormous covering, which opens out to the skies and the view. The Acapulco climate, as well as the fact that this is a holiday home, ensure that Lautner was able to realise an old dream here: the boundary between indoors and outdoors has completely disappeared. In Turner, the concrete shell roof encapsulates the whole house. Carefully chosen cut-outs in the concrete shell connect the cave-like space with the surrounding landscape. Lautner says that this house will definitely survive the test of time because it is too expensive to demolish. In the Pacific Coast house, Lautner goes one step further by having the roof and walls merge into an organic whole.

Once in a while, a good idea is repeated and taken a step further. The swiveling façade with its built-in sofa from Carling comes back in Turner – the swimming pool edge in Marbrisa is repeated in the Pacific Coast house.

Our research in the archive showed that an idea wasn't finished for Lautner until it was built. For example, the pavilion next to Harpel, which was never built, shows strong similarities to the house for Lautner's cousin in Pensacola. And the clerestory from the 1964 design for Goldsmith, which was never built, pops up again two years later in the phenomenal Harpel 3 in Anchorage.

During our visits to the houses, we spoke to the original clients many times. The impression this gives us of Lautner is extraordinarily homogeneous: a large man, eloquent, and very convincing. But there is also the continuous tension between the desire for the best proposal and its financial consequences. The unbuilt 'super houses' after Marbrisa were undoubtedly much too expensive to be carried out. In his focus on the end result, Lautner didn't spare himself either: he was so eager to see his ideas carried out that everything else was of secondary importance, such as his home life and his financial situation. At least the arrival of office manager Christine Tanaka put the organisation and the firm's finances in order.

Looking at other breakthroughs in architecture, it is clear that such dedication and focus are preconditions for success. In Lautner's case, that focus lay on making 'real architecture': a radical functionalism that takes no notice of tradition, regulations, conventions or finances, but simply wants the best.

Because life's complexity doesn't offer us any clear answers, Lautner's work is so complex that it was long ignored by lazy architecture critics. While it was publicised in *Arts & Architecture*, it was not part of the programme of the Case Study Houses to meet the growing demand for houses after the Second World War. Although Lautner's themes were universal, his designs are too specific to serve as prototypes. The loose, rough-outline Googie style became known as the 'roadside Southern Californian Architecture', but changed from an honorary nickname to a term of abuse. More fitting was Frank Lloyd Wright's definition of the term 'organic architecture'. The problem here is that Lautner's work is too broad in scope, and Wright's definition is too vague. This made Lautner difficult to place, which did not help secure his position in architectural history. Actually, general interest in John Lautner has only begun to grow since we started the preparations for our trip. The exhibition in the Hammer Museum, the companion book and the film by Murray Grigor certainly contributed to this. In recent books, Lautner also gets the attention he deserves. He is mentioned in detail in the survey of the development of modern architecture, *The Future of Architecture Since 1869* by Jean-Louis Cohen, and there is a whole chapter on him in Thomas Heinz's *Architecture of the Sun: Los Angeles Modernism 1900-1970*: finally, he is up there with Neutra and Eames. And then there are the people who have always been convinced of Lautner's genius and shouted it from the rooftops, like Alan Hess.

The grassroots movement also seems to be influencing architecture criticism. Thanks in part to the internet, one can search for information oneself, allowing for the exchange of facts and insights. The amount of information about Lautner that can be found on the internet has increased enormously since the beginning of our research, ten years ago. For instance, most addresses can now easily be found online.

Our expectation that visiting unknown works would lead to new insights about the most successful designs came true, but that achievement is overshadowed by the wealth of ideas we found in the archive of the unbuilt work. In each sheaf of papers we pulled out of the rolls, we found new gems. Our attempt to make reconstructions of this unbuilt work with our students is still in its early stages and certainly merits serious future work, although 3D images can never come close to the experience of a real visit. This last fact was proved again and again when we visited works that had been photographed well, but were infinitely much better in reality. In addition, it is interesting to note that often, the houses we got to spend a whole day in ended up being our favourites: Elrod, Pensacola, Turner, Bosustow, Marbrisa and Harpel 3.

Now it only remains for me to explain why Lautner is so attractive to me personally. I was trained at Delft University of Technology at a time when architecture was taught in a strictly pragmatic-functional way. Architecture as a design discipline was only really rediscovered around that time. There was a handful of lecturers who talked about the architecture of modernist heroes, after years of discussion, especially about the social aspects of the discipline. It could happen that you were overloaded with the architecture of J. J. P. Oud and Mart Stam, but that Neutra was already almost a guilty pleasure, and if he was mentioned at all, it was probably for nationalist motives, because of the fact that Dutch architecture enthusiast and patron Cees H. van der Leeuw was involved and loaned him money to build his own house at Silver Lake. My discovery of Lautner was mostly a relief: finally, an architect pulled out all the stops. Private residences, a term of abuse in Delft, designed and detailed in a way that seemed almost sacrilegious. In a country where Calvinism had seamlessly transitioned into a shoddy kind of pragmatism, with a strict system of prejudiced positions, Lautner represented a freedom that is hardly conceivable to contemporary students in the current pluriform field. Lautner did everything that wasn't allowed in architecture. Becoming immersed in his inventiveness and the sheer joy he took in designing, which jumps out at you in all of his projects, is little short of fantastic, and because of the quality of the work, it is both intimidating and an example. It is precisely because there was so little information about his work that the hunter-gatherer in us was awakened. We vowed not to rest until we had found and visited everything.

List of built works

nrs. 01 — 144

№	name	type	start	finish
01	Taliesin West Shelter	temporary sleeping/drafting shelter	1937	1937
02	Lautner, John	house	1939	1940
03	Midgaard	cabin remodel & terrace addition	1939	1939
04	Bell	house	1940	1941
05	Springer	guest house & house extension	1940	1940
06	Astor Farm	guest house	1942	1942
07	Darrow Office Building	office building	1945	1945
08	Embassy Shop	shop remodel	1945	1945
09	Mauer	house	1945	1946
10	Weinstein	house remodel & addition	1945	1945
11	Hancock	house	1945	1946
12	Beverly Hills Athletic Club	club remodel	1946	1946
13	Coffee Dan's Vine St	bar	1946	1946
14	Coffee Dan's Broadway	bar	1946	1946
15	Coffee Dan's 8th St	bar	1946	1946
16	Eisele	guest house	1946	1946
17	Carling	house	1947	1948
18	Bubbling Wells Resort	motel	1947	1947
19	Bubbling Wells Pool	pool house	1947	1947
20	Gantvoort	house	1947	1949
21	Henry's Glendale	bar/restaurant	1947	1948
22	Jacobsen	house	1947	1947
23	Polin	house	1947	1947
24	Tower Motors / Parkway Motors	Lincoln Mercury Showroom	1947	1948
25	Valley Escrow Offices	office building	1947	1948
26	Salkin	house	1947	1948
27	Sheats (L'Horizon)	apartement building	1948	1950
28	Dahlstrom	house	1948	1949
29	Schaeffer	house	1948	1949
30	UPA Studios	office building	1948	1949
31	Brooks	house remodel	1949	1949
32	Googie's	restaurant	1949	1949
33	Alexander	house	1949	1951
34	Baxter-Hodiak	house remodel	1949	1951
35	Foster	house	1950	1950
36	Harvey	house	1950	1958
37	Shusett	house	1950	1951
38	Deutsch	house	1950	1954
39	Harvlan	office building remodel	1950	1950
40	Gootgeld	house	1950	1952
41	Seletz	studio	1950	1950
42	Bick	house	1951	1952
43	Evans & Reeves	exhibition stand	1951	1951
44	Bergren	house	1951	1953
45	Lippett	house remodel	1951	1957
46	Carr	house remodel & addition	1952	1952
47	Howe	house	1952	1953
48	Williams, H.	house	1952	1952
49	Henry's Alhambra	bar/restaurant remodel	1952	1959

current staus	client			place
demolished	Mr	John	Lautner	Scottsdale, AZ
extant	Mr & Mrs	John & Mary	Lautner	Los Angeles, CA
extant	Family		Lautner	Marquette, MI
extant	Mr & Mrs	L. & N.	Bell	Los Angeles, CA
extant	Mr & Mrs	Norman	Springer	Los Angeles, CA
demolished	Ms	Mary	Astor	Indio, CA
extant				Beverly Hills, CA
demolished	Mr	Nouard	Gootgeld	Beverly Hills, CA
extant	Dr & Mrs	Edgar	Mauer	Los Angeles, CA
extant	Mr	Alex	Weinstein	Los Angelcs, CA
extant	Mr & Mrs	Garnett	Hancock	Los Angeles, CA
demolished 1970s				Beverly Hills, CA
demolished	Mr	Joseph	Bulasky	Los Angeles, CA
demolished	Mr	Joseph	Bulasky	Los Angeles, CA
demolished	Mr	Joseph	Bulasky	Los Angeles, CA
extant	Mr	Arthur	Eisele	Los Angeles, CA
extant	Mr	Foster	Carling	Los Angeles, CA
extant	Mr	Lucien	Hubbard	Desert Hot Springs, CA
demolished after fire	Mr	Lucien	Hubbard	Desert Hot Springs, CA
extant	Mr & Mrs	W. F.	Gantvoort	La Cañada Flintridge, CA
demolished	Mr	Glenn	Amundsen	Glendale, CA
extant	Mr & Mrs	G.	Jacobsen	Los Angeles, CA
extant	Mr & Mrs	Ben	Polin	Los Angeles, CA
demolished	Mr	Arthur	Eisele	Glendale, CA
demolished	Mr	Willard	Gilland	Sherman Oaks, CA
extant	Mr	Jules	Salkin	Los Angeles, CA
extant	Mr & Mrs	Paul & Helen	Sheats	Los Angeles, CA
extant	Mr & Mrs	Grant	Dahlstrom	Pasadena, CA
extant	Mr & Mrs	J. W.	Schaeffer	Glendale, CA
demolished 1980s	Mr	Stephen	Bosustow	Burbank. CA
extant	Mr & Mrs	Richard	Brooks	Studio City, CA
demolished 1989	Mr	Mort	Burton	Los Angeles, CA
extant	Dr & Mrs	George & Grace	Alexander	Long Beach, CA
extant	Mrs	Ann	Baxter-Hodiak	Los Angeles, CA
extant	Ms	Louise	Foster	Sherman Oaks. CA
extant	Mr & Mrs	Leo	Harvey	Los Angeles, CA
demolished 2010	Mr & Mrs	David	Shusett	Beverly Hills, CA
extant	Mr & Mrs	George	Deutsch	Los Angeles, CA
demolished 1980s	Mr	Leo	Harvey	Los Angeles, CA
altered beyond recognition, 1980s	Mr	Nouard	Gootgeld	Beverly Hills, CA
extant	Dr	Emil	Seletz	Los Angeles, CA
demolished 1990	Mr & Mrs	Lester	Bick	Los Angeles, CA
demolished 1951			Evans & Ingraham	Inglewood, CA
burnt down and rebuilt 1957	Mr & Mrs	Ted & Betty	Bergren	Los Angeles, CA
altered	Mr	Manny	Lippett	Los Angeles, CA
altered beyond recognition	Mrs	Fern	Carr	Beverly Hills, CA
extant	Mr & Mrs		Howe	Los Angeles, CA
extant	Mr & Mrs	Harry	Williams	Los Angeles, CA
demolished	Mr	Glenn	Amundsen	Alhambra, CA

№	name	type	start	finish
50	Henry's Pasadena	bar/restaurant remodel	1953	1959
51	Payne	house addition	1953	1953
52	Tyler	house	1953	1953
53	Coneco Corp	house	1953	1954
54	Wolf	guest house	1953	1953
55	Beachwood Market	shop remodel	1954	1954
56	Fischer	house	1954	1955
57	Harpel	house	1954	1956
58	Lek	addition	1954	1954
59	Baldwin	house	1955	1955
60	Henry's Arcadia	bar/restaurant remodel & addition	1955	1955
61	Flower Shop for Mr. Samuel Morhaime	shop	1955	1956
62	Zahn	house	1955	1957
63	Kaynar Factory	factory building	1956	1959
64	Reiner (Silvertop)	house	1956	1965
65	Speer	office building	1956	1956
66	Johnson	house	1956	1965
67	Henry's Pomona	bar/restaurant	1956	1957
68	Hatherell	house	1956	1958
69	Bosustow	house remodel	1956	1958
70	Bergren	rebuilt & addition	1957	1957
71	Pearlman	cabin	1957	1957
72	Lautner	house	1957	1959
73	Preminger	house remodel & pool	1957	1962
74	Speer	addition	1957	1957
75	Bergren	studio	1957	1957
76	Garcia (Rainbow)	house	1958	1962
77	Malin (Chemosphere)	house	1958	1960
78	Harpel 2	guest house	1958	2017
79	UPA	addition	1958	1959
80	Concannon	house	1960	1960
81	Midtown School	school building	1960	1961
82	Tolstoy	house	1961	1974
83	Vine Street Offices	multiple office remodels	1961	1962
84	Wolff	house	1961	1961
85	Hinerfeld	house addition & remodel	1961	1961
86	Sheats	house	1962	1963
87	Thiele	addition	1962	1962
88	Henry's Glendale	bar/restaurant remodel	1962	1962
89	Castagna	house remodel	1963	1963
90	Wolfe	pool & house addition	1963	1964
91	Wolff	guest house	1963	1964
92	Conrad	house addition	1964	1965
93	Henry's Alhambra	bar/restaurant addition	1964	1964
94	Rothschild	kitchen remodel	1964	1965
95	Zimmerman	house	1965	1968
96	Harpel 3 (a.k.a. Harpel 2)	house	1966	1967
97	Marina View Heights Headquarters	office building	1966	1967
98	Wolff 2 'Wind Song'	cabin remodel	1966	1968

current staus	client			place
demolished 1980s	Mr	Glenn	Amundsen	Pasadena, CA
extant	Mr & Mrs	John & Janet	Payne	San Dimas, CA
extant	Mr & Mrs	Ted	Tyler	Studio City, CA
extant	Mr	Pat	Hamilton	Sherman Oaks, CA
extant	Mr	Milton L	Wolf	
extant	Mr	Harry	Williams	Los Angeles, CA
extant	Mr	Harry C.	Fischer	Los Angeles, CA
extant	Mr & Mrs	Willis	Harpel	Los Angeles, CA
demolished 1990s	Mr & Mrs	Nico	Lek de Tachinville	Studio City, CA
extant	Mr & Mrs	Joseph	Baldwin	Los Angeles, CA
demolished 1978	Mr	Glenn	Amundsen	Arcadia, CA
extant, demolition pending 2018	Mr	Samuel	Morhaime	Burbank, CA
extant	Mr & Mrs	Paul	Zahn	Los Angeles, CA
extant	Mr	Kenneth	Reiner	Pico Rivera, CA
extant	Mr & Mrs	Kenneth	Reiner	Los Angeles, CA
altered beyond recognition	Mr	Paul	Speer	Los Angeles, CA
extant	Mr & Mrs	Stanley	Johnson	Laguna Beach, CA
demolished 1986	Mr	Glenn	Amundsen	Pomona, CA
extant	Mr & Mrs	George	Hatherell	Sunland, CA
extant	Mr & Mrs	Stephen	Bosustow	Encino, CA
altered beyond recognition	Mr & Mrs	Ted & Betty	Bergren	Los Angeles, CA
extant	Mr & Mrs	Carl K. & Agnes	Pearlman	Idyllwild, CA
extant	Mr	Ernest	Lautner	Pensacola, FL
extant	Mr	Ingo	Preminger	Los Angeles, CA
altered beyond recognition	Mr	Paul	Speer	Los Angeles, CA
demolished	Mr	John	Bergren	Los Angeles, CA
extant	Mr & Mrs	Russ	Garcia	Los Angeles, CA
extant	Mr & Mrs	Leonard	Malin	Los Angeles, CA
under construction	Mr & Mrs	Willis	Harpel	Los Angeles, CA
demolished 1980s	Mr	Stephen	Bosustow	Burbank, CA
demolished 2002	Mr & Mrs	Charles	Concannon	Beverly Hills, CA
extant	Mr & Mrs	Kenneth	Reiner	Los Angeles, CA
extant	Mr & Mrs	Peter & Ann	Tolstoy	Rancho Cucamonga, CA
demolished				Los Angeles, CA
extant	Mr	Marco	Wolff	Los Angeles, CA
extant	Mr & Mrs	Norman	Hinerfeld	Los Angeles, CA
extant	Mr & Mrs	Paul & Helen	Sheats	Beverly Hills, CA
extant	Mr & Mrs	David	Thiele	Sherman Oaks, CA
demolished 1980	Mr	Glenn	Amundsen	Glendale, CA
extant	Mr & Mrs	Joe & Chalya	Castagna	Los Angeles, CA
extant	Mr	Bernard	Wolfe	Beverly Hills, CA
extant	Mr	Marco	Wolff	Los Angeles, CA
extant	Mr & Mrs	David	Conrad	Fullerton, CA
demolished	Mr	Glenn	Amundsen	Alhambra, CA
demolished 1980s	Mr	Harry R.	Rothschild	Beverly Hills, CA
extant	Mr	Wayne	Zimmerman	Studio City, CA
extant	Mr & Mrs	Willis	Harpel	Anchorage, AK
extant	Mr	Morris	Misbin	San Juan Capistrano, CA
extant	Mr	Marco	Wolff	Banning, CA

№	name	type	start	finish
99	Elrod	house	1966	1968
100	Stevens	house	1966	1968
101	Walstrom	house	1967	1969
102	Hilo Campus Life Science Building	laboratory building	1967	1972
103	Henry's Glendale	bar/restaurant remodel	1968	1968
104	Mills	kitchen remodel	1969	1969
105	Familian	house	1969	1972
106	Hope	house	1969	1980
107	Garwood	house	1970	1972
108	Marbrisa	weekend retreat	1971	1973
109	Elrod	remodel	1971	1972
110	Gefsky	addition	1971	1971
111	Elrod	addition	1971	1972
112	Jordan	house	1971	1973
113	Bosustow	cabin	1972	1976
114	Beyer	house	1973	1983
115	Crippled Children's Society	rehabilitation center	1973	1979
116	Little	dental clinic remodel	1973	1973
117	Burchill	completion	1973	1974
118	Goldsmith 2	house	1975	1978
119	Lautner Three Rivers	cabin	1976	1976
120	Barnes	remodel	1976	1979
121	Segel	house	1977	1980
122	Rawlins	house	1977	1980
123	Aldrich	pool & house addition	1977	1978
124	Maloney	house remodel	1978	1978
125	Pacific Coast House	house	1979	1990
126	Goldstein	multiple remodels	1979	1994
127	Crahan	pool	1980	1981
128	Turner	house	1980	1982
129	Schwimmer	house	1981	1982
130	Flowers That Bloom in the Spring Tra-La	house remodel	1982	1982
131	Krause	house	1982	1983
132	Sunset Plaza	entrance gate	1983	1987
133	Shearing	house	1984	1992
134	Stevens	bathroom remodel	1984	1991
135	Segel	studio addition	1986	1986
136	Boykoff	house remodel	1986	1989
137	Nicholas	remodel	1987	1987
138	Beyer	pool & terrace addition	1988	1988
139	Goldstein Properties	office	1989	1989
140	Marina Fine Arts Store	remodel	1989	1991
141	Todd	remodel & addition	1989	1989
142	Eicher	remodel & addition	1991	1991
143	Rodman/Friedberg	remodel	1992	1992
144	Preminger 2	pool	1994	1994

current staus	client			place
extant	Mr	Arthur	Elrod	Palm Springs, CA
extant	Mr & Mrs	Dan & Enid	Stevens	Malibu, CA
extant	Mr & Mrs	Douglas & Octavia	Walstrom	Los Angeles, CA
extant			Hilo University	Hilo, HI
demolished 1980	Mr	Glenn	Amundsen	Glendale, CA
dismantled 2006	Mr & Mrs	Kendall	Mills	La Cañada Flintridge, CA
extant	Mr & Mrs	Gary	Familian	Beverly Hills, CA
extant	Mr & Mrs	Bob & Dolores	Hope	Palm Springs, CA
extant	Mr & Mrs	Donald C.	Garwood	Malibu, CA
extant			private	Acapulco Guerrero, MX
extant	Mr	Arthur	Elrod	Palm Springs, CA
extant	Mr	Harold	Gefsky	Los Angeles, CA
extant	Mr	Arthur	Elrod	Palm Springs, CA
extant	Mr & Mrs	William & Johanna	Jordan	Laguna Beach, CA
extant	Mr & Mrs	Stephen	Bosustow	Westwood (Lake Almanor), CA
extant	Mr & Mrs	Stanley	Beyer	Malibu, CA
extant				Woodland Hills, CA
status unknown	Dr.	E.	Little	San Juan Capistrano, CA
extant	Mr & Mrs	Philip & Jacklyn	Burchill	Los Angeles, CA
extant	Mr & Mrs	Gary	Goldsmith	Sherman Oaks, CA
demolished 2009	Mr & Mrs	John & Elizabeth	Lautner	Three Rivers (Tulare County), CA
extant	Dr	Chester	Barnes	Los Angeles, CA
remodeled	Mr & Mrs	Gilbert & Joanne	Segel	Malibu, CA
extant	Mr & Mrs	Robert & Marjorie	Rawlins	Newport Beach, CA
extant	Mr & Mrs	Robert	Aldrich	Los Angeles, CA
extant	Mr	Roy	Maloney	Manhattan Beach, CA
extant			private	Malibu, CA
extant	Mr	James F.	Goldstein	Beverly Hills, CA
extant	Ms	Elizabeth	Crahan	Los Angeles, CA
extant	Mr & Mrs	Allan	Turner	Aspen, CO
extant	Mr & Mrs	Alden	Schwimmer	Beverly Hills, CA
altered beyond recognition	Mr & Mrs	Dan & Kristi	Stevens	Los Angeles, CA
extant	Mr & Mrs	Bud	Krause	Malibu, CA
extant			private	Los Angeles, CA
extant	Mr & Mrs	Steven & Miriam	Shearing	Coronado Cays, CA
extant	Mr & Mrs	Dan & Kristi	Stevens	Malibu, CA
demolished 2016	Mr & Mrs	Gilbert & Joanne	Segel	Malibu, CA
extant	Mr & Mrs	Harry & Beatrice	Boykoff	Los Angeles, CA
extant	Mr & Mrs	Frederick M.	Nicholas	Beverly Hills, CA
extant	Mr & Mrs	Stanley	Beyer	Malibu, CA
dismantled 2006	Mr	James F.	Goldstein	Los Angeles, CA
extant	Mrs	June	Perez	Marina Del Rey, CA
extant	Mr & Mrs	Michael	Todd	Los Angeles, CA
extant	Mr	Bruce	Eicher	Los Angeles, CA
extant	Mr & Mrs	Howard/Anne	Rodman/Friedberg	Los Angeles, CA
extant	Mr	Ingo	Preminger	Pacific Palisades, CA

With thanks to

The authors would like to thank the following persons and institutions.

First of all, for their patience and support:

Christine M. Yadlowsky Kikkert
Isabelle Kikkert
Julia Kikkert

Catharina Verduijn-Saariste
Maarten & Philip Saariste
Rein & Anneke Saariste

Adam Barr & Sherri
Adele Cygelman
Alan Hess
Alex Dias Texeira
Alison Clark
Andrea Kreuzhage
Andrew Nasser
Andrew Nolan
Anna Thomas
Anne Friedberg & Howard Rodman
Barbara & Dan Abbott
Barry Rosengrant
Bea Boykoff
Benedikt Taschen
Bette Jane Cohen
Bill & Barbara Childers
Bill Rosar
Brent Bolthouse
Carolyn Gootgeld Levine
Chalya Castagna
Charles Carey
Christian Lamb
Christopher Bentley
Crosby Doe
David & Kathy Cuddy
David Lautner
David Zander
Dennis Connor
Donald & Debra Morgan
Douglas & Octavia Walstrom
Douglas Reed
Duncan Nicholson
Eleanor Schrader
Elizabeth Honnold Harris
Elizabeth Chaponot
Frank Escher
George Ng
Grace Alexander
Guy Zebert
Gwen Neidlinger
Hamid Shams
Harold Gefsky
Harriet Selling

Harry Williams
Helena Arahuete
Inge Meijer
Irvin Paik
James Goldstein
James & Kellie Lumb
James Perry
Jamie Rigler
Javier Arango
Jeffrey Richards
Jeremy Scott
Jeronimo Arango
Jill & George Garcia
Jim Langenheim
Jim Preminger
John Knight
John McIllwee
Judith Lautner
Judy & Raimund Brendel
Julia Strickland
June Perez
Karol Lautner Peterson
Katherine Monger
Kelly Lynch & Mitch Glazer
Ko Jacobs
Kristi De Wind
Larry Worchell
Lawrence & Susan Levenstein
Leonard Malin
Marco Alexander
Mark Haddawy
Martin Daoust
Matt Allen
Max Lautner
Melissa Matuscak
Mia Doi Todd
Michael & Patricia Berns
Michael Kilroy
Michael LaFetra
Michael Todd & Kathryn Doi Todd
Mike & Ann Yadlowsky
Milton Sidley
Murray Grigor
Nancy Pearlman
Nathaniel Rothschild
Norman & Else Madson
P. Waverly Davidson III
Page & Myra Wood
Pamela Courtial
Patrick & Gloria Smith
Patrick Newall
Paul Masson
Penelope Spheeris
Peter & Taia Siphron
Peter Tangen
Philip & Jacklyn Burchill
Priscilla Presley
Ravi Gunewardena
Rex Linn

Richard & Cynthia Troop
Richard Turner
Rob Gage
Roban Poirier
Robert & Nina Kotick
Roger Richman
Sam & Helen Zell
Sarah Sackner
Silke Maloney
Sister Christine Machado
Stephen Price
Steve Hayes
Steve Ramser
Steven Maloney
Suzanne Thiele
Ted Sprague
Tee Bosustow
Terry Sanders
Tjeerd Hermsen
Tracy Beckman & Ryan Trowbridge
Trina Turk & Jonathan Skow
Victoria Sork
Vikki Hakkinen
Warren Lawson
William Jordan
Wim de Wit

Participants excursion Louter Lautner, ArtEZ University of the Arts, 2007:
Annemiek Schepers
Arthur Middelkamp
Hayke Zweede
Hugo Bolté
Loe van de Ven
Machiel Spaan
Ralph van Zon
Rudy Jansen

Students project Fontys AAS, 2009:
Barry van Ham
Greg Helder
Gijs Hoeijmans
Biek Nijst
Jimmy Oomen
Gilad Sitton
Amir Tatarevic
Thomas van Weert
Onno van Wensen

Minke Vos
Sabo Day
Werkplaats Typografie
ArtEZ University of the Arts
Stichting Fonds BKVB
The Getty, Los Angeles

Literature

Von Alvensleben, Ludolf, John Lautner: Architect,
Los Angeles: eine Ausstellung zum 80. Geburtstag,
exhibition catalogue, Hochschule für Angewandte
Kunst, Vienna, 1991

Bonvicini, Pierluigi, John Lautner: Architettura
organico-sperimentale, Bari (It.): Dedalo, 1981

Campbell-Lange, Barbara-Ann, John Lautner,
Cologne: Taschen, 1999

Cohen, Jean-Louis, Nicholas Olsberg and Frank
Escher, Between Earth and Heaven: The Architecture of
John Lautner, New York: Rizzoli, 2008

Escher, Frank (ed.), 'John Lautner. A tribute', Journal
of the Taliesin Fellows, 18, Summer 1995, pp. 5-36

Escher, Frank (ed.), John Lautner: Architect,
Princeton: Princeton Architectural Press, 1994

GA Houses #32, Tokyo: ADA, 1991

GA Houses #52, Tokyo: ADA, 1997

Hayes, Steve, Googie's. Coffeeshop to the Stars,
Vol. II, Albany, GA: BearManor Media, 2008

Hess, Alan, Googie. Fifties Coffee Shop Architecture,
San Francisco, CA: Chronicle Books, 1986

Hess, Alan, The Architecture of John Lautner,
photography by Alan Weintraub, New York: Thames &
Hudson, 1999

Laskey, Marlene, 'Responsibility, Infinity, Nature, John
Lautner', interview University of California, 1986

'Outdoors in town', House & Garden Magazine,
July 1949

Wolfe, Bernard, 'Swimming in Red Ink', Playboy
Magazine, July 1964

About the authors

JAN-RICHARD KIKKERT (1963) graduated with honours from Delft University of Technology in 1989, having completed a project in what was then Leningrad. After a few years of practical experience, he continued his studies under Herman Hertzberger at the Berlage Institute in Amsterdam. In 1996 he started his own firm, and while he was running it, he taught at various architecture schools inside and outside the Netherlands. He has been the Head of the Architecture Department at the Amsterdam University of the Arts since 2016. During his studies he visited a lot of architecture, and he has continued to do so; he encourages his students to do the same. He regularly gives lectures about the work of John Lautner both at home and abroad. He is married and has two daughters.

TYCHO SAARISTE (1971) graduated from Delft University of Technology in 1995. His boundless interest in architecture began when he was very young, while visiting classical masterpieces by Le Corbusier, Neutra, Schindler and others with his father (an architect/teacher of architecture). He has worked for various architectural firms, where he specialized in designing complex commercial and industrial building projects. In addition, he has a great passion for the architecture of free-standing residential houses. The discovery of John Lautner's work has had a lasting impact on him. Tycho regularly gives lectures about Lautner, whose influence can be observed in many of his own designs. In his work, he follows Lautner's motto, 'The purpose of architecture is to improve human life.' He lives near Rotterdam with his family.

Colophon

Authors:
Jan-Richard Kikkert
Tycho Saariste
Author 'Introduction':
Alan Hess
Author 'Foreword':
Ko Jacobs
Editorial coordination:
Minke Vos
Picture editing:
Jan-Richard Kikkert
Tycho Saariste
Sabo Day

Translation (Dutch-English):
Hannah Kousbroek
in cooperation with Sarah Hart
and Sarah Welling
Final editing and correction:
Lucy Klaassen
Copy-editing:
Shaun Lavelle

Concept and design:
Sabo Day, Amsterdam

Lithography and production:
Colour & Books, Apeldoorn

Printing and binding:
Wilco Art Books, Amersfoort

Cover:
Elrod House, Palm Springs, CA, 1966-1968

Photo credits:
All photos in this book were made by Jan-Richard Kikkert and
Tycho Saariste, with the exception of:
p. 38-39: Beverly Hills Athletic Club: photographer unknown
p. 44-45: Bick: Jan-Richard Kikkert in the John Lautner Archive
p. 64: Coffee Dan's: Jan-Richard Kikkert in the John Lautner Archive
p. 65: Concannon: ArtEZ Academy of Architecture
p. 94: Embassy: photo archive Carolyn Gootgeld Levine
p. 103: Flowers That Bloom in the Spring Tra La: photo archive
Gwenn Neidlinger
p. 116-117: Gootgeld: Jan-Richard Kikkert in the
John Lautner Archive
p. 140: Henry's Alhambra: Jan-Richard Kikkert in the
John Lautner Archive
p. 141: Henry's Arcadia: Jan-Richard Kikkert in the
Arcadia Public Library
p. 142: Henry's Glendale: Jan-Richard Kikkert in the
John Lautner Archive
p. 144-145: Henry's Pomona: Jan-Richard Kikkert in the
John Lautner Archive
p. 146-147: Henry's Pomona: Bill Rosar
p. 148: Hilo Campus: Jan-Richard Kikkert in the
John Lautner Archive
p. 152-153: Hope: Palm Springs Historical Society
p. 212: Mills: Bonhams
p. 274-275: Shusett: Jan-Richard Kikkert in the John Lautner Archive
p. 288-289: Taliesin West Shelter: photographer unknown
p. 293: Tower Motors / Parkway Motors: photographer unknown
p. 300-301: UPA Studios: Jan-Richard Kikkert in the John Lautner
Archive; original photos by Higgens
p. 302: Valley Escrow Offices: Jan-Richard Kikkert in the
John Lautner Archive
p. 345: Yokeno: Vaughan Trammell
p. 348: Wolff 3: Jan-Richard Kikkert in the John Lautner Archive
p. 349: Wood: Jan-Richard Kikkert in the John Lautner Archive
p. 359: Harpel 2: Jan-Richard Kikkert in the Andrew Nasser Archive
p. 361: Larsen: Jan-Richard Kikkert in the John Lautner Archive
p. 363: Carr: Jan-Richard Kikkert in the John Lautner Archive
p. 364-365: Jan-Richard Kikkert in the John Lautner Archive
p. 367-369: Jan-Richard Kikkert in the John Lautner Archive
p. 385: Sugarloaf Mountain: photo made by a passer-by

The photographs of the work of John Lautner are included in
this book with permission from his heirs. The photographs of the
interiors of the houses were made with the permission of the
residents at the time of the visits.

In memory of:
Ann Friedberg
Bette Jane Cohen
Douglas & Octavia Walstrom
Duncan Nicholson
Jan & Dolores Kikkert
Jim Langenheim
Karol Lautner Peterson
Ken Reiner
Marjorie & Patricia Rawlins
Martin Daoust
Philip Burchill
Tee Bosustow

ArtEZ Press
Minke Vos, Thaïsa de Leij
PO Box 49
6800 AA Arnhem
Netherlands
www.artezpress.artez.nl
ArtEZ Press is part of ArtEZ University of the Arts.

Distribution:
Idea Books
Nieuwe Herengracht 11
1011 RK Amsterdam
Netherlands
www.ideabooks.nl

This publication has been financially supported by the
Stimuleringsfonds Creatieve Industrie, the Academie van Bouwkunst
of ArtEZ University of the Arts, Felix Claus, Machiel Spaan and
Gortemaker Algra Feenstra.

stimuleringsfonds creatieve industrie

ArtEZ University of the Arts

 Gortemaker
Algra
Feenstra

Lautner A-Z. An Exploration of the Complete Built Work
is part 20 in: **ArtEZ Academia**

ArtEZ Press

ISBN 978-94-91444-41-8
NUR 648

This book is also available in Dutch
(ISBN 978-94-91444-43-2).